TANDEM

The Blazing Sout...

The roots of Paul I. Wellman's life are in the
West; he was born in Oklahoma at a time when
settlers were still arriving from the East, his
grandfather was a missionary to the Cheyenne
Indians, and, during one part of his life, he was a
cow-puncher in western Kansas, where he knew
at firsthand the last of the unspoiled West, and
numbered among his friends old-time frontiersmen
and cattlemen.

In recent years he has achieved eminence as one
of the most highly thought-of authors in America,
particularly on Western subjects. Besides THE
BLAZING SOUTHWEST, Paul I. Wellman has
written a companion volume, THE
TRAMPLING HERD, books on the Indian wars,
and numerous novels.

Another book by Paul I. Wellman published by Tandem Books

THE TRAMPLING HERD   40p

The Blazing Southwest

The Pioneer Story
of the American Southwest

Paul I. Wellman

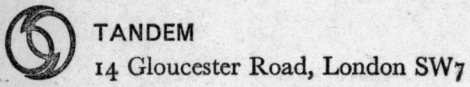

TANDEM
14 Gloucester Road, London SW7

First published in Great Britain by W. Foulsham & Co.
Ltd., 1961

Published by Universal-Tandem Publishing Co. Ltd, 1973

Copyright © 1954 by Paul I. Wellman

To my father
Dr Frederick Creighton Wellman

Made and printed in Great Britain by
Hunt Barnard Printing Ltd., Aylesbury, Bucks.

CONTENTS

List of Maps

Book One

THE TRAVAIL OF TEXAS

CHAPTER ONE

American Rifles and Filibusters

IN less than two centuries, starting with Coronado's expedition from New Spain (now Mexico) of 1540, the Spanish tide had swept northward until it lapped the Platte River in the present state of Nebraska, and the Arkansas River in present Kansas.

Rarely has history seen men of such hardihood, endurance, and grim purpose as the early Spanish captains who, with their soldiers and priests, crossed and recrossed that area — as vast as Europe excluding Russia — pathless, empty, mysterious and filled with perils. Their very names seem to march with banners and music : Coronado, Melchior Diaz, Cardenas, Padilla, Juan de Oñate, Zaldivar, Diego de Vargas, and the rest. In time they learned every route across the wilderness, and encountered every wild tribe in it. Sometimes they fought the Indians, sometimes they converted and enslaved them. The priests may have been concerned with human souls, but the captains sought gold and other riches. Whatever their driving motives, those mighty men succeeded, for a time, in making the American Southwest a Spanish province in good truth.

But then the tide began its ebb. Villasur, in 1720, encountered Frenchmen and their Pawnee Indian allies on the Platte River, and suffered a defeat in which he was killed with nearly half his command. A year later, in 1721, St.

Denis, the French adventurer, by a wily show of power he did not possess, secured an agreement whereby the Red River of Texas became the boundary of French Louisiana.

Their northward thrust thus blunted both from New Mexico and from Texas, and their colonial administration weakened by lack of support from the king and his administrators in Spain itself, the Spaniards found themselves unable to maintain their hold even on the territories north of New Spain which they already claimed.

This was because of the appearance of a new menace. From the mountains over the horizon to the west marched a numerous, lethal, savage people, suddenly become terrible because they had acquired the horse from the white man. In the interior plains they caused a great turbulence among the tribes already living there, and that disturbance created a new warlike spirit and sent other young braves out seeking scalps or loot. To the west, in Arizona and New Mexico, the implacable Apaches were beginning their endless vendetta against the white man.

Missions, *presidios*, and settlements were attacked by these barbaric tribes. San Saba was wiped off the map by the Comanches. A strong Spanish military expedition, commanded by Colonel Parilla, was defeated and routed by a force of savages from confederated tribes.

Retreat became imperative. Interior missions, forts and settlements were abandoned. By 1763 the central plains of Texas were emptied by Spanish establishments. Save for a few weak settlements on the coast of the Gulf of Mexico, in the extreme south of Texas, and on the Rio Grande River in New Mexico, Spanish authority had all but ceased in that area known as the American Southwest.

That year, 1763, when the Spanish tide ebbed in the Southwest, also marked the end of the Seven Years' War. A thin-faced, cold-eyed Prussian soldier, Frederick the Great, won durable military fame in that war by his battles against the united strength of Russia, France and Austria : and a British statesman, William Pitt, who planned in terms of continents and human races, destroyed the power of France on the seas and in her colonies. In India, Clive won control of the subcontinent for England; American colonials and British regulars fought the bloody French and Indian War, which was climaxed by Wolfe's defeat of Montcalm, the fall of Quebec and the passing forever of New France, henceforth called Canada, into British hands; and the English navy swept the seas so that France ceased to exist as a major naval power.

Out of this maelstrom of world conflict Spain might have gained much had she simply remained out of it and waited to pick up the pieces. But Charles III foolishly entered into the celebrated *pacte de famille,* in which all Bourbon rulers, including those of Italy and Spain, joined France in an alliance against Britain. The Spanish king soon rued his blunder. The magnificent English sea dogs devoted themselves to Spanish ships and colonies with such annoying assiduity that by the end of the war they had seized Cuba, the Philippines, Minorca and Florida; had almost swept Spanish commerce from the seven seas; and had even made a landing on the Texas coast, although this project was soon abandoned.

Yet Spain came unexpectedly well out of the Treaty of Paris, which ended the Seven Years' War. With Canada lost, France felt that Louisiana was untenably isolated between the British and Spanish possessions. It had never been profitable and about it still clung the malodorous memory of Law's 'Mississippi Bubble'. Rather than let it fall into Britain's hands, Louis XV of France made a gift of the 'Island of New Orleans' and all French territories lying west of the Mississippi to his cousin, Charles III of Spain, while at the same time ceding all territories east of the Mississippi to England. There were numerous territorial adjustments, including confirmation of Spain in the possession once more of Florida, Cuba and the Philippines. But France's disposal of her continental territories affected most directly and importantly the Southwest.

Thus France, which had for generations been Spain's great adversary in America, stepped forever from the arena. And because of French hatred of Britain, Spain discovered herself possessing – on paper at least – the very territories from which France had so long held her back. And facing, incidentally, across the Mississippi a far more aggressive threat in the restless Anglo-Americans.

That threat became increasingly acute when, twelve years after the Treaty of Paris, the American colonists began their War for Independence, winning it in 1783. And shortly after that Europe once more went into eruption. Out of the French Revolution and the Reign of Terror stepped an undersized young artillery officer who, with the famous 'whiff of grapeshot', ended mob rule in Paris and went on to become Emperor Napoleon I of the French, and possibly the supreme military genius of all time.

In this explosive situation the Spanish rulers, as usual, blundered. Charles IV, 'stupid to the point of imbecility', and subservient to his strong-minded and sexually unvirtuous wife, Maria Luisa of Parma, and her paramour, Manuel de Godoy, at first attempted to aid the old regime in France. But when the French revolutionary army came swarming over the Pyrenees he quickly reversed himself and signed a treaty of peace; and when Napoleon came to supreme power, the Spanish king – under some pressure – secretly ceded Louisiana back to France, on October 1, 1800.

To the people of the Southwest these events seemed distant and vague, although their eventual effects were climactic. Settlers were more concerned with their local problems, not the least of which had to do with the Indians. The record of the last half of the eighteenth century is spiked with Comanche forays on missions and settlements in Texas, and with depredations of Apaches, Navajos and Utes in New Mexico, in which towns and *ranchos* were scourged and many Indian pueblos decimated, destroyed or abandoned.

Yet during this period one Spanish official of energy and daring, Juan Bautista de Anza, first demonstrated a feasible land route from Sonora across the desert to California, and then, in 1775, led a colony of 244 persons over that route to

12

San Gabriel mission near present-day Pasadena, California, and thence north to San Francisco Bay, where he established in 1776 the *presidio* and mission which were the foundations of the city of San Francisco. From that date the true history of California as a whole began, and coincident as it is with the opening of the American War for Independence, it serves as a yardstick whereby the comparatively recent settlement of California can be compared to that of the Southwest, of which California is an offshoot.

Leaving his colony and returning to New Mexico, Anza was appointed governor of the latter province in 1777, and personally recorded one episode which is worth recounting as illustrating the destruction of some of the pueblo peoples.

Sturdiest of all the mesa dwellers were the Hopis, who never fully accepted Spanish authority after the revolt of 1680. In their communal houses, perched on cliffs in their harshly eroded country, they kept at bay the Apaches and Navajos and preserved toward the Spaniards an attitude of peace, dignified and aloof, so long as the Spaniards did not approach too closely.

A few *visitas* were made to them by padres, and on each occasion the friars were well received but had singularly few results insofar as conversions to the Catholic faith or loyalty to the Spanish Crown were concerned. On one such *visita*, about 1774, Padre Silvestre Velez de Escalante counted 7,494 people living in seven pueblos on three separate mesas, the largest of which was Oraibi; and reported that though the Hopis were 'well disposed' their chiefs would not give up their authority, keeping from submission to Spain and the Church not only their own people but the Cosninas (Havasupai) as well. In his enthusiasm for the good work the holy father proposed that a Spanish army be sent to reduce the Hopis, by fire and sword, to a meekness which would make conversion attractive to them.

This was not necessary, for an even more baleful evil than Spanish soldiery shortly made its appearance in Hopi land.

'Viva la viruela!' had shouted Cortés' men when smallpox, brought to Mexico by one of their own number, began to

13

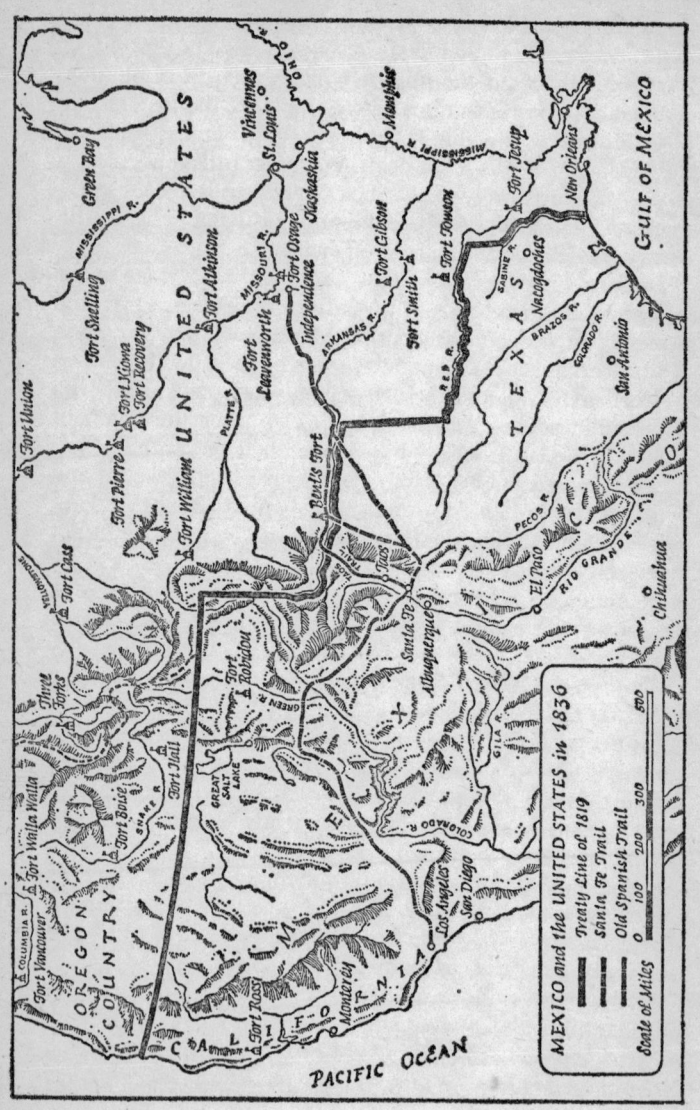

MEXICO and the UNITED STATES in 1836

— — — Treaty Line of 1819
·········· Santa Fe Trail
— ·· — Old Spanish Trail

Scale of Miles
0   100   200   300   500

rage through the valley of Tenochtitlán, leaving the dead by thousands and making Spanish conquest infinitely easier. And *la viruela,* the loathsome disease to which the Spanish tongue gave so beautiful a name, suddenly struck down the Hopi towns where Spanish arms and Spanish priests had proved so ineffective. Through the seven pueblos smallpox swept with dreadful mortality. To the pestilence was added famine. No rain fell in three years and the Apache and Navajo raids never ceased. Where Padre Escalante found 7,494 souls in 1774, there survived only 798 in 1780. And where Hopis once herded 30,000 sheep only 300 remained, while in all seven pueblos were but five horses and not one head of cattle.

Yet when Governor Anza, in that terrible year of 1780, visited the Hopis with a military expedition and offered them a load of provisions to relieve immediate wants, the chief at Oraibi proudly declined the gift on the ground that 'he had nothing to offer in return'. He added that he and his people did not care to hear any preaching by Anza's padres because, since his nation seemed doomed to perish, the few remaining were resolved to die in their own faith. Yet, if any of his people wished to go with the Spaniards and become Christians, he would not hinder them.

Of the 798 Hopis existing so miserably, only thirty families accepted the Spanish food and the Spanish religion. These were taken along by Anza when he withdrew, and were settled near the present Laguna, New Mexico. The Hopis dropped into the limbo of obscurity after that. Yet somehow they managed to survive. And they kept their customs and beliefs, too. Today there are about 2,500 of them, still living on their mesas, the essential pattern and structure of their life changed comparatively little.

Meanwhile, more important events, historically speaking, were taking place toward the east. No sooner had Napoleon secured title to Louisiana (with the solemn promise not to alienate it except back to Spain herself) than he turned about and sold the great territory to the United States. At this time Louisiana included the entire western watershed of the

Mississippi, bounded roughly by the Red River on the south, the Rocky Mountain continental divide on the west, the indefinite Canadian boundary on the north, the Mississippi itself on the east; and including also the 'Island of New Orleans', a strip of land extending east of the Mississippi to the Pearl River, in what is now southern Louisiana.

The young Republic thus acquired at an expenditure of $15,000,000 – which Napoleon needed for his new war with Britain – more than 1,000,000 square miles of territory and 90,000 inhabitants. The historic transaction was completed late in 1803, and President Thomas Jefferson sent William C. C. Claiborne and General James Wilkinson to take over the new territory as governors, Claiborne of the south and Wilkinson of the north division.

So, by a stroke of a pen, almost, the Spanish-Mexican settlers, who had been occupied with Indian difficulties and with bickerings between the Franciscans and Jesuits over jurisdiction, suddenly found themselves cheek by jowl with far bigger trouble on their northwest border.

While Spain held Louisiana, commerce with the American settlers had been forbidden by law. Spanish officials deemed it dangerous to permit a flood of the aggressive, formidable Americans to enter their territory, but it was like trying to turn back a tidal wave. Each year larger numbers of flatboatmen from upriver clamoured for unrestricted commerce in New Orleans, while a smuggling industry of wide proportions sprang up. So great was the irritation created that Kentucky, Tennessee and Illinois frontiersmen made open threats to march in an army and take over New Orleans by force.

With the Louisiana Purchase this long-pent flood was loosed. The sturdy young United States still was unfilled and unformed, and had no idea what its eventual frontiers would be. But down the Mississippi floated the cargo craft of the American settlers – flatboats, arks, broadhorns, even rafts – with crews of boatmen, long-haired, beared, fierce, outlandish and often brutal; frontiersmen accustomed to every danger and hardship, uneducated and uncivilized, yet carrying in them the immense vitality of a new people. And overland came the wagons, with families – a tide which swept over and occupied Louisiana, changing its ways, its tempo of life, the very character of its population.

Land-hungry settlers even began looking over into Texas, and from the very first a cause of quarrel existed – a boundary argument. The United States said that the Sabine River was the boundary of its new acquisition. Spain insisted that the line was along the Arroyo Hondo, a creek half-way between Adaes and Natchitoches – and thus the old 'neutral ground' established by St. Denis and Aguayo back in 1721 became a subject of dispute between the two nations.

But Spanish officials and settlers discovered rapidly that they no longer were dealing with polite French colonials. What they now faced was something more nearly resembling a race of human grizzly bears.

Even before the United States acquired Louisiana the first shadow of the inevitable fell across the Southwest when daring frontiersmen from east of the Mississippi went venturing out on the forbidden Texas plains to see what was there.

There was Philip Nolan, a strange, furtive character, though lacking nothing in courage, who began in 1792 a series of law-defying journeys into Texas. He went ostensibly on horse-hunting expeditions, but he also drew maps and explored uncharted areas, and his real objectives were shrouded in a mystery which has defied time.

It is known, however, that he took council with General James Wilkinson, a very slippery gentleman. During the War of Independence, Wilkinson served in the Revolutionary army, and was a close friend of Benedict Arnold and Aaron Burr. After the war, in 1798, he went west to Kentucky, where he took a secret oath of allegiance to Spain and began to intrigue with the discontented Kentuckians to detach their territory and Tennessee from the United States and join them to Louisiana – and the New Orleans markets. As a Spanish secret agent Wilkinson was known officially as 'Number Thirteen' and for his services he received a Spanish stipend which he continued to collect when, later, he returned to the military service of the United States. Yet even while taking Spanish money he connived against his Spanish friends. Philip Nolan's expeditions almost surely were part of his shadowy plans, which may have schemed as high as a conquest – for his own advantage – of the northern provinces of New Spain.

Thrice Nolan entered Texas, returning each time with horses – and maps and reports based on keen observation. Still he seemed dissatisfied and in 1800, with fourteen American frontiersmen, five Mexicans and a Negro slave, he once more rode out on those forbidden plains, defying the risk of capture and punishment.

This time he pushed his luck too far. Three of his men deserted and returned to American soil. Then, on March 21, 1801, a Spanish force of a hundred and fifty men with a piece of artillery surprised Nolan's party. Nolan and some of his men were killed and wounded, and after a brave fight, during which they defended themselves in an arroyo all day, the survivors surrendered. Nolan's ears were cut from his head 'in order to send them to the governor of Texas', and the prisoners were sent to San Luis Potosí to await trial. Eventually they were tried at Chihuahua, convicted as *filibusteros*, and their final sentence referred to the Spanish Crown.

A long wait. The prisoners had been in custody five years before they learned their fate. The king's sentence was that every fifth man should be hanged. But by that time only nine of the party survived and after due consideration the authorities decided that one life was sufficient to satisfy the royal doom.

One morning a large drum was placed on the ground and the prisoners, blindfolded, were caused to throw dice on the drumhead. He who threw the lowest number would die. The Spanish adjutant-inspector listed those who took part in this lottery as Ellis P. Bean, Lucian García, Jonah Walters, Solomon Cooley, William Danlin, Joseph Reed, Charles King, Ephraim Blackburn and David Fero.

There is a morbid fascination in the numbers these men rolled with the 'devil's bones' in their dreadful gamble with death. In the order they cast – each taking precedence 'according to his age' – here were their throws, as recorded : Blackburn, 3 and 1, making 4; García, 3 and 4, making 7; Reed, 6 and 5, making 11; Fero, 5 and 3, making 8; Cooley, 6 and 5, making 11; Walters, 6 and 1, making 7; King, 4 and 3, making 7; Bean, 4 and 1, making 5; and Danlin, 5 and 2, making 7.

Blackburn, the first and eldest, threw the lowest number. From the beginning he must have known his was a very low cast and one almost suffers with the poor fellow as the others spun the dice and the results were announced – his hopes rising and falling and finally dying when Danlin, the youngest and last, threw a 7.

On the day following, November 11, 1807, Blackburn was hanged 'at the Plaza de los Uranges, in the Villa of Chihuahua'. His comrades were forced to witness his execution.

Of the surviving eight, two escaped to the United States; Cooley was freed and settled at Santa Fe, New Mexico; and Ellis P. Bean, after serving in the Mexican army during the revolution, held several important offices, married a Mexican heiress named Ann Gorthas, and spent his final years in affluence on his wife's large estate near Jalapa. The fates of the other four are not known.

Nolan's full reasons for his expeditions were never publicly explained. But behind him was General Wilkinson. And behind Wilkinson was . . . a network of aims, plans and ambitions, so complicated, secret and often apparently conflicting that they have not been unravelled completely to this day.

Nolan was dead. But Wilkinson turned to Aaron Burr, then in disgrace for killing Alexander Hamilton in a duel, who had a fantastic plan known to history as the 'Burr Conspiracy' to seize the Spanish territories west of the Mississippi and establish there an independent nation. Even while acting as governor of the northern Louisiana Territory,

19

Wilkinson agreed to aid Burr, contrary to his orders and the treaties made by his government.

In 1806 he sent Lieutenant Zebulon M. Pike, who had explored the upper Mississippi, on what amounted to another armed invasion of Spanish territories. Its real object, like Nolan's, was perhaps to survey a favourable route for an armed campaign, but with his usual duplicity Wilkinson couched his orders in terms by which he could clear his own skirts if anyone ever charged him with disloyalty or exceeding his authority.

Pike did his best. Setting out from near St. Louis, July 15, 1806, he reached the Arkansas by October, and sending back part of his expedition, with sixteen men marched up the river and became, with his command, the first Americans to see the great Colorado peak which bears his name. Winter came down, with severe weather, and Pike became entangled among the high mountains, at last being politely captured by a Spanish detachment in New Mexican territory, equally politely deprived of his papers, and sent back to his own country, with all courtesy but with all firmness.

He brought back much information concerning the Spanish territories, but its value for the present had passed. In his absence Wilkinson had betrayed his fellow conspirator, Aaron Burr. Out of the long and important trial of Burr, in which the prisoner at the bar and those charged with him in the end were released 'for lack of sufficient evidence', Wilkinson emerged with a reputation so badly tarnished that he never fully recovered from it.

The next *filibusteros* from the United States were brought in by the Mexicans themselves. Spain at that time had a three-continental empire, of which Texas and New Mexico-Arizona were no more than outposts of one viceroyalty. All through the Spanish provinces in North and South America – and even in European Spain itself – something of the ferment that caused the American and French revolutions was stirring. Administration was loose at the fringes of empire, and even in the capitals corruption had become so universal that a great explosion was building up.

It was brought to a head by the Spanish monarchs themselves. When a popular uprising against the court favourite, Godoy, occurred in Spain in 1807 and Charles IV abdicated, there was a brief period of enthusiasm for his successor, Ferdinand VII, who announced a policy opposing French aggression.

But the Spaniards were dealing now with Napoleon. Ferdinand's reign lasted only from March 19 to April 30, when he was forced to abdicate the throne he had scarcely warmed in favour of his predecessor, Charles IV (at the instance of Marshal Murat, who arrived with part of Napoleon's army), and Charles in turn abdicated May 10, in favour of Napoleon. For this complaisance the two Spanish princes were given estates in France and handsome pensions, and Bonaparte promptly placed upon the Spanish throne his brother Joseph.

Crowning a Frenchman – and a plebian – as king of Spain removed any lingering loyalties the majority of the Mexican people may have had for the mother country, and the inefficiency, venality and arrogance of royal officers appointed from overseas completed the discontent.

'The condition of Mexico at the beginning of the present (nineteenth) century', wrote the historian William Kennedy in the late 1830's, 'was stamped with the repulsive features of an anarchical and semi-barbarous society, of which the elements were – an aboriginal population, satisfied with existing in unmolested indigence; a chaos of parti-coloured casts, equally passive, ignorant, and superstitious; a numerous Creole class, wealthy, mortified, and discontented; and a compact phalanx of European (Spanish) officials – the pampered Mamelukes of the Crown – who contended for and profited by every act of administrative iniquity.'

It was against those officials that the aroused people of Mexico turned their resentment. Napoleon's proclamations were publicly burned, the French emissaries were driven from the country, and Spanish officers who acceded to the new order were deposed and forced to seek refuge from the mobs. Juntas were formed and a plan of revolution adopted.

It was betrayed to José Yturrigaray, the Viceroy, who ordered the leaders arrests. That forced premature action and the revolution began – with a priest at its head.

Padre Miguel Hidalgo y Costilla, *cura* of the small town of Dolores, the population of which was chiefly Indian, had won the esteem of his people by his kindness and his efforts to improve their condition. Around him the rebellious forces rallied and in September 1810 he took the field 'for the defence of religion and the redress of grievances'.

Unfortunately for the good name of his cause, when he saw atrocities committed by royalist troops operating against him, he sought reprisals by turning loose his Indians to wreak all their resentments and natural cruelties on every Spaniard or European who fell into their hands. His 'army' was disorderly and undisciplined and he was promptly defeated, captured and shot. His conqueror, General Calleja, a Spaniard of the most brutal type, eclipsed anything Hidalgo's Indians had done in the ferocity of his massacres in the rebellious towns and districts.

But the avalanche was started. Another priest, Padre José María Morelos y Pavón, stepped into Hidalgo's place as the revolutionary leader. He was defeated by General Agustín de Iturbide, a native-born Spanish-Mexican, in the royal service, who one day would declare himself emperor of Mexico. Betrayed by one of his followers, Ignacio Elizondo, Morelos was captured, degraded from his priestly office by the Inquisition, and, like Hidalgo, shot as a traitor.

Up to this time Texas has not been directly affected by the revolution, although Spanish officials and native peoples alike were deeply interested and excited by the events. But now something happened that was to forecast the future.

Before the defeat of Morelos, Bernardo Gutiérrez de Lara and José Alvarez de Toledo entered the United States to raise a force of Americans to invade Texas on behalf of the revolution. The frontier was filled with men eager to fight, and A. W. Magee, a graduate of West Point and a former lieutenant in the United States Army, had little difficulty in enlisting two hundred riflemen from Kentucky, Louisiana,

Tennessee and Mississippi. He assumed the title of colonel, apointed Samuel Kemper lieutenant-colonel, and marched into Texas with the avowed purpose of 'freeing it from Spanish rule'.

Gutiérrez was the nominal commander – it being policy to give the Mexicans the impression that one of themselves was the leader – but the actual commander was Magee and under him his American subordinates. By the time he neared Natchitoches his hardcore of frontiersmen had been augmented by enlistments from the French, Italian and Spanish populations of Louisiana, and Mexicans from Texas, until he had under him five hundred men.

The 'army' had little organization and no commissary, but it could fight. It now began a career of remarkable activity. At the Sabine River a royalist force appeared, was scattered by the first volley from the frontiersmen, and chased all the way to Nacogdoches, which the Americans occupied August 11, 1812.

From there the invaders marched with unexampled rapidity and audacity on Trinidad – which was evacuated as soon as the first coon-skin caps were sighted – and then toward La Bahía, also called Goliad, which was the key to San Antonio de Béxar.

There they were besieged by Governor Manuel de Salcedo and General Simon de Herrera with fifteen hundred royalist troops. In their first assaults Salcedo's forces had a disheartening taste of the accuracy of the American frontiersmen's rifles, and fell back. Yet the numbers of the enemy and his artillery appeared so overwhelming that Colonel Magee agreed to surrender on condition his men be allowed to return safely to the United States.

These terms, when they were announced, his men promptly and unanimously repudiated, and shortly thereafter Magee was found dead in his tent, apparently by his own hand, since his 'honour' had been besmirched.

Salcedo, perhaps justifiably angered at the failure of his negotiations, ordered a general assault. But the American long rifles began to speak their deadly message and the royalist columns fell back, stunned, with a loss of two hundred men. Salcedo raised the siege and retired.

It was now early March and with confidence vastly increased the filibusters marched toward Béxar – or, as the Americans preferred to call it, San Antonio.

Salcedo, who had been reinforced, attempted to ambush them in the dense chaparral of Salado Creek. What took place, the so-called Battle of Rosillo, is worth looking at, since it set a pattern of combat which would continue – the American rifle's mastery of many fields.

Salcedo's trap was easily discovered by the American scouts, who were accustomed to bush hunting. So the governor brought his army out and arranged it in the open, for better manœuvrability, with his six pieces of artillery in the centre.

When he observed this disposition, Colonel Kemper, who had succeeded Magee in command, assigned Captain Lockett, with a detachment of the finest marksmen in the American ranks, to pick off the artillerymen in the centre. Then, placing Captain Ross in command of the left wing, and taking charge of the right himself, he issued a general order that his men should fire three volleys and then charge.

What followed was a devastatingly bloody demonstration of what accurate rifles could do. Under the withering blaze from Lockett's sharpshooters the royalist artillerymen melted to the ground before they could more than fire their first – and harmless – salvo. Up and down the entire line Salcedo's men were dropping under the relentless marksmanship of the frontiersmen. Suddenly the filibusters charged. The royalists broke and fled. Pursuing, the victors slaughtered them as they ran.

It was a foretaste of San Jacinto. Salcedo's army ceased to exist. Nearly one thousand of his men were killed or wounded, while of the victors only nine were killed and twenty-five wounded. Most of the defeated survivors scattered like rabbits, hid in the chaparral and decamped from the country at night never to be soldiers again if they could help it. Of the two thousand royalists who started the battle only about three hundred fugitives reached San Antonio.

The Americans advanced on San Antonio; and Salcedo and Herrera, with their men, surrendered, on the promise that their lives would be spared. But here appeared a sinister attribute of this sort of Mexican fighting – bad faith. Though they were promised mercy, Gutiérrez had Salcedo, Herrera and some of their men marched out of town to an arroyo of the river half a mile below. The Mexican escort of seventy men did not waste bullets on them. They simply stripped the prisoners, bound them, and cut their throats.

After that horrifying butchery Kemper, Lockett, Ross and many of the better class of Americans abandoned the campaign and returned to Louisiana. Those who remained, with reinforcements which came to them because of their success, defeated Colonel Elizondo, the renegade who had betrayed Morelos; but in turn, badly led by Colonel Toledo, who replaced Gutiérrez in command, were ambushed and almost wiped out by Colonel Arredondo with a royalist army of two thousand men and eleven pieces of artillery, near the Medina River. Only ninety-three of them escaped alive to Natchitoches.

The fight on the Medina ended the revolution in Texas – for a time. Arredondo took possession of San Antonio. Elizondo, the renegade, was given the task of providing a blood bath for the province, to him most congenial. He swept through the country, captured and shot seventy-four men, some on mere suspicion that they favoured the insurgents, and imprisoned a hundred more. Then retribution overtook this treacherous brute. He was shot and fatally wounded by Miguel Serrano, one of his own lieutenants, who lost his reason, it was said, because of the inhumanity of Elizondo's executions.

Royalist troops were once more in control everywhere. Many liberal Mexicans fled to Louisiana, abandoning their lands and homes. Penalties were made stricter and more savage against foreigners who came into Texas without permission. But to hold back the Americans was impossible.

In the succeeding years numerous further efforts were made to gain footholds on Mexican-Texas soil, most singular among which was the piratical colony of Jean Lafitte on Galveston Island. With his brother Pierre, Lafitte long had engaged in smuggling goods up the mouth of the Mississippi to New Orleans, his headquarters being at Grand Terre, a beautiful island in Barataria Bay. From smuggling (winked at by the Creole merchants of New Orleans who profited by it) Lafitte turned to privateering when he found he could obtain letters of marque first from Colombia, then from Venezuela, countries then in revolution and hence at war with Spain.

A very thin line divided the privateer – especially one legalized by such shaky governments – from the outright pirate. Lafitte, however, liked at least a surface semblance of legality and always asserted that his ships captured and looted only Spanish craft.

But it appeared to be difficult for some of his captains – corsairs like Dominique You, Nez Coupé, René Baluche and Gambi – to distinguish between the flag of Spain and those of other nations. Because of their depredations, the Lafittes were declared outlaws; and Pierre, the elder brother was imprisoned in the Cabildo in New Orleans. From this he 'escaped' by virtue of some judicious bribes Jean Lafitte arranged.

At this point the War of 1812 intervened and for a time the Lafittes were submerged in greater events. They refused an offer – with an inducement of $30,000 cash – to aid the British when General Pakenham began his invasion and effort to take New Orleans. Although an American fleet occupied Barataria Bay and Grand Terre, to prevent the British fleet from using the harbour, the Lafittes tendered their services and those of their men to General Andrew Jackson, who commanded the United States forces. The latter, desperately trying to gather his defences, accepted the Baratarians; and their piratical artillery played a conspicuous part in the defeat of Pakenham and his British army at the Battle of New Orleans.

Jean Lafitte and his men were given full pardons as a reward for their services. He attended the victory ball after the battle, and found himself a popular figure. Always dashing in appearance and making friends easily among influential people of the city, he might have become a respected citizen of New Orleans had he chosen.

But a career of peace was not in his nature. Enjoined from using American bases for his attacks on Spain, since the United States was at peace with that nation, he and his followers moved down to the coast of Texas and occupied Galveston Island, from which they continued to scourge Spanish shipping, smuggling their captured goods and slaves into Louisiana. During this period Lafitte was visited by two Louisianans who bought slaves from him and illegally took them across the border into the United States to sell them – a violation of the laws so common that it was hardly condemned. They were brothers, Rezin and James Bowie. Of the latter Texas was to hear very much in the future.

Once again the shadow of General Wilkinson fell across Texas. Dr. James Long, who had married Wilkinson's niece and was firmly attached to that worthy's fortunes and schemes, organized in 1819 an 'army of liberation' to invade the province. With three hundred men – among them young Jim Bowie – he occupied Nacogdoches and in a bombastic manifesto proclaimed a 'republic', complete with a constitution, a system of laws, and himself as president and commander-in-chief. Shortly after, he visited Lafitte on Galveston Island and tried to enlist his aid; but the pirate, while royally entertaining him, thought the project too shaky and gave no help.

Spain lodged a sharp diplomatic protest with the United States and sent an army under Colonel Ignacio Pérez against the filibusters. The 'republicans' at the time were scattered, and far too happily employed enjoying themselves with the wine and women of the country to do much fighting. In separate contingents Pérez defeated them, killed Long's brother David, and drove them across the Sabine.

The defeat, however, did not discourage the 'president and

27

commander-in-chief'. He gathered another 'army' and invaded Texas again; and this was in 1821, after Mexico obtained independence from Spain, which removed the thin pretence of 'liberating' the Mexican people and made it an outright territorial raid. The rash Dr. Long 'captured' Goliad, but promptly was himself captured by his old adversary Pérez – now commanding for the Mexican government – and sent to the City of Mexico. There, though he was not confined, he made himself continuously troublesome and finally was shot by a sentry while trying for some reason, to force his away against orders into the barracks of Los Gallos.

Long's death put a final period to Wilkinson's machinations. Discredited and disgraced, the scheming general died in the City of Mexico December 28, 1825.

The end came also for Lafitte. He had gathered on his island a populous settlement of choice rogues, who, including their women, with whom they lived without benefit of clergy, and the children of these extremely irregular unions, numbered more than a thousand. On the island he had erected a fortified house called the Maison Rouge, and there was a good harbour for his piratical ships. Prosperity was enjoyed by the 'colony', and its chief lived in barbaric splendour that impressed visitors to his fortress-palace.

But nature and the old inability of his captains to distinguish between national flags worked against him. A hurricane swept the island destroying most of its piratical shacks and killing many of the people. Lafitte's mistress, a quadroon girl of considerable beauty named Catherine Villars, received injuries from which she never fully recovered.

To cap this, Lafitte's captains made the mistake of robbing American vessels. One day the brig-of-war *Enterprise*, Captain Kearny, anchored off the island and swung its guns on the settlement. Kearny, with some of his officers went ashore and held a conference with the pirate chief. Lafitte was beginning to age, and was no longer the dashing figure of old. A young officer with Kearny left his word picture of him :

'My description of this renowned chieftain . . . will shock

28

. . . many who have hitherto pictured him as the hero of a novel or melodrama. I am compelled by truth to introduce him as a stout, rather gentlemanly personage, some five feet ten inches in height, dressed very simply in a foraging cap and blue frock coat of a most villainous fit; his complexion, like most Creoles, olive; his countenance full, mild, and rather impressive, but for a small black eye, which now and then, as he grew animated in conversation, would flash in a way which impressed me with a notion that *Il Capitano* might be when roused, a very ugly customer.'

Kearny notified him that he must get off the island and cease his piratical activities. Lafitte might have defied one ship like the *Enterprise*, but he knew now that the full power of the United States Navy was arrayed against him. When the brig-of-war sailed away, he one day, early in 1821, destroyed all the buildings of the settlement by fire, disbanded his men, and sailed away with his ailing mistress and a special crew on his favourite vessel, the *Pride*. Five years later he died in Yucatán and was buried there.

CHAPTER TWO

New Spain Becomes Mexico

SPAIN had repelled every encroachment by peoples other than her own, and Texas, after two centuries, was virtually empty. A few missions and *presidios* had been established but it seemed impossible to colonize the great province.

Chief reason for this was the Indian problem. Of all the wild and warlike tribes in New Spain, the most numerous and fiercest roamed the immense expanses of Texas, where the cannibal Karankawas, the swooping Comanches, the ever treacherous Caddos, Wacos and Tawakonis, and the Apaches of endless bloody guile, created a peril so continuous that Mexicans and Spaniards alike shunned the area.

Even the first Spanish *conquistadores*, who feared nothing, failed to bring the country into submission. Save for such strongholds as Nacogdoches, Goliad and San Antonio, most of the missions and *presidios* by 1820 had been destroyed, their very locations sometimes forgotten.

It now occurred to the Spanish administrators that there might be merit in changing a policy of centuries. In 1819, therefore, after the 'Treaty of Amity', whereby, in exchange for the cession of Florida, the United States confirmed Spain in her possession of Texas, the restrictions against Americans and other non-Spaniards entered the province as colonists were removed.

It appeared safe enough to do so : the revolution seemed ended and royalist power strongly established. Development of Texas lands by the industry of American colonists would bring welcome revenue in taxes to the Crown. Furthermore the officials of New Spain considered that in the Americans, self-reliant and formidable, they might have a solution to the Indian problem. Let Americans form a buffer for the rest of New Spain.

The danger in which they were placed must have occurred to the Americans, but that land hunger which always has characterized the Anglo-Saxon race made them willing to undertake any risk and they were not slow in taking advantage of the new dispensation.

First to apply for a tract of land, on which he agreed to introduce three hundred families as colonists, was Moses Austin, a native of Connecticut, who made a fortune producing lead from mines in Missouri, then lost it when the Bank of St. Louis, in which he was a large stockholder, failed in 1818. With his remaining resources, Austin sought opportunity in Texas and, travelling to San Antonio in 1820, offered his petition. His journey back to Louisiana was one of great hardship, and shortly after Missouri he died, June 10, 1821, probably of pneumonia resulting from exposure.

Moses Austin did not live to learn that his petition had been granted, the news arriving a few days after his death. But anticipating success, he had charged his son, Stephen

Austin, to carry out the venture. The latter did so in the troublous years that followed, to the best of his abilities and strength.

Between the time the father visited Texas and the son took over the colonizing enterprise, however, a startling change took place. Without warning the supposedly quiescent revolution broke out again in New Spain. Under Vicente Guerrero, who had been a lieutenant of Morelos, the insurgent Mexicans won victory after victory over royalist forces.

General Iturbide, who had put down the Morelos revolt, was sent with the principle royalist army against Guerrero. He found his antagonist superior to him and, after losing several skirmishes, resorted to treason. Making a secret compact with Guerrero, he transferred himself and his army to the revolutionary cause, and the two of them issued the so-called 'Plan of Iguala', which declared Mexico independent of Spain, but accepted a Bourbon prince as a ruler, proclaimed the pre-eminence of the Roman Catholic Church, and 'social and racial equality'. The agreement was signed in February, 1821, just a month after Moses Austin had started his return journey from San Antonio, about the time Lafitte was destroying and abandoning his settlement on Galveston Island, and some time before Long's second expedition of 'liberation'.

With his army and general gone over to the other side, Viceroy O'Donojú, by the Treaty of Cordova, recognized the independence of the nation. In this treaty, incidentally, the country was given the official name *Mexico*, for the first time in history.

Spain's power was ended, but no Bourbon prince could be found who was willing to accept the 'throne' of Mexico. In this impasse Iturbide, who may have been working toward this end the whole time, had himself proclaimed emperor in May, 1822. The 'empire' lasted less than a year. In March, 1823, Iturbide was forced to abdicate by a new revolution launched by a figure destined to loom large in Mexican history – General Antonio López de Santa Anna. It was the beginning of a long succession of revolutions, counter-

31

revolutions, massacres and bloodshed through which Mexico and Texas were to pass.

A look into the future: This Santa Anna, who would manage to lose for Mexico slightly more than half her territory – the states of Texas, New Mexico, Arizona, Nevada and California contain 765,540 square miles, while Mexico today contains 760,372 square miles – was to be the only one of the early Mexican leaders of note who escaped being shot. Iturbide was exiled to Europe, but when he returned to Mexico he was convicted as a traitor and shot. Hidalgo, Morelos, Leonardo and Nicolás Bravo, Matamoros, Mina, Guerrero, Victoria, Mexia, Pedraza, Santamanet, Herrera and Paredes – all, sooner or later, faced firing squads in the turmoil that overwhelmed the country until the rise of Benito Juárez, who himself executed Maximilian, the emperor installed by Napoleon III during the American Civil War. But Santa Anna, perfidious, vain, bloodthirsty and so selfish that he did not hesitate to sell out his country to save his own pusillanimous hide, lived out his life and died in bed.

So Mexico was free – at least from the bonds of Spain. It meant vast and sweeping changes in administration and politics. Stephen Austin, confronted by radical alterations in government, whereby his father's grant from Spanish authorities became ineffective, nevertheless undertook with the stubborn courage which was his great characteristic to carry on the task assigned to him.

The senior Austin's proposal was the foundation of what became known as the Empresario System – the word *empresario* meaning contractor. Under it, heads of colonizing families were to receive 640 acres of land, with 320 acres additional for their wives, 100 acres apiece for each child, and 80 acres for each slave. A premium thus was placed on procreation and slaveholding.

The Spanish government specified that all colonists must be Catholics, or become Catholics before entering Spanish territory; that they must show credentials of good character;

and that they must take the oath of allegiance to the king of Spain.

Already, by December, 1821, when Mexico was still trying to induce a Bourbon prince to come and rule her, some colonists had been gathered by Stephen Austin and were settling on land along the Brazos River, which though dangerous Indian country was fertile and productive. But it was necessary to induce the new government of Mexico to validate their claims, so Austin decided to go to the City of Mexico.

In a journey of extreme difficulty and danger – Mexico was chaotic and murder and robbery common episodes of every day – disguised in ragged clothes and a blanket, he finally reached the capital in April, 1882. There he spent a year – twelve months of patient negotiation, frustrated again and again, until after the abdication of Iturbide he at last saw his grant confirmed by the Mexican Congress.

He even gained some extra concessions. The decree, dated February 18, 1823, increased land grants to the colonists. To the head of each family was granted one *sitio*, or square league, of grazing land, and one *labor* of tillage land, in all adding up to 4,605 American acres. Unmarried men received one fourth of a *sitio*. The new arrangements encouraged matrimony, without putting any particular stress on big families.

At the same time *empresarios* were given various authorities, including the civil government of their colonies, the administration of justice and the command of militia, with the rank of lieutenant-colonel. They could make war on Indian tribes which molested them, and import supplies free of duty through Galveston Harbour. Compulsory Catholicism, evidence of good character and an oath of allegiance were required as before.

From the first the Austin colony in Texas was a success. Other *empresarios* flocked in, among them Robert Leftwich, Hayden Edwards, Green De Witt, Ben Milam, James Powers and David G. Burnet, most of whom were prominent in later Texas annals. By 1835 the map of Texas was virtually covered by grants, some of which were never carried into effect, while others merged with stronger concessions. But the colony in the Brazos Valley remained chief; and its leader, Stephen Austin, was recognized as the head and spokesman of the American settlers, who came in such numbers that, whereas in 1821 the population of Texas, exclusive of Indians, did not exceed 3,500, by 1830 it was almost 20,000.

The newcomers accepted unhesitatingly the role of facing the hostile Indians which was thrust upon them. In the spring of 1823 the Karankawas attacked the settlements in the lower Colorado Valley, killing two men and wounding two others. The colonists responded with a celerity and deadliness that must have astonished the aborigines. With a party of determined men Robert Kuykendall pursued the hostiles, surprised them on Skull Creek, killed nineteen of them, and destroyed their encampment.

It was an augury of unpleasant things to come for the Indians, yet the Karankawas continued their depredations until in a few bitter campaigns, some of which were led by Austin himself, they were almost exterminated and driven into Mexico, where they since seem to have disappeared entirely.

Other Indians, notably the Wacos and Tawakonis, were troublesome, for the lands surveyed and appropriated were their hunting grounds. To attempt to recite the small raids, ambuscades, skirmishes, pursuits and battles of this frontier war would be impossible, but one action deserves mention, because it forms one of the most mysterious and at the same time thrilling episodes in all frontier history.

Mention has been made of Miranda's discovery of silver in the San Saba country in 1756, and the *presidio* and mission established there. Following the destruction of the mission in 1758 by the Comanches, the *presidio* was abandoned also and for sixty years the silver workings reported on the San Saba lay idle, their very location forgotten.

About 1828 a remarkable adventurer arrived in Texas to become a permanent resident – big Jim Bowie, six feet two inches tall, weighing two hundred pounds, all hard muscle, bone and gristle, and active as a cat; a man with reactions so instantaneous that they made him the most celebrated duellist this country ever knew, and with the deadliest of all close-combat weapons – the knife.

Bowie was a rimrock American of his day, cut from the same piece of granite as Andy Jackson, Sam Houston and Davy Crockett. It was said of him that he respected nobody but the ladies, and feared nothing but running out of drinking liquor. Yet he was no drunkard, for though he drank like all men of his time, his exploits were those of a superbly trained athlete. He never lied. He loved to make money; but it was the making of it, and not the money itself, that was the prime attraction. And he loved danger better than money-making.

Legends persist of him in every part of the land where he ever passed. He was born on the frontier about 1799, roped and rode huge alligators in the bayous of Louisiana, and made dangerous cruises to deal with the pirate, Jean Lafitte, in his buccaneer's roost on Galveston Island. He was with Long's first filibustering expedition, but not the second. He speculated largely in land deals and made a fortune.

During this time he gained the reputation of being the most terrible duellist in American history. His favourite weapon was the bowie knife, a fighting blade with a cross hilt and remarkably tempered steel, to which he gave his name. That he invented the knife has been disputed – no fewer than thirteen persons have claimed the honour. But it is notable that none of these claims was advanced until after Jim Bowie was dead and could not refute them. By the best evidence, he got the idea from an ordinary butcher knife his brother Rezin gave him, which was equipped with a brass cross guard. Working from that, he devised the fighting weapon which later was forged for him by James Black, an Arkansas blacksmith, and became the archetype for the most universal and deadly weapon of the frontier until it was supplanted by the nimble six-shooter.

Numerous duels were fought by Bowie, all under ferocious

circumstances. Once he was locked with his antagonist in a pitch-dark room, he with a knife, the other with a sword, to feel for each other's lives in the blackness. He killed his enemy. On another occasion he fought a Spaniard with knives, the two of them seated on a log, their leather breeches nailed to it. Again he killed. Bloody Jack Sturdevant, chief of the Hole-in-Rock outlaws of the Ohio River, met him in a ten-foot chalked circle, their left wrists strapped together. Bowie crippled the outlaw's weapon arm for life. In the Vidalia sand bar duel, one of the most celebrated in history, he wounded two men and killed Major Norris Wright, after the latter had stabbed him with a sword-cane when he was down with a pistol wound. Three assassins, sent to murder him by Sturdevant, waylaid him at night on a lonely wilderness road. He slew all three with his terrible knife. On another occasion he varied his fighting method by using pistols in a duel in which he killed a crooked steamboat gambler he had exposed. There were other episodes, some legendary, some attested, but contemporaries agreed that Bowie was never a bully and fought only when challenged. When he did fight, however, he was apt to stipulate conditions of combat so grim that the next man might hesitate to seek trouble with him.

John Myers Myers, writing in *The Alamo*, said, 'Most dangerous men are apt to be either men of no control or men of limited emotions; men who are passionate lechers or drinkers, or men possessed of abnormal asceticism. Bowie atonishes investigation by his soundness. He was self-controlled but warm-hearted; he drank but he had other things to do; he got along with the women but he was no skirt chaser.'

When he arrived in Texas Bowie already was a man of considerable property. Yet when he heard stories of the lost San Saba mine his old craving for adventure took possession of him. Making friends with the Lipan Apaches, he lived with them as a hunter and warrior for months, and eventually was shown, according to his own statement, the hidden workings, which he entered, appraised, and found very rich.

Returning to San Antonio, he made his plans, and on November 2, 1831, set out with ten other men, including his brother Rezin and Cephas Ham, an old Indian fighter. By November 19 they were within two days' travel of their destination, when Bowie was warned by friendly Indians that a large party of hostile warriors was on their trail. The night of the twentieth they camped in a grove of live oaks on a point of land made by the sharp bend of a creek. The neck of the little peninsula was heavily grown with thick chaparral brush and in this they took the precaution of cutting passages, with an open space in the centre.

Next morning as they started the last day's ride, which would take them to the San Saba mine, the exact location of which only Jim Bowie knew, the Indian war party which had been trailing them appeared – 164 hostile savages, Caddos, Wacos, Tawakonis and probably Lipans, since Bowie's old friends had turned against him.

David Buchanan, who could speak the Caddo tongue, advanced with Rezin Bowie towards the Indians, to parley. But the savages fired, wounding him in the leg. Replying with his double-barrelled rifle, Rezin Bowie took Buchanan on his back and bravely began carrying him back to camp.

Yelling, the hostiles pursued, intending to spear the two men; but Jim Bowie, with Cephas Ham and some others ran out to meet them, and with accurate fire killed four, whereupon the others fell back.

A battle to the death was now certain. Protecting themselves as well as they could behind the trunks of the live oaks on their little peninsula, the Texans fought off the Indians until some of the savages crept behind and opened a raking fire on them from the rear. One man was killed and another wounded before Bowie could get what was left of his party into the chaparral thicket, where they could move about in concealment through the passages they had cut.

From this screened defence, under the keen leadership of Bowie, the handful of white men repelled charge after charge throughout that day. Twice the Indians tried to burn them out by setting fire to the prairie. The second time flames got into the brush which concealed the defenders, so that they had to beat it out with their coats and what little water was left in their canteens.

But by evening the Indians had had enough of the deadly Texas rifles. They withdrew, taking their dead. In the day's furious fight, by their own account, they lost fifty killed and thirty-five wounded. Of the Texans, one was dead and three wounded.

Taken all around, this is possibly the most brilliant fight against heavy odds in the history of the West. In the battle the Texans were armed only with muzzle-loading rifles; whereas in some other notable fights against great odds, such as Forsyth's victory over the Cheyennes at the Arickaree, and the Wagon Box defeat of the Sioux, the white men used repeating, breech-loading Spencer carbines and six-shooters.

Because most of their horses were killed and their wounded men needed medical care, Bowie's party was unable to continue on to the mine after the battle. Instead they returned to San Antonio. No second attempt was ever made to reach the San Saba, and the secret of the location of the mine died with Jim Bowie when he was killed at the Alamo. J. Frank Dobie, in *Coronado's Children*, has recorded the many efforts since made to locate it. People still believe it is there, somewhere in the vicinity of the present town of Menard. But if there was a mine shaft, it was filled in – persumably by the Indians – and so overgrown with brush tha nobody has even been able to find it again.

After the San Saba fight the Waco-Caddo-Tawakoni confederacy never again was a serious menace, and the Texas settlements were thereby relieved of one peril.

CHAPTER THREE

Mexican Autocrats and Texas Fire-eaters

THE character of the Texas settlers was by no means uniform. Among them were insolvent debtors, adventurers, soldiers of fortune, even fugitives from justice. It was during this period that 'G.T.T.' – 'Gone to Texas' – became a byword in the United States when a defalcator with his bank's funds in his carpetbag disappeared overnight, or someone made a hasty exit from a community when the law began to smell too closely at his heels on a suspicion of horse larceny, highway robbery or murder.

The overwhelming majority of settlers, of course, were honest, capable, hard-working and law-abiding (within limits). They were the builders of Texas, the solid community which, in spite of an infinity of different modes of thought, personalities and ways, managed to cleave together and in the end create out of the wilderness a land in which their descendants take a pride almost inordinate. Illustrative of the divergencies among Texans at this time, two men, at opposite poles in policy and motive furnish an interesting comparison.

Stephen Austin, head of the Brazos colony, was a composition of contrasts. A slender man of moderate height, he had a face suggesting thought rather than action and a temperament somewhat in keeping with that appearance. His forehead, slightly balding, was too high; his eyes were too wide, almost femininely so; his nose was too long, taking away from his small mouth and making his chin appear weak by comparison.

He had accepted the responsibility of the Texas colony when he was only twenty-seven years old, and he bore that responsibility like a burden. His habits were abstemious, he cared neither for the humour nor for the rough talk of the frontiersmen, and kept much to himself when it was possible to do so. He never married, living in the home of his sister and her husband, James F. Perry.

In the Indian wars of the early colony he proved his courage as also in the journeys of hardship and danger he made to the City of Mexico on behalf of his colonists. But when called upon to command the forces of Texas later, his unhappy irresolution and overcaution showed he was not by temperament a soldier.

He was charged with being overfond of debates, oratory, rostrums, gavels and rules of order. Yet this was a manifestation of his desire to be in all things fair and just.

Of himself he once wrote, 'My temper is naturally hasty and impetuous; the welfare of the settlement required that I should control it effectually, for one in my situation, falling suddenly into a fit of passion might do hurt to the interests of hundreds. My disposition is by nature, also, open, unsuspecting, confiding and accommodating almost to a fault. I have been, therefore, subject in a peculiar manner to imposition. Experience has enlightened me as to this latter deficiency, I fear, almost too late, for I am apprehensive of having fallen somewhat into the opposite extreme.'

Austin took in all sincerity the oath of allegiance to the Mexican government, and strove honestly and earnestly to live as a loyal citizen of his adopted country. Constantly confronted, on a frontier between two clashing civilizations, with the necessity of restraining his over-zealous compatriots, he received much abuse. But his selflessness, which was heroic, enabled him to accept persecution with all patience and forgive his detractors. Though a conservative in the affairs of Texas, his sole interests were those of his people, and even when he was repudiated by them he accepted their rebuffs and faithfully tried to carry out the subordinate duties they assigned to him.

If Austin was at one extreme of the Texas body-politic in his conservatism, the opposite extreme was William Barret Travis, a sandy-haired lawyer with a blazing blue-grey eye, who arrived in Texas sometime in 1831. He was a gentleman, obviously of the type produced by the Deep South, given to rhetoric, with a touchy sense of honour, and if need be, a subscriber to the *code duello*. He also was possessed of more than his share of courage, and more than his share of willingness to promote and participate in any excitement that would enliven the dull routine of life.

His early history was shrouded in some mystery. One version was that his real name was William Barr, not Barret, and that he was a foundling, the name (with defective spelling) being conferred on him when he was discovered, one morning in 1809, as an infant, tied to a bar of a gate on the farm of a man named Travis – who adopted him – near Saluda, South Carolina. This yarn has been denied by persons who said variously that he was born in Alabama and North Carolina.

Whatever the truth about his origin, he was a rebel by nature from his childhood. He attended school in a South Carolina academy, which he left – at the urgent request of the faculty – for fomenting a student riot against what he considered 'tyrannical rules'.

In the 1820's he appeared in Alabama, read law, was admitted to the bar, and practised successfully in the somewhat rough and ready courts of the period. He married and was the father of a son and daughter; but in 1831, believing that 'he had reasons to suspect her of unfaithfulness', he left his wife – who retained custody of their daughter and his entire bank account – and with his son went to Texas, penniless, to begin life over again. Mrs. Travis obtained a divorce and promptly remarried, but Travis never again attempted the rocky path of matrimony.

By 1831 the entry of Americans into Texas had been made illegal by Mexico. Travis refused to take the ban seriously, coolly took up headquarters in Anahuac, and began there to practice the very law he was violating. A born intransigent with high-flown notions, an eloquent tongue and a flair for leadership, he was as if bound by destiny to become a focal figure in the troubles about to take place in Texas.

41

Already, when he arrived, there was much discontent evident in the colony, and that discontent was hastened and increased by events. Left without any support, military or otherwise, to shift for themselves on the frontier, the American colonists found it difficult to work up any great enthusiasm for the Mexican government. For one thing, changes occurred so frequently and unpredictably in the palace of Chapultepec that it was hard to keep track of them.

So the Texans kept their own modes, language and traditions, and refused to absorb Mexican customs and habits, and remained in all essentials Americans. Their towns were laid out on the American plan; their systems of local government were American, although they used Mexican names – *alcalde* for mayor, *ayuntamiento* for town council, and so on. Their notions of justice and freedom were American. Farming and business methods were American, and more successful than those of the natives. The bustling, aggressive spirit was American . . . that universal Mexican habit, the *siesta*, was never adopted by the colonists, they had no time for it.

Mexico had, in 1824, adopted a constitution which has been called 'the most complex form of government ever devised by man'. Though it was better than nothing, and reflected only Mexico's lack of training in self-government after three centuries of subjugation to Spain, the constitution was a constant irritant to many Texans, who in particular resented the denial of trial by jury and absence of religious freedom.

Nevertheless, the time would come when Texas-Americans would pour out their blood in copious quantities for that poor, limping, imperfect constitution, when it became the symbol of freedom in the unhappy land.

As early as 1826 an abortive effort was made to set up an independent state by Hayden Edwards, an *empresario* whose licence had been cancelled. Some colonists were willing to help him and he gained the support of the Cherokee Indians who lived in the Red River Valley, through their chief, The Bowl, and John Dunn Hunter, a white man who had been taken by them as a child, grown up among them, and gained great influence over them.

The 'Republic of Fredonia' was proclaimed in east Texas, but it was extremely short-lived. Ellis P. Bean – he of the Nolan expedition – was in Nacogdoches as Indian agent for the Mexican government. He persuaded the Cherokees that Edwards' cause was already lost before it started, and The Bowl and his warriors withdrew, murdering Hunter and his aide, a half-breed named Richard Fields, to show their good faith and repentance.

At this juncture a Mexican force of three hundred men under Colonel Matio Ahumada appeared, the 'revolutionists' were demoralized by the sight of all those uniforms, Edwards skipped over the border, and the so-called Fredonian War collapsed after a single skirmish.

Brief as it was, the disturbance set some men to thinking. What would happen if *all* Texas should decide to break away from Mexico? It became a subject of considerable speculation and to some, particularly the politically-minded, it presented some highly advantageous prospects.

Throughout the Fredonian trouble Stephen Austin and other American *empresarios* maintained strict loyalty to the Mexican government. Austin even arrested one of Edwards' emissaries who came to the Brazos colony seeking recruits. It was, of course, only good business policy to thus underline fealty toward a government under which the *empresarios* all held their contracts.

In spite of this, however, Mexican officials became increasingly suspicious of American settlers. And perhaps not without reason, for the United States at this time began to behave in a somewhat alarming manner.

General Andrew Jackson was elected President in 1828. The old war horse was a confirmed and avowed expansionist, whose illegal military activities in Florida had been condemned in Washington, but ended in the cession of that territory to the United States by Spain. Now, many Mexicans believed, his eye was on another former Spanish province, Texas – perhaps even the whole of Mexico! Their apprehen-

43

sion was strengthened when Old Hickory gave his forthright support to the theory that under the terms of the Louisiana Purchase the United States was entitled to all lands as far as the Rio Grande. And this apprehension coloured their attitude when the President instituted negotiations for the purchase of Texas, authorizing Ambassador Poinsett to 'go as high as five millions' for the province.

Mexico had no desire to sell and was offended by the offer. At just about this time, in 1829, owing to a revolution engineered by Santa Anna, General Anastasio Bustamente became *presidente*. One of his first acts was to issue a decree aimed directly at the American colonists in Texas. At a single stroke it prohibited further entry of Americans into Mexican territory, suspended *empresario* contracts, stopped further introduction of negro slaves (without mentioning Mexico's parallel peon system), placed heavy duties on imported goods, and laid down other rigorous restrictions on the colony.

As if he anticipated that his decree would meet opposition, Bustamente simultaneously began to strengthen Mexican garrisons in Texas, placed new commanders at many posts, and gave them authority to supersede civil with martial law. At Nacogdoches, San Antonio, Goliad, Anahuac, Galveston, Velasco, Victoria and other posts, about thirteen hundred Mexican soldiers were distributed.

The new troops were of the worst description. Finding that it could not keep up an army on volunteer enlistments, the Mexican government had adopted the policy of filling its ranks with convicts from its prisons. Since not even by this method of putting uniforms on criminals could enough men be secured for regiments, *ayuntamientos* (village councils) were instructed, 'with the assistance of armed force, to proceed to make levies; vagabonds and disorderly persons shall be taken in preference for military service; recruits may be obtained by entrapment and decoy'.

Such villainous soldiers, further brutalized by the harsh and often cruel methods of 'discipline' to which it was deemed necessary by their officers to subject them, had hitherto been quartered in the subservient villages and cities

44

of Mexico. There they had things very much their own way and learned such arrogance, viciousness and light-fingered activity that, when they were transferred to garrisons in a free-minded province like Texas, trouble was inevitable.

It came to a head in May, 1832. And, oddly enough, it was not a native Mexican whose oppressions brought on the conflict, but an American – a Kentuckian by birth – Colonel Davis Bradburn, a soldier of fortune then serving as an officer in the Mexican army. A hard, self-important man, Bradburn believed he knew how to handle insubordination and he seemed to hold some sort of a grudge against the people of the land of his own birth. From the beginning, when he was placed in command at Anahuac, he was offensive, sneering and dictatorial toward the settlers.

Those who complained of his numerous injustices, which included dispossessing some persons of their land and property on various pretexts, found themselves nursing their wrongs behind the bars of Bradburn's specially built prison. He refused any redress for thefts, robberies and other crimes committed by his rascally troops. On the other hand, to stop smuggling – which since Bustamente's decree had vastly increased – he closed all the ports of Galveston Bay, except Anahuac, where no vessel of more than six feet draft could enter, and where he could personally inspect every cargo that came in or went out. This caused such protest that on the orders of his superior, General Mier y Teran, Bradburn reluctantly allowed the port of Brazoria to remain open.

Late in May a woman, unnamed but presumably American, was seized one night, dragged to a vacant house on the outskirts of Anahuac, and brutally raped by five of the criminal soldiers of the *presidio*. A worthless and depraved Texan witnessed the outrage, and either participated in it or at least made no effort to prevent it.

When the victim's story became known, Texans, who held the virtue of their own women in high esteem, quickly gathered in an angry mob. The Mexican soldiers had escaped to their barracks, but the Texan who had been present was seized. Because there was some doubt as to his actual participation in the ravishment, lynching was decided against in favour of that ancient and accepted rite – tar and feathers. The prisoner was stripped naked. In a cauldron tar was heated to a fluid (and scalding) state, smeared over the naked body of the wretch, and feathers dumped over him which, adhering to the tar, caused him to assume the ludicrous appearance of some obscene and disgraceful fowl. Then he was told to get out of town.

At this point a detachment of Bradburn's soldiers appeared, fired several shots, and arrested some of the leading spirits of the crowd. As might be expected, one of those leading spirits was William Barret Travis, who in a few months had become a conspicuous resident of Anahuac. The prisoners were locked in Bradburn's jail, and when citizens demanded their release the colonel sneeringly refused.

Anahuac was thoroughly aroused and angry. Texans transplanted from the bayous of Louisiana and the forests of Tennessee and Kentucky, always had a long rifle handy, over the door or mantel or leaning in a corner. Down came the guns from the racks, and Texans swarmed angrily toward the *presidio*, capturing a squad of Mexican cavalry on the way.

In the streets a few tentative shots were fired. Before anyone was hurt, however, Bradburn called a parley and agreed to surrender his prisoners in exchange for the Mexicans held by the Texans, on condition the Texans withdrew six miles out of town. The prisoners held by the Texans were released in good faith, but no sooner did Bradburn have his men than he opened fire and drove the settlers out of Anahuac, still keeping Travis and the other captives under lock and key in his jail.

It was now war between Anahuac and Bradburn. The colonists, however, were Americans, and to Americans of that day no tenet was more cherished than the belief that the proprieties should be maintained : which meant that before the shooting began a meeting must be held, proper officers elected, and a set of resolutions drawn up and passed.

The resolutions adopted in this instance were interesting

46

in one respect. The name of Santa Anna bulked large in them. And to explain this a short discussion is necessary.

Bewildering changes in government had taken place in Mexico. Since 1822, when Juan O'Donojú, the last Spanish viceroy, left the country, the following successions had occurred : Augustín de Iturbide, emperor, 1822; Guadalupe Victoria, president, 1824; Gómez Pedraza, president, 1828; Vincente Guerrero, president, 1828; Anastasio Bustamente, president, 1829. During this time an almost continual turmoil of revolts and counter-revolts went on in interior Mexico, so that one never knew, quite, from night to morning, who would be head of the government.

It might have been noticed that there was a certain bug under the chip in most of these revolutions, *coups d'état* and blood purges. The name of that insect was Antonio de Santa Anna. He fomented almost every revolt, made and unmade presidents, and gradually was working toward his own great ambition, which was to be dictator, with unquestioned and absolute authority over Mexico and perhaps – who could tell? – vast regions beyond Mexico, if fortune smiled on him.

The most recent series of manipulations by Santa Anna's dexterous political hand had included the following : Under the constitution of 1824, Pedraza was elected president in 1828. But Guerrero, who was defeated in the election, began a revolution – his chief general being Santa Anna, who had previously overturned Iturbide.

Santa Anna was defeated by Pedraza's troops, but the dogged half-Indian Guerrero fought and captured the capital. Pedraza, the lawfully elected president, fled into exile and Santa Anna, who had been hiding in mountainous Oaxaca, came out from his refuge.

His reputation was tarnished, but shortly after this he regained his popularity by defeating at Tampico a weak Spanish force which made an abortive effort to resubjugate Mexico. Santa Anna returned to the capital a conquering hero and almost at once turned against Guerrero, forced him to evacuate his office late in 1829, and assisted Bustamente to become president January 1, 1830.

Bustamente was a usurper. He seized the presidency from Guerrero, whom he captured and shot. But Guerrero was a usurper also, having seized the government from Pedraza. After two troubled years, resentments against the Bustamente administration culminated in a tardy realization that Pedraza was, after all, the lawful president. In the summer of 1832 revolutionary forces sprang into being in Vera Cruz, Zacatecas, Jalisco, Durango and elsewhere, declaring for 'legitimacy'. And who suddenly appeared as leader of the revolt against Bustamente? The slippery Santa Anna, who had himself helped drive into exile this very Pedraza.

The Texans could hardly be expected to understand these kaleidoscopic changes. Mexican politics were too volatile. Yet, out of the turmoil, Santa Anna somehow managed to appear to the settlers as a champion of democracy. So, at Anahuac, the resolutions duly moved, seconded and passed by the Texans 'adopted' Santa Anna's 'cause'.

Having adjourned, they went into action and the action flamed all around Galveston Bay. It even involved a 'navy' – consisting of a single schooner, the *Brazoria*, commandeered at the town of that name by John Austin, who incidentally was no relation to the *empresario*.

Austin was a man of action. He mounted a single cannon on the deck of the little ship and provided it with 'bulwarks' of cotton bales. Then he sent it sailing down the Brazos River to Velasco, which lay above the mouth of the stream, while with 112 men, all experts with the rifle, he marched overland for the same destination.

Velasco was garrisoned by one hundred and twenty-five Mexican soldiers commanded by Colonel Ugartechea. The latter, a good officer and loyal to his country, rejected Austin's demand that he surrender.

Thereupon a curious battle began. Placing on the schooner forty men, all good marksmen, who were protected by the cotton bales, Austin had the ship brought to anchor within two hundred yards of the fort, her single cannon bearing on it. The rest of his men he disposed on the landward side.

The schooner really won the fight. All day her cannon

blasted away at the *presidio*, while her riflemen prevented the Mexicans from using their own solitary piece of artillery with any effect by dropping the men who served it until they flinched from the duty. At last only Colonel Ugartechea himself would point the gun. His courage was so admired by the Texans that they let him live.

But by nightfall fifty of Ugartechea's one hundred and twenty-five men were on the casualty list – thirty-five killed and fifteen wounded. The large proportion of dead was due to the fact that the Mexicans were fighting behind walls and exposed only their heads. The head was sufficient target for the Texas riflemen, and a bullet striking that mark usually was fatal.

Meantime, the Texans had lost but seven killed and nineteen wounded, little more than half the Mexican casualties.

In the evening Ugartechea surrendered. He was permitted to evacuate Velasco with his surviving men, who were allowed to carry their arms and baggage, and even provisioned for their march to Matamoros.

While this was going on at Velasco, a rather surprising series of events took place at Anahuac. Colonel José de las Piedras, commandant at Nacogdoches, arrived there July 1 and, as Bradburn's superior officer, ordered the immediate release of Travis and the other prisoners. Offended by this Bradburn threw up his command. Thereupon Piedras appointed Lieutenant-Colonel Cortinas to succeed him.

No sooner had Piedras returned to Nacogdoches than the Mexican soldiers at Anahuac mutinied, declared for Santa Anna 'the liberator', evacuated the city, and marched south. Bradburn, his life now in peril from both Mexicans and Texans, slunk out of Anahuac, boarded a ship for New Orleans, escaped arrest there by saying he was seeking aid for the Texans to drive the Mexicans out of the province, and eventually reached Vera Cruz by sea, where he was reinstated in the Mexican army. He entered Texas again in 1836, as an officer in Santa Anna's invading force.

These victories by no means appeased the Texans. By midsummer Santa Anna's revolution against Bustamente

49

was in full career and it seemed as good a time as any to the Texans, who already had declared for 'the liberator', to expel the garrison at Nacogdoches.

The action there was notable for the fact that one of its leaders was James Bowie, he of the famous knife, and afterward a spearhead of the Texas revolution.

Colonel Piedras was faithful to Bustamente. When, August 2, an 'assemblage' of about three hundred men, including prominent Mexicans as well as Texans, entered Nacogdoches 'peacefully' to invite the garrison to declare for the constitution of 1824 (which had become quite a sacred symbol), Piedras trotted out his cavalry and fired on the crowd. A distinguished old Mexican, Encarnación Chirino, the *alcalde* of the town, was killed, thus becoming an early Texas martyr.

The 'peaceful' nature of the assemblage disappeared about as rapidly as that of a community of Texas red-tailed wasps when someone inconsiderately prods their nest with a stick; and the circumstance that most of those present had their shooting irons with them suggests something or other about their real original intentions.

Bullets began to sing up the streets and the cavalry retreated hastily, while the Texans – more a posse than an army – took possession of the houses around the central plaza, where stood the church into which Piedras had withdrawn most of his troops.

Adobe walls now hung out curtains of smoke and the keen crackle of rifles, with the duller reports of Mexican muskets, made the streets echo with ear-shocking clatter. Leaden slugs probed and searched the Mexican defences, and here and there men began to crumple up in the church. By nightfall Piedras had forty casualties. He took advantage of the darkness to get out of there, retreating without bothering to remove his dead and wounded.

Here Bowie, who had just arrived in Nacogdoches, took charge. As soon as he learned from a wounded prisoner what direction Piedras was taking, he rode with twenty men 'on good horses' by a lower road, circling Piedras and heading him off at the crossing of the Angelina River. His plan was to delay the Mexicans while the main force from Nacogdoches overtook them and hit them from the rear. But somehow the people in Nacogdoches got involved in passing more resolutions and never did arrive in time to help Bowie.

Of this Bowie was unaware. He hid his twenty men in the brush down by the ford and when Piedras' advance guard came to the river it was fired upon and retreated with some losses to the main body.

Piedras, thoroughly confused and convinced he was surrounded by an overwhelming force, camped a considerable distance back from the river. Next morning Bowie, tired of waiting for reinforcements that did not come, boldly sent two messengers to the Mexican camp demanding surrender. Piedras complied. His men stacked arms and it was not until then that Piedras discovered to his chagrin that he had given up three hundred soldiers to Bowie's twenty Texans.

The Mexicans were marched back to Nacogdoches, where the soldiers unanimously declared for Santa Anna and his 'Plan of Vera Cruz', and were allowed to return to Mexico. Piedras was held for a time at Brazoria, but later was released also and returned to Mexico by way of Tampico. In the entire Nacogdoches action the Texans lost only three killed and five wounded.

By the end of August not a Mexican soldier remained in Texas, except a small force of about seventy men in the *presidio* at San Antonio.

Down in Mexico, Santa Anna defeated Bustamente's army and saw the 'rightful' president, Pedraza, reinstated to serve out the remainder of his term – which had but four months to run. From Santa Anna's point of view, that was just about enough time to build up sentiment to which he could in due time turn a responsive ear, when the people of Mexico would 'call' him to the presidency – from which he envisaged an even higher step for himself.

CHAPTER FOUR

The Leaders and the Revolt

THE affairs at Anahuac and Nacogdoches made marked men of several persons, including Bowie, Travis and John Austin. But late in 1832 another arrived who was more important than any of them, more important than Stephen Austin – a strange giant named Sam Houston.

Born in Virginia in 1793, of Scotch-Irish ancestry, he went to Tennessee as a boy when his widowed mother took her brood of children across the Alleghenies to the new land. His educational opportunities were meagre, but so all encompassing was his mind and so retentive his memory that whatever he read he digested and kept. His taste in literature was in itself notable for an untrained youth of the frontier. The Bible, the *Iliad*, Shakespeare's works, *Pilgrim's Progress* and Caesar's *Commentaries* were the books over which he pored and from which, throughout his life, he was able to quote profusely, exactly and appositely.

He did not admire labour unless its rewards were exceptional and as a youth, tiring of clerking in a country store, he left civilization and went to the Cherokee country. There he lived and became a member of the tribe, being adopted as a son by Oo-loo-te-ka, a chief, who gave him the Indian name Co-lon-neh (the Raven) – a complimentary title, for the Cherokees considered the bird not an evil omen but the most sagacious of the feathered kind.

Among the Indians he took part in hunting, dancing and the game of lacrosse, in the rough sport of which he excelled with his size and athletic ability. But this did not stop him from reading, for when his brothers came from the settlements to try to persuade him to return home they found him beneath a tree, immersed in the lines of the *Iliad*, a translation of which he had taken to the woods with him.

He refused to return with his brothers and remained with the Indians for some time. In this period he acquired the curious habit of speaking of himself in the third person – a trait of the Indians, and, be it noted, also of Julius Caesar, whom he read continuously. He learned also the trick of forensic imagery which the red-men used in their speeches, and which later gave a distinctive flavour to his public oratory as well as his private conversations.

In 1812, when he was nineteen years old, he returned to civilization and for a time taught school; but with the outbreak of the war with Britain he enlisted in the Tennessee infantry. His regiment never faced the redcoats. Instead it was led by General Andrew Jackson against the Creek Indians, who had been stirred into hostility by Tecumseh, the Shawnee chief, and who under their chief Weatherford captured Fort Mims with a great massacre and terrorized the whole frontier of Alabama.

At the Battle of the Horseshoe, Houston, already an ensign, led a charge of the Tennesseeans against the Indians behind their barricade, and was the first man to leap down from the parapet among the savages. His bravery brought in his men after him, the ramparts were taken, and Houston, wounded by an arrow, caught Jackson's attention. It was the beginning of Houston's career.

Later in the day the young ensign was again wounded, leading an attack on a covered blockhouse. Such zeal solidified Jackson's regard for him. Houston was hospitalized at home while the general went to New Orleans and defeated Pakenham's British army, but when Jackson returned to Tennessee and to politics Sam Houston was one of Old Hickory's bright young men. Under the aegis of that leader he went to Congress, fought a duel with General William A. White – and put his opponent in bed for four months with a well-placed bullet – became a general of militia, and was elected governor of Tennessee.

His method of campaigning was remarkable. Each frontier

community of that day had its 'bully' — its acknowledged champion, who could whip every man in the country round and lorded it over all. Houston would go into a village and challenge the town bully to a wrestling match. When the match was over, he would address the crowd which had quickly assembled to see the contest. It is said that Sam Houston — who was, according to at least one account, in the neighbourhood of six feet six inches tall and perhaps weighed 240 pounds of bone and muscle — never lost a wrestling match, or a precinct which he addressed.

Jackson was elected President and Houston, at the height of his career, was generally considered Old Hickory's political heir, who should go to the White House after him. Then disaster came, and through a woman.

Houston married a young lady of an aristocratic Tennessee family named Eliza Allen. She was very much younger than he and it is said that she preferred another suitor, marrying the governor at her father's command. Exactly what happened probably will never be known, but shortly after the wedding the bride, weeping, returned to her father's home; and Houston, evidently severely shaken, resigned his governorship and disappeared, eventually showing up among the Cherokees, who had in the interim moved to what is now Oklahoma.

It created a political sensation such as never before had been known in America. Everywhere were rumours but neither Eliza nor Houston offered any explanation of the separation. Before departing, however, Houston left a notice that 'if any wretch ever dares to utter a word against the purity of Mrs. Houston, I will come back and write the libel in his heart's blood.'

All this happened in 1829. For three years he lived with the Cherokees near Fort Gibson, drinking far too much for his own good. Once he travelled to Washington as 'ambassador of the Cherokee Nation', presenting himself at the White House in a buckskin coat, blanket, moccasins and other habiliments of the Cherokees. President Jackson received him with joy and embraced him publicly. Before Houston

54

returned to the Cherokees there may have been a strong understanding between them on certain matters concerning the Southwest. A year later Houston was in Texas.

The episodes above form only the briefest outline of his extraordinary career, but now in Mexican territory, ostensibly as a private lawyer, his presence could not fail to produce enormous speculation. Sam Houston was such a man of tumbling passions and mighty achievements as comes not once in a generation, but perhaps once in a people's history.

At San Felipe de Austin he encountered Bowie, now married to Ursula, a daughter of Juan de Veramendi, vice-governor of Texas, and living in San Antonio. From the beginning they were friends and understood each other. With Bowie, Houston visited San Antonio, and when he returned to Natchitoches, Louisiana, he wrote on February 13, 1833, a letter to Andrew Jackson which is at least significant. It began:

'Having been as far as Béxar, in the province of Texas ... I am in possession of some information that . . . may be calculated to forward your views, if you should entertain any, touching the acquisition of Texas by the United States.'

The letter continued; its writer believed Texas would be transferred to some other power than Mexico – perhaps England – within the near future, unless the United States intervened; and added that nineteen twentieths of the people of the province desired union with the United States. Perhaps all this was only a suggestion : but it may also have been a report.

Disturbing news sifted up from south of the Rio Grande as Santa Anna began the final devious series of shifts whereby he became dictator. In May, 1833 he became president, elected as a proponent of religious freedom, liberal political rights and equality between races. Almost at once a *coup d'état*, promoted by him to give him dictatorial powers, was attempted but failed. By December it was clear that he had changed his political beliefs and was on the reactionary side of the *ricos* and the Church.

55

The Texas settlers wanted their province separated from Coahuila, to which it had been joined since the days of that French genius of disruption, St. Denis, and from which it was badly administered. Other reforms were desired also and a state constitution was drafted which embodied them. With this document Stephen Austin, the patient and long-suffering leader of the colony, travelled to the City of Mexico, to present it to the government for ratification.

Texas did not see him again for two years. When he reached the capital his petition was heard and he was allowed to begin his return journey. But on the way he was arrested at Saltillo and sent back to the City of Mexico, where he was lodged in the dungeon of the old Spanish Inquisition. Though later he was transferred to a better prison, he was not released to return to Texas until September, 1835, never having been tried on any charges.

Meantime Santa Anna at last came out in his true colours. By the 'Plan of Cuernavaca', proclaimed in May, 1834, he made a public apostasy of his declared beliefs; joined the clergy in pronouncing against religious reform; supported the wealthy property owners; discarded the slogan of equality between races on which he had been elected; repealed the constitution of 1824 and substituted a new constitution written by himself; and in October seized absolute power as president-dictator.

In all Mexico only Zacatecas, Coahuila and Texas opposed this usurpation. The rebellions in the first two named states were put down bloodily, but Texas proved a nut somewhat harder to crack.

Though most of the colonists as yet wished only to have the constitution of 1824 restored and a true liberal in Chapultepec palace, firebrands like Travis began urging complete independence. Santa Anna recognized the danger he faced and, acting before Texas resistance was fully formed, sent a strong force to occupy it at once.

It was Bowie who gave the first warning. He had lost his wife and two children in a cholera epidemic which swept Texas and Coahuila in 1833; and had since wandered, rest-

less as a lost soul, drinking heavily, indulging in land specu-
lations and political manœuvrings in the unstable legislatures of Coahuila, for which later he was severely criticized
– a man deprived of purpose and aim in life by the grief that
overwhelmed him.

Early in June, 1835 he was in Matamoros, across the Rio
Grande near the gulf, when the Mexican provost marshal
posted notices forbidding all foreigners to leave the city.
Bowie, however, took his horse from the stable of the inn
where he was staying and escaped by night back across the
river into Texas. At Hatch's plantation on the Lavaca River,
a hundred and sixty miles away, he wrote a letter to Dr. J. B.
Miller, the *jefe politico* at Brazoria :

I have just arrived here from Matamoros, and as all communication is cut off between Texas and all other parts of
the republic, I take this opportunity of giving you some
information that may be useful to Texas. I left Matamoros
on the 12th of the present month. All the vessels in the port
were embargoed for the purpose of transporting troops to the
coast of Texas. The commandant, General Cos, forbid all
foreigners from leaving the city under any circumstances. I
run away and succeeded in getting this far safe. Three
thousand troops had reached Saltillo on their way to Texas.
All this may or may not be news to you.

It *was* news to Dr. Miller – and to all of Texas. The substance
of Bowie's letter crossed Texas with a celerity which only fear
could impart. Committees of Safety were formed and men
began gathering at night to drill as informal companies of
volunteer soldiers.

Houston had recently returned from Washington, Phila-
delphia, New York and elsewhere, where he had been engaged in some mysterious business which, it was whispered,
had to do with financial and manpower help for Texas. He
received a letter from Samuel Swartwout – Aaron Burr's go-
between in the conspiracy with General Wilkinson – in which

57

that worthy said, 'If I mistake not Texas will be U States in 5 years, or an independent Empire, when you'll be King.'

But Houston had no ambitions to be a king. He had a different aim, and it was linked closely to the policies of Andrew Jackson. He began organizing the Department of Nacogdoches, set up a Committee of Vigilance and Safety, and was in turn commissioned by it 'Commander-in-Chief of the forces of the Department to sustain the principles of the Constitution of 1824.'

Trouble started quickly. An armed mob, led by the ever turbulent Buck Travis, in June expelled Captain Tenorio and his twenty Mexican soldiers from Anahuac. Disarmed, the Mexicans were marched to San Felipe de Austin, the colony's capital. Some of the council there denounced the proceedings as high-handed. Tenorio and his men, their arms restored, were treated well and sent on to join the garrison under Colonel Ubartechea in San Antonio, where the Mexican forces, including the first detachment from Cos's army across the border, now numbered five hundred men.

There were some clashes at sea between Texas ships and Mexican ships, and a Mexican armed schooner, the *Correo*, was captured by the *San Felipe*, a hastily converted ship manned by Texans and commanded by Captain Hurd, and brought into Anahuac as a prize of war in July.

Then, early in September, Stephen Austin arrived back in Texas. He had been released by Santa Anna, who believed he could keep Texas in line as previously. But Austin had had his fill of the dictator and his methods. At a banquet honouring him in Brazoria he gave an address urging unity, then offered a toast, 'To the constitutional rights and the security and peace of Texas – they ought to be maintained.'

When word came that General Cos was sending substantial reinforcements Ugartechea, the Committee of Safety of the Austin colony, at Austin's direction, drew up a circular for the direction of the colonists, in which these fateful words occurred :

* * *

This committee deem it to be their duty to say that, in its opinion, all kind of conciliatory measures with General Cos and the military at Béxar are hopeless, and that nothing but the ruin of Texas can be expected from any such measures. They have already and very properly, been resorted to without effect. War is our only recourse. There is no other remedy. We must defend our rights, ourselves, and our country, by force of arms.

The great *empresario* had declared for war and called on the people for unity. Texas rallied around him.

But though Texas was at last united, Texas was hardly prepared. Without opposition General Cos occupied San Antonio.

Shortly after, hostilities began. The town of Gonzales, on the direct road between San Antonio and San Felipe, had for four years been the proud possessor of a six-pound cannon. Ugartechea demanded that it be surrendered and sent Lieutenant-Colonel Francisco Castañeda with two hundred cavalry to seize the piece. Texans gathered to repel this 'invasion'. When, September 20, Castañeda tried to cross the Guadalupe River, he met a hot fire from eighteen riflemen under Captain Albert Martin and fell back from the ford and camped on a hill.

That night one hundred and sixty-eight Texans, of whom fity were mounted, led by Colonel John H. Moore, crossed the river to attack the Mexican position. At four o'clock on the morning of September 21, under a heavy fog, the assault began. With the disputed cannon booming in the centre and the rifles of the Texans crackling, the Mexicans were routed and fled all the way back to San Antonio. A few of them remained behind, dead. The Texans lost not a man.

Militarily the affair at Gonzales was insignificant, but to the Texas revolution it was what the Battle of Lexington was to the American War for Independence. Every Texan knew that from this time forth he would be treated as a rebel. There was no alternative but to fight.

Men came flocking to Gonzales, each bringing his own

arms and ammunition – long rifles, chiefly, though some carried shotguns loaded with buckshot, a few bore muskets, and almost all had, sheathed at their hips, the sinister bowie knives which had become almost a symbol of the frontier fighting man. So many camped about the small town that Ugartechea, who was about to march with five hundred men to wipe out Castañeda's disgrace, decided not to attempt it.

From Goliad, on October 9, came word that Captain Collingsworth, with about fifty men, had by a surprise night attack captured that important point, which commanded lower Texas – and with it $10,000 in money for the payment of the Mexican troops, two pieces of artillery, three hundred stands of arms, and the entire garrison, including its commander, Lieutenant-Colonel Sandoval.

Perhaps as important as any of the foregoing was the finding by Collingworth's men of Colonel Ben Milam, hiding in a thicket. He was an *empresario*, and a veteran of the War of 1812, of the Mexican revolt against Iturbide, and of various Indian battles – a proved fighter and a man with capacity for leadership. Milam had been captured by Santa Anna's troops in Monclova, escaped from his prison in Monterrey, and had ridden six hundred miles through enemy country to join his fellow Texans.

Soon after, Austin arrived at Gonzales and was elected commanding general of the Texas army. It was an 'army' by courtesy title only, for Austin had less than 350 men, ill armed and undisciplined, without organization, commissary or proper officers. He did what he could to form them into companies with commanders, to organize a commissary, and otherwise to bring order out of confusion; and on October 13 he moved south to the San Antonio River, where he took up a position eight miles below the capital and sent couriers to San Felipe begging for reinforcements.

Sam Houston and others had been appealing for aid in the United States – and not in vain. In New Orleans two companies of cavalry, calling themselves the New Orleans Grays, were sent to Texas at their own expense, while volunteers hurried in from elsewhere, notably Arkansas, Tennessee and Louisiana. Austin's army grew.

An interesting development of this period was the first organization of that famous body of fighting men known as the Texas Rangers. It was authorized by the Texas General Consultation at San Felipe, October 17, 1835, and was at first limited to three companies: one of twenty-five men under Silas M. Parker on the Indian frontier between the Brazos and the Trinity; a second under Harrison Greenwood, of ten men, patrolling east of the Trinity; and the third, of twenty-five men, under D. B. Frayer, to guard the territory between the Brazos and the Colorado. The organization would eventually take on far broader duties and grow in strength, and would win fame not shared by any other similar organization on the continent, save the Royal Canadian Northwest Mounted Police.

The Consultation also adopted a bill of rights, appointed Henry Smith governor, and outlined the powers of a provisional government in a declaration of twenty-one articles. It is to be noted that this was not a declaration of independence. Many of the delegates were in favour of that step, but the majority were not yet ready.

CHAPTER FIVE

"We Will Rather Die in These Ditches"

HAVING reached Salado Creek, which enters the San Antonio River just below San Antonio, Austin ran into excitement. One of his officers was Jim Bowie, now bearing the rank of colonel. A turbulent and restless adventurer, but a notable fighting man, Bowie did not enjoy the entire confidence of Austin, who regarded him as a disturbing influence.

Nevertheless, when it was necessary to send forward a scouting expedition of some peril, Austin selected Bowie for

61

the task. So on October 27, with Captain James W. Fannin as second in command, and ninety-two men, Bowie rode out to reconnoitre the old missions which formed a sort of ring around San Antonio, and to find a suitable advanced camping place for the main army. His instructions were to choose the site, send back a messenger announcing its position, and await there the coming of Austin.

As ordered, the detachment advanced, encountered no enemies at the San Juan Capistrano and San José missions, and went on to Concepción mission, a two-towered century-old Franciscan church situated only about two miles south of San Antonio's main plaza. There Bowie chose a camp site in a bed of the San Antonio River, and sent back his courier to Austin expecting immediate support.

But Austin failed to move as he had promised. That night Bowie lay with his small force in his terribly exposed position, wondering how soon the Mexicans would discover him. Morning came, with a heavy fog that obscured all vision. Suddenly a rifle cracked out – a warning signal from a sentry, placed in a tower of the mission. A Mexican force had arrived and was already deployed before them, pinning them against the river.

Bowie made his dispositions coolly. The shelving bank of the river behind his camp offered protection and there he posted some of his men. The rest, in two companies, he sent into the woods which stretched out on either side of a level plain in front like extending arms.

All at once the fog lifted. Before them, occupying the triangular plain between the wooded areas, Bowie's men saw the long rank of blue uniforms with white crossbelts in an X pattern – Mexican infantry. The Texans were in a trap from which they must fight their way out.

Frontier habits paid dividends. Many of the men that night had slept cold so that they might wrap their blankets about their guns against the foggy damp. The keen crackling of Texas long rifles sounded, and empty places began to appear in the blue line.

From the Mexican array crashed a heavy volley. Then a

small brass cannon was wheeled forward and grapeshot began tearing through the woods.

Making his way through the timber in which Fannin's men lay firing, Bowie directed several sharpshooters to devote themselves to the cannoneers. Rifles began looking at the brass gun. Gunner after gunner spun to the ground, and the rest fell back, leaving the loaded cannon standing alone, far out ahead of the infantry line.

'Boys, let's get that gun!' shouted Bowie. Waving his great knife over his head, he bounded from the woods.

After him leaped his men. They did not march forward in an orderly line, according to the rules of the military textbooks then current. They ran, stopping now and then to fire with deadly effect, then dashing on again. Blue-clad Mexican soldiers in increasing numbers began to flop and kick on the ground.

First to reach the cannon, Bowie ordered it swung around, himself seized the burning fuse stick from the dead hand of the gunner who last had held it, and applied it to the vent.

At the roar of the gun a great hole was torn in the Mexican front. Onward whooped the Texans.

The Mexican soldiers, though well drilled in close-formation manœuvres, had little stomach for the fight. They were mostly impressed into the service, being convicts, or peons who had been waylaid and kidnapped, or vagrants forced to don uniforms. With sudden, overwhelming panic, they broke and stampeded before the Texas charge.

Jim Bowie had won the first pitched battle of the war. The Mexicans suffered a loss of sixty-seven killed and almost as many wounded, while the Texans had one dead and no wounded. The deadly shooting of the frontiersmen, the furious charge and the ferocious pursuit which followed foreshadowed once again the decisive Battle of San Jacinto.

After the battle Austin moved up the main army, but instead of occupying the ground defended by Bowie, he passed on north and took a position on the river above the city. Though he now had more than a thousand men, including the New Orleans Grays, he hesitated, too cautious to follow the urgings of his officers and attack the town itself. The indecision enabled General Martín Perfecto de Cos, Santa Anna's brother-in-law, who was now in command in San Antonio, to strengthen his position by barricading the streets, erecting batteries, and sending to Laredo for a reinforcement of five hundred more soldiers.

With all his great qualities, Austin was not by character a soldier. He spent his time quarrelling with some of his commanders, once receiving – and refusing to accept – the resignation of Bowie, perhaps the best of them, while he lay idle, fearing that he could not long keep his army together.

Meanwhile the Consultation at San Felipe took some decisive actions. General Sam Houston was named commander-in-chief of all the Texas forces – over Austin's head – and Austin himself was appointed on a commission to visit the United States to gain help. It must have been a bitter disappointment to Austin. Smith was governor in his stead, and Houston commander-in-chief, replacing him. Nevertheless, with the patience and self-sacrifice which were his nature, he surrendered the command of the army before San Antonio to Colonel Edward Burleson, and on November 25 departed for his new duties.

The day following, November 26, there was another skirmish and again Bowie was the leader. Erastus Smith, better known as Deaf Smith, a giant who, in spite of defective hearing, was the army's best scout, brought word that a Mexican convoy of loaded pack mules was approaching San Antonio from the south. It was believed to be Ugartechea, returning from Laredo with the five hundred soldiers, and with pay for the troops.

Bowie galloped with his company to intercept them. Some shooting took place, the convoy was driven back, and when Cos sent out a detachment from the city to relieve it Colonel Burleson arrived with the main force of Texans and turned the affair into a rout. But when the loads of the pack mules were examined they did not contain silver, as expected, but only grass-fodder for the animals in the San Antonio garrison. This occasioned mirth among the Texans, and the sharp little battle has always been called 'the Grass Fight'.

Still the Texas army lay idle, and discontent grew. Tired of doing nothing, many of the free and easy 'soldiers' walked out of camp and went home, until not more than eight hundred remained before San Antonio. At last, December 3, Burleson announced that he intended to attack. This was received with enthusiasm by the army. Almost at once, however, Burleson rescinded his plan on the ground that the enemy had learned of it, and proposed instead to withdraw.

Before the men, drawn up in ranks, stepped Colonel Ben Milam, carrying his rifle on his shoulder. He waved his rakish hat and cried out in a humorous, drawling voice, 'Who'll go with old Ben Milam into San Antonio?'

A roar greeted the words. Followed one of the strangest assaults in history. Virtually ignoring Burleson, the Texans moved forward the night of December 4 in two columns, led by Milam and Colonel Francis Johnson. Before dawn, December 5, the attack began. Military precedent was ignored, and each Texan was, in a manner of speaking his own commander.

While Colonel J. C. Neill made a noisy diversion before the Alamo – the old mission church which had been converted into a fort – the attacking columns, carrying in addition to their firearms crowbars to break through the walls of adobe houses, surprised the garrison of San Antonio and gained entrance into the city.

A tremendous cannonade began, Cos directing his artillery to sweep the streets. But the Texans did not use the streets. Instead, they worked their way from one house to another, by opening holes through the soft adobe walls, and from the windows the deadly rifles did their work so effectively that several times that day enemy guns within range had to be abandoned.

Night came. The attackers strengthened their positions by opening trenches for communication and defence. With dawn the battle was resumed. Working their way steadily forward, the Texans penetrated almost to the *presidio*, the centre of the Mexican defence.

During this assault Ben Milam, the moving spirit of the attack, while crossing the courtyard of the Veramendi house was killed by a bullet which struck him in the head. But the Texans fought on. By night they were near the central square, making their progress from house to house, almost fighting their way from room to room.

The night of December 7 once more interrupted the fighting. In the darkness Ugartechea arrived with his reinforcements. The lack of quality in these is seen by the fact that four hundred of the soldiers were uniformed convicts, who had to be guarded on the march by the other hundred regular and trustworthy soldiers. Their arrival did not daunt the Texans, who with the first light of day began again their attack.

That morning of December 8 was signalized by a charge of the New Orleans Grays and a company from Brazoria, which captured buildings that commanded the plaza and the *presidio*. During this day intense cannonading continued. It did little harm to the attackers, but under its cover Cos withdrew from the city into the Alamo. His troops by this time were demoralized, many deserting and fleeing from the city. Disorganization grew so complete that on the morning of December 11 Cos sent a flag of truce to Burleson, and gave up the fort and city to the Texans.

In the four-day assault the Texans lost two killed and twenty-six wounded, while the defending Mexicans suffered casualties never fully enumerated, but estimated at between three hundred and four hundred, counting dead, wounded and desertions.

Cos marched south across the border into Mexico, having given his parole of honour that he would not again fight the Texans. He took with him 1,105 men, provisioned but carrying no arms – except for the hundred regular soldiers who were to guard the convict troops. He had surrendered the city, the Alamo fortress, twenty-one pieces of artillery, five hundred muskets, much ammunition and other booty of military value.

As far as it went, the victory was complete. Not a Mexican soldier was now left north of the Rio Grande and many Texans were so sanguine as to believe the war was over. But their leaders, especially those who knew anything of the nature of Santa Anna, were under no such delusion. In addition to the rebellious nature of the capture of San Antonio, a personal affront had been given the Mexican dictator, for his brother-in-law, General Cos, had suffered a deep humiliation. Already Santa Anna had displayed bloodthirstiness in crushing a revolt in Zacatecas. He could be expected to be even more ferocious against the *Americano* Texans, whom he detested anyway.

One who realized the danger most keenly was Houston, who had the responsibility of rallying an army to meet the expected invasion. He had managed to get the Consultation to pass ordinances under which an army might be organized, including land bounties for soldiers who served in it. But the capture of San Antonio, rather than strengthening, seemed to weaken his position. He had not been present at the fighting. Not Houston, but Colonel Johnson and Dr. James Grant, an adventurer who had been wounded, were the idols of the army.

This pair, and many other officers and men, overconfident after the victory, began to propose an invasion of Mexico itself; to capture Matamoros and from it campaign into the country which, it was represented by schemers like Grant, contained thousands of 'liberal Mexicans' who would rise to join them, perhaps to the halls of the Montezumas themselves. Grant had a heavy personal interest in promoting such a campaign – he had mines below the Rio Grande which had been seized by Santa Anna, and he wanted the army to get them back for him.

Houston knew that the Mexicans would resent rather than rejoice at the projected invasion, and opposed the Matamoros expedition. So also did Bowie and many other thinking Texans, who knew the Mexican temperament. But the majority in the army – now increased by many new recruits – believed in an easy victory and a march supported by the spoils of rich cities : a looting expedition in every sense.

To check this move, Houston sent an order to Bowie to organize a force and proceed ahead of the army to Matamoros. At least a seizure of that city under Bowie's direction would be at the command of the recognized authorities. In some manner the order was not delivered to Bowie, so he did not move. Then a message came from Colonel Neill, who had been left in command of the Alamo with eighty men, mostly sick and wounded, that Johnson, Fannin and Grant already had marched with the army on their expedition.

A sorry and humiliating condition of affairs confronted the commander-in-chief at this news that he had lost his army. Houston rode hard to Goliad, where he found Bowie. He also found Grant, styling himself 'Acting Commander-in-Chief', and the runaway army in high fettle, so cocksure and determined on its course that he did not even attempt to assert his authority as it marched away.

At this grave moment another messenger came spurring from Neill at the Alamo, saying that the Mexican army again was invading Texas, and Santa Anna in person, with a large force, was about to attack San Antonio.

The despairing Houston had only one man on the spot on whom he could depend – Bowie. Raking together a handful of men, about twenty in all, the commander-in-chief sent Bowie with them to San Antonio, with orders to demolish all fortifications, blow up the Alamo, abandon the place, and bring all cannon north for the use of the Texas defence.

While Bowie marched to take command of the Alamo under these orders, Houston rode on, overtaking the army at Refugio, where Colonel Johnson informed him that the General Consultation had deposed both Governor Smith and himself, and that Fannin was the new commander-in-chief.

There was little Sam Houston could do. He did what he could, addressing the soldiers with such a gloomy yet realistic picture of what they would face in Mexico that he greatly reduced the enthusiasm for the venture. Then he rode back to San Felipe. Deprived of his command, he announced himself as a candidate for the new convention which was to meet March 1 to reorganize the government. Beaten at one point, Houston was always ready to fight at another, and he had equal facility in politics and war.

Meantime Bowie, of whom Houston had written Governor Smith, 'There is no man on whose forecast, prudence, and valour I place a higher estimate than Colonel Bowie,' reached San Antonio. He conferred with Colonel Neill and saw that it would be impossible to transport the cannon. Furthermore, he became convinced that the Alamo was a key defence point, where Santa Anna might be checked. He perhaps felt also that he had some latitude to act, owing to Houston's removal from command.

He therefore took the responsibility of disobeying the orders given him and began to prepare the place for defence. On February 2, 1836, he sent to Governor Smith, who still held his office in the absence of a successor, the following message :

Relief at this post in men, money, and provisions, is of vital importance. The salvation of Texas depends on keeping Béxar out of the hands of the enemy. Colonel Neill and myself have come to the conclusion that we will rather die in these ditches than give up to the enemy. The citizens deserve our patriotism, and the public safety demands our lives rather than evacuate this post to the enemy. Again we call aloud for relief. Our force is small. The returns of the day show only 120 men and officers. It would be a waste of men to put our brave little band against thousands. I have information just now from a friend that the forces at Presidio is 2,000 complete. He states further that 5,000 more are a little back and marching on. The informant says that they intend to make a descent on this place in particular, and there is no doubt of it.

Thus was made the decision to fight it out at the Alamo, and Bowie made it. He generously gave equal credit to Colonel Neill, but that gentleman rather eliminated himself from the

69

consideration shortly thereafter by taking leave and departing from the doomed place on a plea of illness in his family. On Bowie alone was the responsibility.

The harried Governor Smith did what he could to help the Alamo garrison. He could not give orders to officers with any assurance that they would be obeyed, but he wrote to William Barret Travis, now a lieutenant-colonel and on recruiting duty, telling him to go to the Alamo with as many men as he could gather. Buck Travis disliked the assignment. Twice he wrote Smith, begging to be relieved of the order, once complaining that he was being 'sacrificed', and once threatening to resign his commission. But in the end he unwillingly went, reaching San Antonio a few days after Bowie had written his decisive letter and bringing with him thirty men.

From the outset there was friction between Bowie and Travis. When he left the Alamo, Colonel Neill had taken it upon himself to 'appoint' Travis to the command of the post – which he had no authority to do, since Bowie had written orders giving him that authority. The act created endless trouble. Travis was ambitious, a politico-soldier who possibly had his eye on future prestige, and he used Neill's unauthorized appointment to divide the loyalty of the men. In the end he was to prove himself flawless in bravery and self-sacrifice, but at this time his personal rivalry with Bowie took the form of letters of complaint to the governor, in which he accused Bowie of drinking too much, and of leaving him to shoulder the whole burden.

At this juncture an unexpected and welcome reinforcement of eighty men from Tennessee arrived, bear and deer hunters all, and led by one of the legendary characters of the frontier – Davy Crockett. The Tennesseean and Bowie had heard of each other before, and from the beginning they were friends.

Crockett later told of how he asked to see the original hand-forged knife, and when Bowie handed it to him, he said, 'Tarnation, if the very sight of it ain't enough to give a man a squeamish stomach, specially before breakfast.'

To which Bowie replied, grinning, 'You might tickle a fellow's ribs a long time with that before you'd make him laugh.'

An election was held to settle the disputed question of command. The Tennesseeans swung it in favour of Bowie. He was declared commander of all the volunteers and Travis commander of the 'regulars and cavalry' – his own thirty men whom he had brought. Thenceforth they signed all orders and communications together.

But a stroke of fate intervened to put all the authority in one man's hands and avert a divided command. While supervising the mounting of a cannon on the wall of the Alamo, Bowie made a mis-step and fell fifteen feet to the ground. One hip was smashed and some ribs broken, evidently with a penetration of the lungs. Confined to a cot in the infirmary, with pneumonia setting in because of his lacerated lungs, Bowie could no longer be a leader. Travis took over.

Shortly thereafter, on February 23, the vanguard of Santa Anna's army, four thousand strong, appeared before the Alamo.

The Texas convention had begun to gather at Washington-on-the-Brazos – up the river from San Felipe – and the vanguard of refugees from the Mexican invasion was beginning to appear, when on February 28 a courier rode in with what has been called the most heroic message in American history. It was dated February 24, and read as follows :

Fellow Citizens and Compatriots : I am besieged by a thousand or more of Mexicans under Santa Anna. I have sustained a continual bombardment for twenty-four hours and have not lost a man. The enemy have demanded surrender at discretion; otherwise the garrison is to be put to the sword if the place is taken. I have answered the summons with a cannon shot and our flag still waves proudly from the walls. I shall never surrender or retreat. Then I call upon you, in the name of liberty, of patriotism, and of everything dear to the American character, to come to our aid with all dispatch. The enemy are receiving reinforcements daily and will no doubt increase to three or four thousand in four or five days. Though this call may be neglected, I am determined to sustain myself as long as possible and die like a soldier who never forgets what is due to his honour or that of his country. Victory or death!

W. Barret Travis, Lt.-Col. Commanding

Thus the gallant Travis endorsed Jim Bowie's equally gallant decision to 'die in these ditches,' in order to halt, or at least delay, Santa Anna's overwhelming invasion.

After that, silence closed about the Alamo as far as the rest of Texas was concerned. March 2 came and the convention went into session. Houston, attending as a delegate, was the dominating figure, his personality such that in that hour of great crisis all, even his enemies, turned despairingly to him.

A harebrained resolution to adjourn the convention and march in a body to the relief of the Alamo was defeated by Houston, who was grimly determined to have here created a government, without which to fight a war would be impossible. Through the first night, with a 'blue norther' howling down so that they shivered in the cabin where they worked, the delegates laboured. Next morning, March 2, they completed a declaration of independence, by which all political connection with Mexico was ended, and Texas proclaimed a free, sovereign and independent nation.

In its statement of grievances, the document included charges of despotism of the sword and priesthood; unlawful overturn of the constitution of 1824; depriving the colonists of right of trial by jury and representation in the legislatures; inciting the savages to massacre inhabitants on the frontier; and armed invasion of Texas for the purpose of driving the colonists from their homes.

The declaration was adopted and signed without a dissenting vote, and on it Houston's signature was the most prominent. Among the signatories were three Mexicans of prominent family and political influence, Antonio Navarro, Lorenzo de Zavala and Francisco Ruiz.

Two days later General Sam Houston was once more appointed – this time unanimously – commander-in-chief of the Texas military forces.

CHAPTER SIX
Santa Anna's Blood Bath

A DREAD though heroic tragedy was being enacted at the Alamo. The mission, which stood across the river and just east of San Antonio, was poorly designed for a fort. Its main plaza was a long parallelogram, about 50 by 150 yards in extent, with the major axis north and south, enclosed by a wall of adobe bricks eight feet high and three feet thick. Within the west wall stood a row of one-storey buildings, and at the middle of the east wall a two-storey convent. East of the convent was a yard, enclosed by an embankment built by the Mexicans under General Cos during the Texan siege of San Antonio, and southeast of this second enclosure stood the church, built of stone, cruciform and properly oriented, its walls five feet thick and two storeys high. The Church had long been dismantled and part of its roof had fallen in. A log stockade connected the corner of the church with the corner of the main plaza wall. Along these defences at various places were distributed fourteen pieces of the artillery captured from Cos.

Military experts have agreed that it would have required at least a thousand soldiers to man properly the extensive walls of the Alamo. Yet the garrison consisted of less than 190, including Crockett's Tennesseeans and thirty-two brave volunteers from Gonzales, who cut their way through the Mexican lines to join the defenders. The exact number is not known; according to various counts, it ranges from 181 to 187. Seven of these were Mexicans, fighting valorously with the Texas-Americans against the oppressor. Man for man, the Alamo's defenders were as courageous and deadly a group of fighters as existed, but they were far too few.

From the first day of the investment, the defenders knew what their fate would be, for on that day, February 23, Santa Anna displayed on the tower of San Fernando church, in full view of the Alamo, the blood-red flag that signified 'no quarter'.

There was some bombardment and skirmishing but no direct assault in the days that Santa Anna waited for the bulk of his army and his artillery to come up. Though the walls were thin and of adobe, the cannon did not greatly damage them because they were light field-pieces rather than siege guns. By March 3 – the day after the Texas declaration of independence – the Mexican dictator had completed his dispositions. On that day the last courier went out from the Alamo. He was Captain John W. Smith. The following day he reached Washington-on-the-Brazos, and the convention gathered to hear the message. A few lines reveal the feelings of Travis, who wrote it:

'The spirits of my men are still high, although they have had much to depress them. . . . Col. Fannin is said to be on the march to this place . . . but I fear it is not true, as I have repeatedly sent to him for aid without receiving any. . . . I hope your honourable body will hasten on reinforcements. . . . Our supply of ammunition is limited.'

The reference to Fannin needs elaboration. He did not, after all, accompany Johnson and Grant towards Matamoros but, considerably chastened in spirits, begged Houston to permit him to redeem himself as an obedient 'company officer'. Repeated messages came to him at Goliad from Travis, imploring assistance; and as he had under him at the time 402 men, he might have changed the course of events at the Alamo. But he seemed rooted by indecision to Goliad. Once he began a march with part of his forces, but returned to Goliad quickly, explaining that he did not have sufficient provisions.

74

It was Colonel James Butler Bonham, a South Carolinian and a personal friend of Travis, who on this last occasion brought the appeal for help. Fannin tried to persuade Bonham to stay with him, but the courier, a magnificent horseman, said, 'I will report to Travis or die in the attempt.' After a long and very dangerous ride he actually succeeded, at one o'clock on the morning of March 3, in reaching the Alamo, where he must have known he faced certain death.

The news Bonham brought of Fannin's return to Goliad convinced Travis that hope was ended. That was the day called by Sidney Lanier 'one of the most pathetic days of time', when the legendary drama occurred within the walls of the Alamo. Travis, according to tradition, assembled his men in ranks, explained to them the doom that awaited them and that he no longer hoped for aid. He added that he left each man to his own choice, but would himself remain to die in the fort. Then with his sword, he drew a line on the ground, and invited those who would die with him to step across it.

They stepped across – every man but one. Even Bowie, who had been carried out on his cot, dying from pneumonia and helpless with his smashed hip, asked that his cot be lifted across the line. The one who did not cross was Moses Rose, who climbed the wall and succeeded in making his escape, to bring the story to the world. It has been discredited by some historians and upheld by others. But even those who say it is not fact, being based on a story published many years after, agree that it is at least plausible. Certainly it is a part of the heroic legend of the Alamo.

His main army having arrived, and rested for three days, Santa Anna ordered the stubborn Alamo to be taken by direct assault, a decision later condemned even by Mexican writers, such as General Vicente Filisola, who wrote :

'In our opinion the blood of our soldiers as well as that of the enemy was shed in vain, for the mere gratification of the inconsiderate, puerile, and guilty vanity of reconquering Béxar by force of arms, and through a bloody contest.'

The night of March 5 the Mexican dictator formed his

infantry into four columns for the attack. One was commanded by General Cos – who had broken his parole of honour. Another was led by Colonel Francisco Duque, a third by Colonel José Romero, and the fourth by Colonel José Morales. The cavalry, under General Ramirez y Sesma, was arranged at places in the rear of these columns, to prevent escape of any fugitives from the Alamo – and, incidentally, to prevent their own troops from fleeing, if a rout occurred.

At three o'clock the morning of March 6, without any preparation by artillery, the four-pronged assault began. Francisco Ruiz, the *alcalde* of San Antonio, who witnessed the entire battle, stated in writing that 4,000 men took part in the attack. They were provided with scaling ladders, axes and crowbars, in addition to their weapons.

Shouts of the Mexican soldiers crying '*Viva Santa Anna!*' must have been the first warnings to the defenders. Immediately every able-bodied man in the Alamo was at his post. The sinister assassin notes of the *degüello* – a bugle call meaning 'no quarter' announced the charge. Then through the gloom the Mexican columns were seen approaching.

The principal assault was against the north wall – the weakest part of the Alamo's too extended defences. It was led by Colonel Duque. Simultaneous attacks were directed against the east and west walls, and from the south on the church and convent yard.

From the Alamo every piece of artillery slammed grapeshot and the snarling rifles of the Texans and Tennesseeans began spraying death. Forward rolled the dark lines of Santa Anna; then hesitated; and finally recoiled in retreat.

The first attack had been repulsed; the ground was covered with Mexican wounded and dead. The east and west columns of assault fell back toward the north, and Colonel Duque, a gallant officer, formed them on his own brigade.

Again the Mexicans charged, and once more the Texas rifles began their crackling. So rapid was the fire that, according to Santa Anna's own report, it 'illuminated the interior of the fortress and its walls and ditches'. Colonel Duque, leading his men, was mortally wounded. The second Mexican attack swirled up to the walls, halted before the deadly blast of Texas lead, and fell back.

Now the fatal weakness of the Alamo became apparent. The thinning numbers of Travis' men were not sufficient to defend the walls. Santa Anna rushed forward his reserves and the increased attacking forces once more returned to the assault, coming at several points at once.

Crockett and his Tennesseeans fought behind the log stockade that connected the church with the plaza. Travis himself directed the artillery. This time the attack, overwhelming in its weight and numbers, was pressed remorselessly home. As the Mexican troops reached the walls the cannon were rendered useless because their muzzles could not be sufficiently depressed to bear on the assailants. The few Texans, scattered along the walls, suffered heavily for, as Filisola said in his latter account of the battle, 'because the wall having no inner banquette, [the defenders] had, in order to deliver their fire, to stand on top where they could not live one second'.

Over the west barricades of the plaza lapped the Mexican horde; and turned the cannon on that side against the houses along the eastern wall where some of the defenders had taken refuge. Travis died, shot through the brain and falling across the trail of a cannon he was trying to fire. Bonham, also serving a gun, was likewise slain. Crockett, hemmed in, his men all dead about him, fought like a cornered wolf, using his clubbed rifle to smash heads until he was bayoneted.

The Mexicans burst into the church, which was the last redoubt, and the wounded and those fighting within it were ruthlessly slaughtered. It is probable that the last fighting man in the Alamo was Jim Bowie. His cot was in the baptistery of the church, where he lay coughing and spitting blood, very weak, but indomitable, with four pistols and his famous knife beside him. The Mexicans broke in the door. How many of them died before they reached him is a matter of dispute; it ranges from two to nine, according to different accounts. In the end they got Bowie. Five bayonets impaled

77

him; one, through the neck, breaking off short and pinning him to his bed. Then they lifted the magnificent dead body on their bayonets and carried it out, dumping it on the ground.

Lieutenant-Governor James W. Robinson of Texas, who made an investigation based on the testimony of all available witnesses – a few women and children, and a slave, who were spared – was convinced that Bowie was the last fighting man in the Alamo. Others died after him, but these were fugitives, no longer fighting, hunted out where they sought refuge, dragged forward, and slaughtered.

When it was over Santa Anna viewed the carnage with mixed feelings. These were, according to Ruiz, the *alcalde,* 182 dead Texans. *El Presidente* ordered them burned, and Ruiz was told to oversee the task of gathering them up and consuming them on two huge funeral pyres, so he had the best chance to make a complete count.

Santa Anna asked to be shown the bodies of Travis, Crockett and Bowie. He had been godfather to Bowie's wife, Ursula de Veramendi, and when he saw the dead man, he said, *'Era hombre muy valiente, no déjale como un perro* [This was a very valiant man, he ought not to be treated like a dog].' Then he changed his mind, shrugged his shoulders, and added, *'Pero no importe; échale dentro* [But it's of no importance; throw him in].' So Bowie's body was consumed on the pyre with his comrades, as no doubt he would have preferred.

Santa Anna had wiped out the Texans; but when he looked over his own army, the results must have shocked him. He admitted later that he lost 600 killed and wounded, but his total loss must have been much greater. Ruiz, who had charge of disposing of the Mexican bodies as well as burning the Texans, said the Mexican loss was 1,600 killed and wounded. After the Battle of San Jacinto, Ramón Caro, Santa Anna's private secretary who was captured, made the following statement which has the flavour of authenticity, since Caro certainly knew his chief's personal records and correspondence :

'We brought to San Antonio more than 5,000 men and we lost during the siege 1,544 of the best of them. The Texans fought more like devils than like men.'

Part of the Mexican loss was due to their own gunfire, for the arrangement of the assault was such that sometimes Mexican columns were cross-firing into each other. Ruiz, finding himself unable to bury all the Mexican bodies, had many of them thrown into the San Antonio River. For weeks afterward great flocks of buzzards hung over the city and river, feeding on the corpses that lodged against the banks, and many people left the city, fearing a pestilence.

Some military writers have said that the Alamo was a useless sacrifice. But others have pointed out that Santa Anna's forces suffered a serious loss in morale from the battle; that he was forced to reorganize his units; and that the loss of so many of his best troops weakened some of his enterprises afterward. At a minimum, the heroes of the Alamo bought the time which gave the convention its chance to make the all-important declaration of independence and the constitution of legal authority to which Houston relentlessly led it. And the cry, 'Remember the Alamo!' was of priceless value in giving fury to Texas arms in future conflict.

Houston received first news of the fall of the Alamo at Gonzales, where he went after his appointment as commander-in-chief. He hurried orders to Fannin, at Goliad, to blow up his defences and retreat; and in a letter to a friend he severely censured Fannin for failing to relieve the Alamo. Fannin failed to move as ordered. At Gonzales Houston gathered up a small force of 374 men, camped under the command of Colonel Moseley Baker, which was rapidly increased by volunteers who came hurrying in.

Word came that Fannin, after all his vacillations, had decided to remain and defend Goliad. When he heard it, Houston, with a groan, gestured at his handful of men and remarked, '*There* is the last hope of Texas. We shall never see Fannin or his men.'

The prediction was correct. Poor Fannin could not make up his mind and he and his men died for it.

Farther south, Grant and Johnson, with what remained of their 'invading force', were experiencing fatal vicissitudes. These two had intended to capture Matamoros but the effect of Houston's oratory at Refugio had so dampened the ardour of their followers that most of the latter abandoned the invasion project. On March 2, General José Urrea, with one of Santa Anna's columns, surprised Grant on the Nueces River. The flamboyant physician and forty-one of his men were lanced to death. Only one of the company survived, Reuben R. Brown, who was saved by the intercession of a priest and a Mexican woman, and eventually escaped to bring the story to the Texas lines.

Johnson, at San Patricio, was attacked the morning of February 27 in a driving rain. Though his men fought stubbornly the place was carried. Forty Texans died in the defence, but Johnson and three companions managed to escape. Johnson afterward wrote a memoir of this ill-fated and ill-advised expedition and a history of the early Texas republic.

In his cleaning-up operation, Urrea continued northward toward Fannin's post at Goliad. He had between nine hundred and a thousand men, against whom Fannin, who now had about five hundred men, might successfully have defended himself. Unfortunately Fannin took this time to divide his forces.

He sent Captain King with 28 men to bring away several terrified families of Texans at Refugio; then sent Colonel Ward with 120 men to rescue King.

Unhappily for this movement, Urrea was a skilful and decisive officer. He attacked Ward and King, killed the latter and many of the Texans; and, though he suffered severe losses himself, forced Ward, who had retreated into a swamp, to surrender, when his men exhausted their ammunition. The prisoners were taken to Goliad by the victorious Mexicans.

When Fannin learned the fate of Ward and King, March 17, he changed his mind once more. He now began to retreat from Goliad as Houston had directed him to do in a dispatch three days before. But he had waited too long. The enemy appeared in force March 19 and when Fannin began to fall back it was in the face of the opposing army. He had now only about three hundred men and nine pieces of artillery, having frittered away the rest of his force. Though he made his withdrawal safely under cover of a fog, he failed to use the ordinary military precautions of scouts and outriders. Suddenly, near the Coleto River, he found himself surrounded by overwhelmingly larger forces.

Nevertheless he prepared to fight. His soldiers, consisting chiefly of several companies from the United States with high-sounding names – the Red Rovers, the New Orleans Grays, the Kentucky Mustangs, the Mobile Grays and so on – were formed in a hollow square. Urrea attacked. Three times his troops were beaten back. Night came, but when the main battle ceased, Campeachy Indian auxiliaries crept forward in the long grass and harassed the Texans with destructive fire, wounding Fannin himself.

Morning dawned at length – Sunday, March 20. With its early light a strong reinforcement was seen coming up to join the Mexicans. After some fighting Fannin surrendered, on the promise the lives of his men and himself would be spared. The Texans were marched to Goliad, where they joined as prisoners the survivors of Ward's detachment.

Santa Anna, who was still at San Antonio, was apprised by Urrea of his success. Some time prior to his invasion of Texas the dictator had caused a law to be passed by the Mexican Congress, by which all foreigners found in Mexico with arms in their possession were considered pirates, to be punished as such. Many of Fannin's men, from Tennessee, Kentucky, Mississippi or Louisiana, fell under this heading. Santa Anna sent an order to Lieutenant-Colonel Nicolás de la Portilla, whom Urrea had left in command at Goliad, to execute the prisoners.

His officers were horrified. Urrea, who had outmanœuvred and captured the Texans, personally asked mercy for them – and received for doing so a sharp reprimand. Portilla, directly commanded to perform the executions, hesitated

81

and spent a whole night wrestling with his conscience and his duty, before he decided to follow what were, indeed, peremptory orders. Colonel Garay withdrew four Texan doctors from the hospital and, with one company of Texans which did not come within the massacre orders, held them apart; and even concealed two doomed soldiers in his own tent to save their lives. Señora Alvarez, a Mexican woman, hid several men in her home, so that they escaped.

But as to Santa Anna, Hubert Howe Bancroft, the historian, wrote, 'No ray of mercy or of pity illumined the dark and cruel soul of the general-in-chief. He was the incarnation of an inhumanity at once revengeful and cowardly. The slaughter of his troops at the Alamo still rankled in his mind, and he would not have spared a single life.'

What followed was the worst of the crimes charged against Santa Anna. On the morning of March 27, Palm Sunday, the Texas-American prisoners were marched out of their barracks. Knowing nothing of their doom, they were in good spirits, expecting soon to be allowed to return to their homes.

Instead, guarded by files of soldiers, they were led into a field and there halted. At a sudden order, the soldiers raised their muskets and began shooting down the unarmed victims. Most fell at the first treacherous fire. A few tried to escape but were mercilessly hunted down. Those who were wounded were put to death. Fannin and Ward were both shot, their bodies left to the wolves and vultures. In this massacre more than three hundred men were murdered without warning; and without sentence being pronounced upon them.

Santa Anna, with the Alamo reduced, Johnson's and Grant's men slain, and Fannin's force massacred, possibly believed that the war was over and Texas under his foot. But there was another with different thoughts.

Sam Houston was yet in the field. Though he had only a handful of men and no supplies, he still had to be defeated.

CHAPTER SEVEN

"Remember the Alamo!"

WITH the fall of the Alamo and Fannin's failure to join him at Gonzales, Houston had but one alternative. Mexican forces to the south and west were too great for him to face with the little force he had called 'the last hope of Texas.' He must keep this small handful from being engulfed with the others, and use it as a nucleus with which to build an army that might have some chance against Santa Anna's thousands.

Retreat was his only possible strategy. He did not yet know what had happened to Fannin, but by withdrawing he could hope for two advantages: as he passed through east Texas he might pick up additional men and arms; and by drawing on Santa Anna into lengthening his lines of communication, he might weaken the Mexican forces through the necessity of leaving garrisons and the difficulty of transporting supplies, artillery and ammunition.

Yet retreat would not be popular. He would have to abandon Texas towns and plantations to an enemy who looted and destroyed invariably. Furthermore, the Texas instinct was to stand and fight, whatever the odds – a headlong trait exemplified by Travis, Bowie and Fannin, with results so disastrous that of all the available men under arms and regularly organized in Texas, totalling perhaps eleven hundred, more than seven hundred had been lost at the Alamo, Goliad and San Patricio.

Houston was almost the only man in Texas with any conception of strategy as against tactics. He was so much alone in having military training that in his little army only he knew how to play the usual signals on a drum, and it was the general who acted as drummer-boy in the Texas camp and on the march.

He gave the order to retreat. Almost instantly it set in motion what Texans still call 'the Runaway Scrape'. The families at Gonzales – thirty of which had lost fathers and husbands at the Alamo – accompanied Houston's army with what they could carry in baggage wagons. The 'government', headed by the new president, David G. Burnet, a Bible-reading adventurer who had been an *empresario,* decamped in some trepidation to Harrisburg, on Buffalo Bayou, which ran into Galveston Bay. Everyone else in Texas seemed to be running also. Wagons, carts and animals, bearing women and children and household effects, choked the muddy roads in terrified flight from the Mexicans. Behind the refugees columns of smoke showed where homes and property were being destroyed by the invaders.

As the army left Gonzales a series of explosions was heard. A momentary panic – Santa Anna's artillery must be coming up! But Houston smiled and shook his head. Some over-zealous persons had poisoned a quantity of liquor and left it, hoping the Mexicans would drink it. Houston had his own ideas of the conduct of civilized war. He had detailed Deaf Smith and a rear guard to gather that liquor and blow it up.

Hampered by the fleeing settlers, his army angry and humiliated by the retreat and almost insubordinate, the general doggedly continued his withdrawal, explaining his plans to nobody. He did, however, seek to encourage his men, who by now numbered some four hundred. Riding beside his column, as if counting them, he said to them, 'We are on the rise of eight hundred strong and with a good position can whip ten to one of the enemy.'

Probably nobody believed him, but his cheerfulness and courage won the loyalty of most of his men. Some deserted in discouragement, but more came in. By the time he reached the Colorado River, where he remained several days to see that every refugee family was safely across, he had about seven hundred in his 'army', and had sent his aide-de-camp, William T. Austin, far ahead to the mouth of the Brazos, to fetch from there cannon and ammunition. He meant to fight

– when conditions made it possible. Not before, no matter what anyone might say or think.

He was still at Beason's Crossing of the Colorado on March 23, when the advance guard of the pursuing Mexicans, under Generals Sesma and Woll, reached the river and camped across it, about two miles above him. Detachments under Captain Karnes and Colonel Sherman were sent to prevent their crossing, and for six days the Texas and Mexican forces lay in striking distance of each other, with only one skirmish, in which Karnes's men killed one Mexican and captured another.

Houston's forces were increasing daily. By March 25 he had more than a thousand men. Sesma and Woll, with only about eight hundred, preferred to wait for their main body before attacking him.

In his army orders of March 21, Houston had said, 'In a few days I hope to have force sufficient to capture the enemy before he can reach the Guadalupe.' And he told Captain Shape to 'tell the people not to run any farther . . . there would be no more retreating; and that the next news they will hear from the army would be of a battle, the result of which no one could doubt.'

This sounded like immediate action along the Colorado. But on March 25 dread news came. A man named Peter Kerr rode in to tell of the capture and massacre of Fannin's command at Goliad. It ended the last hope of junction with that force; and furthermore it indicated that Urrea, the victor over Johnson, Grant and Fannin, must be pressing close on the Texan's rear. While Houston might have beaten Sesma and Woll, such a victory would not have been decisive, for he dared not pursue them under present conditions.

He therefore ordered another retirement March 26. The command was received with bitter dissatisfaction by his men, who wanted to fight, and had no conception of the problems being faced by their general. Many asked for furloughs to move their families to places of safety. Houston invariably granted these requests. As his retreat continued, more and more asked, until his force was reduced by half. And when

85

he reached San Felipe and decided to leave it and move up the Brazos River, there was outright insubordination.

Many of the angry Texans said that the chief settlements which should be protected were *down* this river, instead of up; and two companies, under Colonel Moseley Baker and Captain Wylie Martin, refused to come into line.

Houston knew all too well the weakness of his position. The 'authority' by which he acted as 'commander-in-chief' was, at the moment, almost as shadowy as the future of Texas appeared to be. Thus far he had kept his army together solely by force of personality, and he could not risk a clash which might divide the loyalties of his men, for he was in no position to deal with mutiny.

He therefore made as much of a virtue of necessity as he could, gave 'orders' to Baker to guard the crossing at San Felipe, and to Martin to go downstream – in other words to do exactly what they wanted to do – and with only 520 men remaining to him, pursued his own plan. On March 31 he camped on the right bank of the Brazos, opposite Groce's plantation, where he planned to cross. But exceptionally heavy rains raised the river to a height never known before, so high that the Texan camp ground was at one time converted into an island by the flood and there was no possibility of crossing it until the waters receded which was not until April 13.

Meantime Sesma and Woll were reinforced at the Colorado by a force under General Tolsa, raising their division to fourteen hundred men. Sesma, the chief commander, decided he was strong enough to pursue the Texans and crossed his force over the river in rafts.

This was a time of peril for Houston, caught with reduced forces on the wrong side of the Brazos. Fortunately, however, Sesma received orders to wait for Santa Anna, who had decided to take personal charge of pursuing and annihilating the last Texas military force.

El Presidente, flushed with the success of his early operations, had been a little surprised to learn that there still remained a stubborn concentration of insurgents in the

Colorado and Brazos area. With his peculiar vanity, he wanted to be present and take all the credit for finally crushing the rebels. He had also a feeling, perhaps, that his own role thus far had been none too brilliant or admirable. His useless battering against the Alamo, with the loss of a large part of his best army, when he might easily have reduced it by starvation, smacked of bad strategy; and revealed a kind of arrogant impatience as well as a disregard for human life. He must have known that his own officers, such as Generals Filisola and Urrea, were criticizing his wasteful and bloody tactics. Furthermore, his massacres of prisoners who fell into his hands found dissent among his best officers and many influential Mexicans in private life. To a nature like his, such censure, even though not openly spoken but only felt by him, would further stimulate his fury against the Texans who, in one way or another, had placed him in a bad light. All in all, *El Presidente* felt he needed to recoup his lost prestige by obliterating personally the last of the rebels.

This vanity saved Houston, who had sufficient time to get over the Brazos before he was caught by overwhelming forces, and further to build up his army beyond that flooded river.

Santa Anna started from San Antonio, where he had been reorganizing his forces, with his army proceeding in three divisions to sweep up all possible lingering insurgent bands and concentrate with the advance division under General Sesma. General Ganoa took the northern route, crossing the Colorado at Bastrop. Urrea marched by the southern coastal route, to take possession of Matagorda. Santa Anna, with his staff, including General Filisola, and a considerable part of the army, took the most direct, central route, by way of Gonzales and San Felipe, to join Sesma and proceed – as he believed – triumphantly on.

Now Houston's strategy – to drain the Mexican strength in the Texas distances – at last began to tell. The rains which had held him at the Brazos continued and proved now as much of a help as they had been a hindrance. Finding the Guadalupe too swollen to move his main command across it, Santa Anna left it with Filisola, who was to bring it along as

87

soon as possible, and with only his staff and an escort proceeded rapidly to join Sesma.

Meantime his left wing, under Ganoa, after crossing the
Colorado, became entangled in the canyons, mesquite and
mud of the intervening country, lost its way, and failed to
arrive at the concentration point until too late. Urrea, with
the right wing, found Matagorda vacated and marched on
down the coast, capturing Brazoria April 22, with a large
quantity of supplies and goods. Urrea was the best of Santa
Anna's commanders, and the celerity of his march was in
itself excellent; but its very boldness placed him out of the
immediate field of action.

Filisola took days getting the central army across the
Guadalupe to follow his commander. And Santa Anna,
having found Sesma's advance division, impatiently began
pressing forward with it, his impatience increased by the
report that the Texas seat of government had been moved
to Harrisburg, on Galveston Bay. If he could capture the
president and congress of the rebellious state and execute
them, he might end the revolution at a single stroke.

Baker's detachment opposed his crossing at San Felipe.
Leaving Sesma with 489 men to occupy the colony's capital
and with orders to follow as soon as Filisola came up with
the main command, Santa Anna proceeded down the river
and put his force of 700 men and a six-pounder gun across at
a point where Wylie Martin's force was too weak to prevent
him. From there, by forced marches, Santa Anna proceeded
to Harrisburg.

Only another very prompt decampment by the Texas
government prevented his capturing it. President Burnet,
indeed, almost was overtaken by a flying squadron of Mexican lancers early on the morning of April 17; but he displayed considerable nimble-footedness on this occasion, and
with his cabinet and congress managed to get across the bay
to Galveston Island, where, at the extremist limit of Texas,
the forlorn government again set itself up and waited
anxiously for news from Houston.

Santa Anna burned Harrisburg to the ground. His only

captives were three printers. From them he learned that Houston and the Texas army were near; and also – this was mere rumour – that Houston intended to fall back to the Sabine River, at the border of Texas, where he expected to be reinforced by volunteers from the United States and make his final stand. Houston actually never had this design, but he did not deny it, and report of it, reaching Santa Anna, affected the latter's movements, since he expected to have to extend his pursuit farther.

While *El Presidente* was thus marching his forces across Texas, Houston experienced troubles sufficiently serious. He himself beat the reveille and mess calls, as well as all other signals, on an old drum – the only one in camp. He also turned his hand to many other tasks usually assigned to subordinates, including helping the farriers in repairing rolling stock and in cutting up old horseshoes for artillery ammunition.

A young recruit complained to a blacksmith he saw working at an improvised forge that the lock on his gun would not work.

'Leave it and come back in an hour,' said the smith.

Later the youth returned with a stammered apology. 'I was told you were the blacksmith, sir. I didn't know you were the commanding general.'

'You were told quite right,' said Sam Houston. 'I'm a damned good blacksmith. Here's your gun. The lock works all right now.'

But there were greater problems. Part of the army was almost mutinous. President Burnet was Houston's enemy, continuously wrote critical letters, and even kept a spy in camp to report on the general.

When things reached a crisis, Houston caused two graves to be dug and nailed notices to the trees at the foot of which they lay, to the effect that they would be occupied by the first men who mutinied. It quietened the threatened insubordination and, when he ordered, the men marched. Another triumph of personality could be chalked up for Houston, for he was not even backed by a shadow government now, since

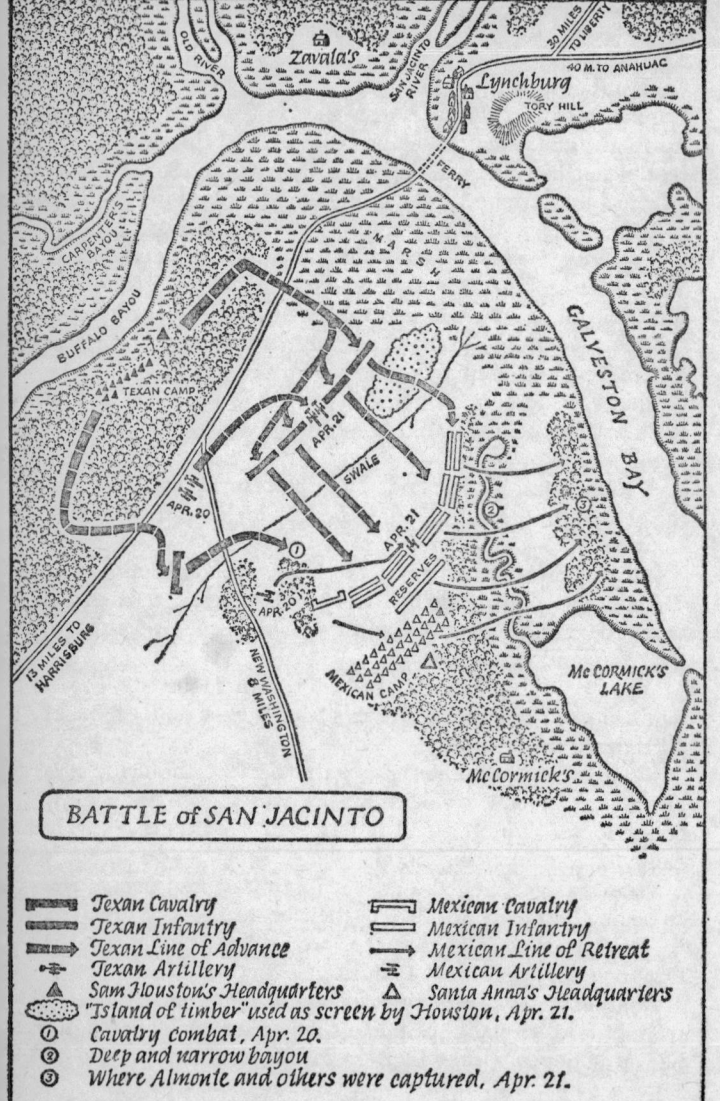

BATTLE of SAN JACINTO

⬛⬛⬛ Texan Cavalry
⬛⬛⬛ Texan Infantry
⬛➤ Texan Line of Advance
⊷ Texan Artillery
▲ Sam Houston's Headquarters

⬜⬜ Mexican Cavalry
⬜⬜ Mexican Infantry
→ Mexican Line of Retreat
⊤ Mexican Artillery
△ Santa Anna's Headquarters

"Island of timber" used as screen by Houston, Apr. 21.
① Cavalry combat, Apr. 20.
② Deep and narrow bayou
③ Where Almonte and others were captured, Apr. 21.

it was no secret that the president of the republic wished to have him replaced by a commander who 'would fight'.

At last Houston received two field pieces – six-pounders which his men christened the Twin Sisters – and volunteers came drifting in, making up for the defections in his ranks and more, so that he had perhaps eight hundred men. Some of these, among themselves, accused him of incompetence, timidity or worse. Burnet's spy, in a letter to the president – which was intercepted – quoted a report that Houston had 'given up drunkenness in favour of the opium habit'. Yet in spite of all the discontent and criticism, Sam Houston somehow compelled his men to march through the incessant rain and mud, explaining himself to nobody, telling them nothing.

He arrived at Buffalo Bayou, opposite Harrisburg, April 18. The town was in ruins, still smouldering. Santa Anna had been there only the day before.

That evening the indefatigable Deaf Smith and a few scouts swam the bayou and captured two prisoners, one of them a courier. The saddlebags of the courier bore the name of W. B. Travis – a memento of the Alamo. But the saddlebags contained something more important at the moment – letters to Santa Anna from Filisola, who was marching to join his chief. For the first time Houston learned that the Mexican force immediately confronting him was commanded in person by the dictator.

It crystallized his determination. Other armies were converging on him and there was risk in fighting just at this point. But the arch enemy was there – just on the other side of the river. Houston would seek personal conclusions with Santa Anna.

The morning of April 19 he assembled his soldiers and made a short speech, telling them that Santa Anna, the murderer of their comrades, was across the bayou and that they were to cross and meet him. He concluded his speech with these words :

'The army will cross, and we will meet the enemy. Some of us may be killed, must be killed; but, soldiers, remember the Alamo ! The Alamo ! The Alamo !'

The army took up the words with a roar. *'Remember the Alamo!'*

Texas at last had a battle cry.

Leaving his sick and the baggage with a small guard, Houston moved down the bayou two miles and got his army across, using an old boat and the floor torn from a cabin which served as a raft, the horses swimming. By nightfall the crossing was complete and in the darkness the Texans pushed forward to Lynch's Ferry – toward which Santa Anna also was marching, from the south. Houston reached the ferry first; and captured a boatload of flour which, with some cattle that were grazing in the vicinity, provided his men with a welcome barbecue to strengthen them for the battle to come.

With a choice of positions, Houston arranged his men in a fine belt of timber which ran along Buffalo Bayou just above the place where the San Jacinto River ran into it and very close to Galveston Bay. In front of the position was an open prairie broken by a few clumps of trees; to its left a marsh prevented its being flanked; and behind it ran Buffalo Bayou itself. It was a position from which there could be no retreat and Houston's selection of it proved his deadly determination to conquer at this point or perish with his army.

About two o'clock in the afternoon of that day, April 20, Santa Anna's vanguard appeared. *El Presidente*, who had been at the hamlet of New Washington the previous night, had a bad scare when a false report came that Houston was upon him. He is said to have ridden like a madman out of the town, crying out at the top of his voice that the enemy was coming and knocking down and riding over people in the street as he galloped out of the place. He was tactfully informed that the report was unfounded and, somewhat shamefaced, formed a column and marched toward Lynch's Ferry.

Near there he at last found Houston. There was a brief skirmish, in which the Texas guns called the Twin Sisters disabled the one Mexican piece of artillery and a few men fell on each side. Colonel Sidney Sherman – who was Burnet's

candidate to succeed Houston as commander-in-chief – made
a charge to capture the Mexican gun and failed. It was just
the chance Houston had been awaiting. He gave Sherman
a tongue-lashing which was heard by the whole army and
took away from him the command of the cavalry – consisting
of fifty-three mounted men. In his place he promoted to
colonel a private with the flamboyant name of Mirabeau
Buonaparte Lamar, and put him in command of the mounted
force. It was the beginning of a career for Lamar, who would
one day become president of the Texas republic on the
strength of this day.

Night fell. The Mexicans camped to the southeast, across
the plain, with the marsh to their right and a wooded ravine
to their left. Morning dawned with no movement from either
army. For some reason Houston was waiting – nobody knew
why – and again there was bitter complaint from the men,
who were anxious to get at their enemies.

In the middle of the morning Deaf Smith rode into camp,
saying that reinforcements were arriving for Santa Anna.
Houston spoke to him aside and the scout went out again. As
Houston watched him go, he remarked aloud, so that a group
of soldiers heard him, that it wasn't often that Deaf Smith
got fooled like that – Santa Anna had been marching his men
around a grove of trees to make it look like a reinforcement.
Smith came back at a gallop and said that the general was
right – the whole thing was a fraud and no reinforcements
had come. But having thus carried out Houston's instructions,
he privately told him that it *was* a reinforcement – General
Cos, with 500 soldiers, raising Santa Anna's force to 1,300
men, against whom the Texans could oppose exactly 783
men.

Later, Houston told Santa Anna that the reason he did
not attack before the arrival of Cos was that he did not want
to make 'two bites of one cherry'.

As a precaution – to prevent Filisola, who was approaching with another large force, from joining Santa Anna during
the battle – Houston sent Deaf Smith to destroy Vince's
Bridge, over which Cos had marched. By this he also cut off

the last slender chance of his own men to escape if they were beaten.

About noon Houston held a council of war; his first and last during the campaign. The question was, 'Whether they should attack the enemy in his position, or await his attack on theirs.' Opinion was divided and Houston said nothing. Instead he sounded out the captains of his companies as to whether they should attack at once or wait until just before daybreak of the morrow. The captains voted overwhelmingly in favour of immediate attack.

Thereupon Houston mounted a great white stallion and deployed his men in battle formation. On this day of days he wore 'an old black coat, a black velvet vest, a pair of snuff-coloured pantaloons, and dilapidated boots', with his trousers tucked in them. 'His only badge of authority during the campaign was a sword with a plated scabbard which he tied to his belt with buckskin thongs.'

Thus the leader of one of the most forlorn hopes in history prepared to fight a battle which, for all the small numbers of combatants involved, deserves to rank among the decisive battles of the world, for it would decide the mastery of half a continent between two rivals not only in race but in basic ideals. As Marquis James wrote in his magnificent biography of Houston, *The Raven*, 'On an obscure meadow . . . wet steel would decide which civilization would prevail . . . in the clash of men and symbols – the *conquistador* and the frontiersman, the Inquisition and the Magna Carta, the rosary and the rifle.'

In the shelter of the small groves of trees before his position, Houston placed Burleson's regiment in the centre, Sherman's on the left, and the Twin Sisters on the right, supported by Millard and Lamar with his cavalry. Then he rode out in the van on his white stallion, raised his hat, and gave the order to advance. A single fife struck up a then popular air, 'Will You Come to the Bower?' and the Texans went forward to come at last to grips with the foe from whom they had so long retreated.

As they broke into view of the Mexican camp, Deaf Smith

careered down the line on a foaming horse, shouting in his high-pitched voice so that all could hear, 'Fight for your lives, boys! Vince's Bridge has been cut down!'

Not a man missed the significance. It was grim victory or death for those ragged Texas fighting men. Not one of them broke stride or paled. Instead they began running forward, and across the plain into the Mexican camp thundered the cry, 'Remember the Alamo! Remember Goliad!' It was the voice of a new people, a cry of fury and deadly retribution.

So suddenly came the attack that the Mexican camp was caught completely by surprise. Cos and his men were sleeping off the weariness of their forced march. Santa Anna, who campaigned in style, was taking his *siesta* in his tent, which was carpeted and furnished in something like splendour. A few sleepy sentinels drowsed, for nobody dreamed that the Texans would advance at this hour.

A bugle sang sudden alarm and Mexican soldiers, hastily buckling on ammunition belts and seizing muskets, ran to a low barricade of pack saddles and carts, and began to fire. Some Texas rifles replied.

'Hold your fire! God damn you, hold your fire!' roared Houston, spurring forward.

The white stallion reared and fell under him, killed by a bullet. He took the horse of a cavalryman, threw himself on it, and resumed his riding up and down the line.

The Twin Sisters bellowed and part of the barricade was blown flat. Now Houston loosed his Texans. Their rifles began to speak; and, howling, they swept over the torn barricade.

Everywhere Mexicans were fleeing. After them roared the avenging Texans, mad with rage and lust for revenge. Without mercy they slew all upon whom they came.

Some of the Mexican officers died bravely, notably General Castrillon, who vainly tried to rally his men, then stood on an ammunition box, his arms folded, sternly awaiting death, which came to him there. General Almonte managed to hold together a body of four or five hundred soldiers by sheer coolness and intrepidity; though later in the day, hemmed in the morass at the rear, he had to surrender them.

But among those who did not await the onslaught of the Texans were Santa Anna and his shifty brother-in-law, General Cos. Both fled at the first attack.

Hardly ever in history was an army so completely obliterated as was Santa Anna's that day at San Jacinto. The figures reported by Houston showed 630 of the enemy killed, 208 wounded and 730 prisoners. The wounded probably were included among the prisoners, but even that adds up to a loss of 1,360 – the entire force Santa Anna had after he was reinforced by Cos.

Six Texans were killed and twenty-five wounded, of whom two later died. Among the wounded was General Houston. He had a musket ball in the ankle, but continued to ride with his boot full of blood until the Mexicans were in full rout.

Captured were all the Mexican arms and ammunition, several hundred horses and mules, all the baggage and camp equipment (including Santa Anna's carpeted tent) and the military chest, containing $12,000.

Next day there was an even more important capture. Santa Anna had mounted a fine horse to save his precious hide, taking the road to Vince's Bridge, hoping to join Filisola's oncoming force. He found to his consternation that the bridge was destroyed. Nevertheless he tried to cross the creek, only to mire down his horse. Abandoning the animal, he hid until night, then got across the little stream, stripped off his gaudy general's uniform, and donned instead the garb of a common soldier – the blue cotton jacket and linen trousers, with a leather cap – which he found, as he said, in a house, but more likely took from the body of one of his own men who had been killed. Thus disguised, he tried to escape on foot.

But a detachment of Texas riders, headed by Joel Robinson soon scooped in the undersized, mud-spattered and abject little figure and took him back to Houston. Santa Anna tried to hide his identity, but a group of Mexican prisoners, seeing him, took off their hats and murmured among themselves, 'El Presidente! El Presidente!'

Thus unmasked, he was conducted to where Houston lay under a tree in the captured Mexican camp, his shattered leg stretched out before him. The Texans had spent the night roistering and captured liquor had left many an aching head, while discipline was almost lost. Well did Santa Anna know that these people held him responsible for the butcheries that had taken place, and he must have felt a choking dread as he stood before the victorious commander who, though too crippled to move about, was writing dispatches, questioning prisoners, and trying to restore some sort of order in his army.

Calmly Houston looked over his unwilling guest and told him to be seated on a box. Even while he trembled for his life, Santa Anna could not help being grandiloquent.

'That man may consider himself born to no common destiny who has conquered the Napoleon of the West,' he said. 'It now remains for him to be generous to the vanquished.'

Houston gave him a grimly piercing look. 'You should have remembered that at the Alamo.'

It shook the Napoleon of the West. He asked for some opium and swallowed a piece of it when it was furnished him from one of the Mexican medicine chests. With his composure somewhat restored, he began to try to excuse his crimes, saying he had only followed the dictates of the Mexican Congress, which had made the laws under which he acted. He did not mention that the Mexican Congress, in enacting those laws, had obeyed his own commands. So much was he in terror of his life that he was willing to do anything – sell his own country if necessary – to save himself. Around him crowded the Texans with hate in their eyes and his fear rose.

But he need not have felt such trepidation. One man present saw past this moment of triumph and revenge and already was planning the future. To Sam Houston, Santa Anna was worth much more alive than dead.

Keeping the dejected little Mexican dictator seated before him, Houston called for pen and ink and paper, and dictated to Santa Anna orders, which the latter eagerly wrote and signed, commanding all his armies to evacuate Texas immediately. Filisola was at the Brazos, where at last he had been joined by Gano. Urrea was at Brazoria. There were other Mexican contingents.

When Urrea joined Filisola, April 25, after news of the disaster at San Jacinto, their combined forces totalled 2,573 men of all arms. There were besides 1,505 more, stationed at San Antonio, Goliad and Matagorda. The numbers were more than sufficient, if promptly brought to bear and well led, to defeat the jubilantly victorious army of Houston, which still numbered less than 800 men.

But these officers were loyal to Santa Anna; and, though he was a prisoner, still regarded him as their commander. When Deaf Smith arrived at their camp the afternoon of April 27, bearing dispatches with Santa Anna's authentic signature, they obeyed. The retreat began as ordered.

Now President Burnet and his cabinet – after sufficient reassurances – felt it safe to return to the mainland from Galveston Island. They did so, and caused trouble of every annoying kind, from the moment they arrived at Houston's camp. Some of them, and a good many of the soldiers, were for lynching Santa Anna at once – and also General Cos, the parole violator, who had been captured. Both richly deserved the fate. But Houston calmly resisted all suggestions along this delectable line. His judgment in saving the two prisoners was presently vindicated.

Nobody understood Santa Anna's perilous situation better than *El Presidente* himself. He agreed rather precipitately to a treaty when Houston proposed it – he would have agreed to almost anything at the moment. The sense of the treaty which Houston dictated was that Texas was independent, and Mexico renounced all claims to it, territorially or otherwise. With a copy of this treaty Colonel Benjamin F. Smith and Captain Henry Teal, as commissioners, set out on horseback after Filisola's retreating army, overtook it between

Goliad and San Patricio, and had the Mexican generals ratify its provisions.

It was a very informal treaty. Some time was going to pass before a formal treaty would be made. But for the present it would do and never again would Mexico seriously threaten to repossess its lost province.

Houston, his wounded leg badly infected, was taken by ship to New Orleans for treatment. When he returned to Texas, still on crutches and far from recovered, he found the republic in turmoil and Burnet, his enemy, unable to control either the government or the people.

Santa Anna was still a prisoner. An attempt had been made to assassinate him by shooting at him through the window of a house in which he was confined, but the bullet missed. A plot also had been made to rescue him via the connivance of a Spaniard named Bartolomé Pages, but it was discovered and failed.

Burnet threw up his hands, announced his resignation from an office he could not cope with, and called an election to ratify the constitution and elect a new president. Some difficulty was experienced in finding a copy of the constitution for ratification, but candidates for the presidency were not so hard to discover. Stephen Austin and Henry Smith, the former governor, offered their names. At the last minute friends of Sam Houston persuaded him to become a candidate. In the election, September 5, Houston received 5,119 votes, Smith 743 and Austin only 587.

To Austin it was a crushing humiliation. Though he accepted the post of secretary of state – as Smith accepted that of secretary of the treasury – and laboured conscientiously on the problems of the infant nation, he died December 7. Houston's announcement gave him the fitting recognition he deserved : 'The Father of Texas is no more.'

With Houston as president, affairs moved in Texas. Santa Anna was saved again from lynching – this time by New Orleans volunteers under General Thomas J. Green. Thoroughly cowed, the Napoleon of the West, at the suggestion of Stephen Austin, then in the last days of his life, wrote a letter to President Andrew Jackson, filled with flowery compliments and humbly appealing to Old Hickory to exert his good offices. Jackson, who had received with every evidence of joy a report of his favourite subaltern's victory at San Jacinto – written on the field of battle and in his own hand by Houston while he lay wounded – replied with a carefully worded message, disclaiming any intent to interfere, but expressing willingness to assist in working out matters if the government of Mexico so desired.

The 'government' of Mexico – Santa Anna – did so desire, and said so, promptly. He was most eager to leave the uncomfortably perilous soil of Texas where people organized impromptu lynching parties in his honour. So he was conveyed overland to the Mississippi, passed by steamboat up that stream and the Ohio to Louisville, Kentucky, and thence by coach to Washington.

Crowds everywhere gathered to see 'the illustrious prisoner'. One who saw him described him thus : 'A graceful figure, with a small oval face, stamped by thought and energy, a bilious complexion, with closely set eyes brilliantly reflecting an impulsive nature and talented mind. A sprinkling of grey hair added dignity . . . when enraged his face changed into repelling fierceness. His character for licentious indulgence was well known, and he abandoned himself to every form of dissipation. He was an inveterate gambler and his favourite form of diversion was the cockpit.'

He conferred with Jackson, agreeing to the treaty terms setting Texas free. From Washington he was liberated to return home by sea. He landed at Vera Cruz July 26, 1837, discredited in his own country and very soon displaced as Mexico's ruler.

In the last days of the Jackson administration the United States recognized the new Republic of Texas, a mighty milestone in its history. Sam Houston turned grimly to the inevitable reorganization work and the administration of his new nation.

Book Two

THE GIANT OF THE NORTH

CHAPTER ONE

The Strange Story of Cynthia Ann Parker

WHILE Houston enacted the drama of the Mexican campaign in the south, northern Texas suffered its own tragedy. Indian hostility in the Red River region was somewhat chronic, but in the Texas revolution agents of the Mexican government were among them, and the plans of the warlike tribes were directed by representations and gifts made by those agents, so that the danger was something bigger and more terrifying than mere horse-stealing raids with incidental scalping.

Particularly active and ferocious were the Comanches. On April 14, 1836, seven days before San Jacinto, a band of those vicious raiders massacred the Horn party of refugees — fleeing before the Mexican invaders — killing nine men and three children and carrying away two young wives who saw their husbands and babies murdered before their eyes. The two unfortunate women, Mrs. Horn and Mrs. Harris, after the usual treatment accorded to captive women by the Indians, were ransomed months later and one of them wrote a pamphlet recounting her experiences, which were not pretty.

Other depredations of like nature occurred. Most important of these was the massacre at Parker's Fort, on the Navasota River, about forty miles east of the present city of Waco.

That rainy April nobody dreamed of trouble at Parker's Fort. For the time and place it was strong, consisting of a group of log cabins, the outer walls of which formed a stockade with blockhouses at the corners and loopholes for rifle fire. Elder John Parker and his wife 'Granny' Parker were the patriarchs of the settlement. Parker was seventy-nine years old, a Virginian who had moved his family to Georgia, Tennessee, Illinois and finally to Texas. One of his sons, Silas M. Parker, was captain of one of the first Texas Ranger companies organized and was at this time away on frontier duty.

So long had this part of Texas been free from hostile incursions that the people of the settlement became careless, preferring to sleep in their cabins on their farms, which were scattered about, rather than go to the fort each night as was the original plan. Most of the men and many of the women were thus scattered when, on the morning of May 19, a large party of seven hundred Comanches and Kiowas, led by Peta Nokoni, a celebrated Comanche chief, suddenly appeared about the fort.

As soon as the Indians made sure that the place was open and undefended, they rushed the fort. Screams, shots, yells, the trampling of feet and the sound of blows made the morning hideous. When the Comanches drew off they had killed and scalped Elder John Parker and several other persons; and carried with them as prisoners two women, Mrs. Elizabeth Kellog and Mrs. Rachel Plummer, and three children, James Pratt Plummer, Mrs. Plummer's little son, and the two children of Silas M. Parker, the Ranger captain, Cynthia Ann Parker, nine years old, and her brother John, some years younger.

The adventures of these prisoners hold interest as revealing what commonly happened to captives of this kind among the Plains Indians.

With their loot and scalps the Comanches and Kiowas rode back toward the Staked Plains. The first night they held a scalp dance and the two white women came in for the usual abuse. A little later the party was divided, Mrs. Plummer and her child were separated, and Mrs. Kellogg and the Parker children distributed among the Indians according to the custom when children were intended for adoption. As for adult women under such circumstances, General Richard I. Dodge, writing in *Our Wild Indians,* published in 1882 and relating his thirty years' frontier service against primitive tribes, said :

Cooper, and some other novelists, knew nothing of Indian character and customs when they placed their heroines as prisoners in their hands. I believe I am perfectly safe in the assertion that there is not a single wild tribe of Indians in all the wide territory of the United States which does not regard the person of the female captives as the inherent right of the captor; and I venture to assert further that, with the single exception of the lady captured by the Nez Percés, under Joseph, in Yellowstone park, no woman has, in the last thirty years, been taken prisoner by any wild Indians who did not, as soon after as practicable, become a victim to all the brutality of . . . her captors.

When a woman is captured by a party, she belongs equally to each and all, so long as the party is out. When it returns to the home encampment . . . she becomes the exclusive property of the individual who captured her. In some instances he takes her to wife, and she has protection, as such; but in the very large majority of cases she is held by him as a slave, for the vilest purposes, being sold by her owner to anyone who wants her. In nearly all the tribes there are more or less of these slaves.

The life of such a woman is miserable beyond expression, for the squaws force her to constant labor, beating her on any, or without provocation. . . . She brings her owner more or less revenue, dependent on her beauty; and, as property, is worth quite as much as an equally good-looking girl of virtue. She is a favorite stake at the gambling-board, and may change masters half a dozen times a day, as varies the fortune of the game; passing from hand to hand; one day the property of a chief, the next, of a common warrior. . . .

Indians always prefer to capture rather than kill women, they being merchantable property. White women are unusually valuable, one moderately good-looking being worth as many ponies as would buy from their fathers three or four Indian girls.

From which it is evident that, if the Indians had no general understanding of slavery when Coronado entered the Southwest, the enlightening influence of the white man had so illumined these ignorant savages by now that they fully comprehended the institution in its worst forms.

Mrs. Plummer and Mrs. Kellog both eventually were ransomed. The former died shortly after she was freed from captivity, February 19, 1839. The unhappy woman did not live to learn that her little son, James Pratt Plummer, was ransomed also, late in 1842.

But what of the two Parker children, Cynthia Ann and John? Continuous efforts were made to trace them, but their particular band, the Quahada Comanches, went so far out into the plains that these efforts failed.

There is a fairly authenticated story that a party of traders, including Colonel Len Williams, a man named Stoal and a Delaware Indian guide, Jack Henry, saw her in a Comanche village on the Canadian River in 1840. She was then thirteen years old. Williams asked to talk with her. This was granted. The girl came to him and sat down at the foot of a tree. She did not reply to any question he asked, but remained perfectly silent as if she had been told to refrain from speaking and was being watched. By this time also she was becoming pretty thoroughly Comanche in her thoughts and ways and perhaps did not wish to return to the settlements. Williams' offer to ransom her was refused by the Indians.

Once more she was seen, fifteen years after her capture, by a party of white hunters, in a Quahada village on the upper waters of the Canadian. At that time she was twenty-four years old and had been married for several years – by Indian custom – to Peta Nokoni, the chief who led the sack of Parker's Fort. By him she had several children, but only one survived to maturity. This was a son, who came down in history as Quanah Parker, the greatest of the Comanche chiefs.

On this second occasion Cynthia Ann was asked if she would like to return to her people. She shook her head and was quoted as saying, 'I am happily wedded. I love my husband, who is good and kind, and my little ones, too, are his, and I cannot forsake them.'

If she did make such a speech it must be a very free (and stilted) translation of something she uttered in the Comanche tongue, for five years later, when she again appeared, she knew not one word of English.

In 1856 – twenty years after the massacre at Parker's Fort – Captain Lawrence Sullivan Ross, later a Confederate general, governor of Texas and president of Texas A. & M. College – with a force of U.S. dragoons, Rangers and armed civilians, surprised a Comanche hunting camp on the Pease River in the Texas Panhandle. A few Indians were killed and the Rangers captured a 'squaw' whose face was bronzed by the elements, but whose hair was blonde and whose eyes were blue. In her arms she carried a baby girl.

The 'squaw' was taken to the settlements by Ross, who sent for Isaac Parker, one of the survivors of the massacre at the fort, and brother of Silas M. Parker, deceased, thinking the woman might be the lost Cynthia Ann. The old account of the meeting in the Ranger camp says :

'Her age and general appearance suited the object of his [Parker's] search, but she had lost every word of her native tongue. Colonel Parker was about to give up in despair, when he turned to the interpreters and said very distinctly that the woman he was seeking was named Cynthia Ann. The sound of the name by which her mother had called her, awakened in the bosom of the poor captive emotions that had long lain dormant. In a letter . . . Captain Parker says, "The moment I mentioned the name she straightened herself in her seat and patting herself on the breast, said, 'Cynthia Ann, Cynthia Ann!' " . . . Her countenance changed and a pleasant smile took the place of sullen gloom.'

In spite of this recognition she was unhappy and considered herself a captive. When she was exhibited to the state convention at Austin she showed distress, thinking the assemblage was a meeting of 'war chiefs', sitting to decide how to put her to death. The legislature appointed her uncle, Isaac Parker, her guardian and voted a pension of $100 a year for her support. Yet every effort to reconcile her to civilized life failed. She had become so thoroughly a Comanche that she desired only to return to her savage people. Three times she tried to escape with her child, and each time she was pursued, recaptured, and brought back. At length her little girl, who bore the name Topsannah – Prairie Flower – died. Soon after Cynthia Ann also died. I have been told by her descendants, the children of Quanah Parker, that she starved herself to death in despair at being prevented from joining the people she considered her own.

John Parker, her brother, also grew up among the Comanches and became a warrior. During a Comanche raid into Mexico, his party captured a Mexican girl. On the trail back to the Staked Plains, John was stricken with smallpox. In consternation the other warriors fled from him, for smallpox was worse feared by the Indians than bullets. He would probably have died alone and neglected, had not the Mexican girl remained with him and nursed him back to health. When he recovered he took the girl back to her people south of the Rio Grande, married her, and remained there. During the Civil War he served in a Mexican company in the Confederate Army, and after the war died on a ranch in Mexico.

The experiences of this group of prisoners, and particularly Cynthia Ann's adoption and love of the savage life of the Indians, are by no means exceptional. Many white men, of course, took up Indian life, married Indian women, and gave up any thought of returning to civilization. This can easily be understood when one considers the adventurous and rather lawless nature of some frontiersmen. But there are also numerous instances where white women, though at first unwilling participants in the barbaric existence, at last so fell under its strange spell that they were unwilling to leave it, even when given the opportunity.

As far as Texas in general was concerned, the immediate effect of the massacre at Parker's Fort in 1836 produced a minor international incident. Shortly after that Comanche raid, an alarming report was circulating that a Mexican army, seven thousand strong, had been mobilized to march into Texas, Bustamente, who had succeeded Santa Anna as president, having repudiated the latter's treaty.

General Edward Gaines, commanding the United States troops on the Louisiana border, was under orders to observe strict neutrality, but to give aid if needed against hostile aggression by Indians 'against either Anglo-American or Mexican states'.

The Parker's Fort incident, Gaines felt, gave him freedom to act under his orders and early in July, 1836 he moved a detachment of regulars under Colonel Whistler across the Sabine, to occupy and fortify Nacogdoches. At this the Mexican ambassador in Washington made strong representations, refused to admit that Texas was independent, asked for his passports, and returned to Mexico. Shortly after, diplomatic relations between the two nations were broken off.

General Arbuckle relieved Gaines in October, but Arbuckle's orders were the same, giving him discretion to maintain troops in Nacogdoches; which he did, and there they remained for some time.

However one may look at it, this was an act of aggression by the United States, covered by a subterfuge and given technical legality by a provision of the treaty with Mexico, whereby both contracting nations agreed to prevent hostilities of Indian tribes against the citizens of either. Nacogdoches, however, was not threatened by any Indian tribe. Gaines's occupation of the town, therefore, was nothing less than an extension of military support to the Texans, who feared another Mexican invasion – under a bland pretext of a 'neutral' protective move.

It caused Bustamente to reconsider his invasion plans, if he had made them, and the march of the Mexican army did not materialize, perhaps owing to the indication of the attitude of the United States. Mexico felt affronted, and the occupation, with other incidents, developed a national spirit of hatred against the United States. The Parker's Fort massacre and the Nacogdoches occupation to which it gave excuse were among the steps which led to war later between Mexico and the United States.

CHAPTER TWO
The Scalp Hunters

It is time to return to New Mexico-Arizona, leaving Texas for the time being struggling in the usual throes of disorganization and jealousy which seem always to afflict a new nation.

Indian troubles had become acute along the northern frontiers of Mexico, particularly in the settlements in the Rio Grande and Gila valleys, where the Apaches never ceased raiding. Mexican weakness was responsible for Apache aggression. There never had been much control of the wild tribes, even during Spanish rule, although some of the Spanish military governors did campaign against and sometimes punish foraying bands. Under Mexican administration – which lacked organization and firmness, since there was a constant changing of presidents and consequent confusion in the lower echelons of government – the Apaches had almost a free hand and became more and more insolent and bloody-minded in their operations against the villages and ranches.

In spite of this agony the Mexicans clung to their fringe of settlements in the Rio Grande Valley and along the southern border of New Mexico-Arizona, where missions like San Xavier del Bac and La Purísima Concepción, and towns like Tucson and Santa Rita del Cobre were buttresses.

The copper mines of Santa Rita were discovered about 1800 by Lieutenant-Colonel Carrisco, who, however, had little benefit from them, since the Mimbreño Apaches considered them the heart of their country and made impossible not only the working of the mines but the conveying out of the ore. In 1804 Carrisco sold the mines to Francisco Manuel Elguea, a *rico* of Chihuahua, who began negotiations with the Apaches. By dint of gifts and promises he succeeded in gaining the consent of the Mimbreño chief, Juan José, for the working of the mines under certain conditions: the Mexicans were not to leave the mining towns of Santa Rita del Cobre without permission; and even then they must follow only two specified trails back to Mexico, one toward Chihuahua and the other toward Sonora. Under these restrictions mining began and before long the *conductas* carrying copper were making regular journeys, while the population of Mexicans at Santa Rita del Cobre continuously increased.

An unusual Indian was Juan José, the Mimbreño chief, in that he had enough education to read, having been taught in his youth by a Mexican priest who hoped to win him to Christianity. The Apache, however, returned to his people and used his learning by causing messengers and carriers of mail to be intercepted, reading the letters and dispatches, and thus forestalling by lightning escape or well-planned ambush the military movements against him. For this reason he was so respected by his people that when he forbade hostilities against Santa Rita del Cobre the injunction was scrupulously obeyed.

In no way, however, did the Apaches consider themselves hampered by this in their activities elsewhere. They carried on their great raids deep into Sonora and Chihuahua, bringing back horses, plunder, scalps and captives.

Although Mexican authorities for a time continued the Spanish policy of forbidding aliens – particularly Americans – to enter their territories, the inevitable mountain men, or free trappers, could not be kept out. Records of their furtive visits are scanty because the men who made them often were totally illiterate. It is certain, however that Ceran St. Vrain of the famous fur company of Bent & St. Vrain trapped on the Gila River in 1826, with a company including the famous mountain man, Bill Williams. The appearance of this party near Tucson caused a diplomatic protest by Mexico to the United States; but since St. Vrain had taken the precaution of getting passports to Santa Fe, he was not arrested. One of his trapping parties, headed by Michel Robidoux, was, however, almost exterminated by Indians on the Gila.

George C. Yount trapped in the same district in 1828; and Ewing Young with a party in 1832. One of the best-documented expeditions was that of Sylvester Pattie, in 1827, when with six men, including his son, James Ohio Pattie, he worked clear down to the Santa Rita copper mines. The party was arrested by the Mexicans and the elder Pattie died in prison. James Ohio Pattie left a colourful account of the expedition, its hardships and its failure.

These were only a few of many. One such party, headed by James Johnson, precipitated bloody history.

The activities of Juan José and other Apache chiefs became so maddening that in 1837 the *junta* of Chihuahua promulgated the *proyecto de guerra* (the project for war) against the Apaches. It was a barbarous law, a law conceived by men who despaired of ever meeting the Apache menace by civilized means. It was a last-ditch law, dictated by fear. The state promised to pay a bounty for *human scalps* : a sum equivalent to $100 for the scalp of every Apache man; $50 for the scalp of each woman; and $25 for the scalp of each child. Sonora also adopted such a law.

It must not be supposed that the Mexicans invented this kind of a law. They had excellent precedent. The British and French colonial governments both had offered rewards for enemy scalps. The Massachusetts colony once offered as high as £100 for the scalp of a grown warrior, and the Pennsylvania colony in 1784 offered 134 pieces of eight for the scalp of a male enemy and 50 pieces of eight for each female. As for the United States, the former Grant County, Arizona, as late as 1866 offered a bounty of $250 each for Apache scalps.

At once, with the *proyecto de guerra* in force, the scalp hunters grew busy, Johnson, the mountain man referred to above, hit upon a plan of wholesale collection of scalps, which eliminated the labour of bushwacking individual Indians. He took his party of trappers to Santa Rita del Cobre and arranged to have the Mimbreño Apaches invited to a feast, which took place probably in the village plaza, though one account says it was on the Gila River, perhaps in present Arizona.

J. P. Dunn, whose facts usually were pretty straight, placed it at Santa Rita del Cobre; and added that in addition to the scalp bounty Johnson was to be paid a bonus for dead Indians by the owners of the copper mines, making the transaction doubly attractive to him.

To quote Dunn, in *Massacres in the Mountains* : 'He [Johnson] made a feast and invited to it a number of Mimbreño warriors who accepted his hospitable bidding. [Squaws and children were invited to the feast also, and shared its tragic and brutal aftermath.] To one side of the ground where his feast was spread, he placed a howitzer, loaded to the muzzle with slugs, nails and bullets, and concealed under sacks of flour and other goods. In good range he placed a sack [or sacks] of flour which he told the Indians to divide among themselves. Unsuspicious of wrong, they gathered about it. Johnson touched his lighted *cigarillo* to the vent of the howitzer, and the charge was poured into the crowd killing and wounding many. The party of trappers at once followed up the attack with their rifles and knives. A goodly number of scalps were secured, that of Juan José among others, but the treachery was terribly repaid.

The surviving Apaches stampeded to the hills. But there they soon rallied, and sought revenge. A new leader stepped forward to take Juan José's place. He was Mangus Colorado, which means (in defective Spanish) 'Red Sleeves' – a name he is said to have won when he robbed a cache of furs left by a trapping party, and appropriated for himself a red flannel undershirt with the rest of the loot.

Mangus Colorado was that anomaly among the short-statured Apaches : a giant. According to Charles F. Lummis, he was six feet six inches tall, with the strength of two or three men. He had won renown in a number of exploits, one of which was the following, vouched for by Captain John C. Cremony, in his *Life Among the Apaches* : Although he already had two Apache squaws in his *jacal,* Mangus captured a beautiful Mexican girl and added her to his household. This was contrary to custom, under which he should either have killed her or turned her over to his wives as a slave. But Mangus Colorado made his own customs. He was challenged by a brother of each of his wives to a duel with knives, accepted both, and before the assembled tribe slew both his challengers. After that nobody dared question his right to bring anyone he desired into his lodge.

Under Mangus Colorado the Mimbreños set out to exterminate every Mexican and white man in the country. Two trapping parties were on the Gila River, one of twenty-two men under Charles Kemp, another of three under Benjamin Wilson. They were surprised and wiped out, only Wilson living to tell the story.

But Santa Rita del Cobre was the chief objective. Mangus placed about it his warriors in a kind of siege made the more fearful in that the besiegers never were seen by those they surrounded. War parties waylaid and destroyed *conductas* bringing supplies to the village. Provisions were almost exhausted and the supply of ammunition nearly gone. Weeks passed, and it dawned on the people at the copper mines that they were cut off from the world – doomed to starve or die at the hands of their deadly enemies, the Apaches.

At length a retreat had to be attempted. The whole population of the village began the march southward, most of them on foot, the soldiers of the *presidio* trying to guard the non-combatants. But the Apaches hung about them, cut off stragglers, and waylaid them in every gorge through which they had to pass. There is no detailed account of this tragic

114

via dolorosa, but this much is known : of the three or four hundred who left Santa Rita only half a dozen or so ever reached Janos, the first military post in Chihuahua to the south. A very full payment indeed had been made for the massacre of Apaches by Johnson.

Yet Mexican bounties continued in force for some time and caused many unscrupulous and villainous men to operate in the Indian country, sometimes with results hardly expected by the authors of the laws.

John Glanton (also called Gallantin and Gallatin) made the gold rush to California in 1849. As conscienceless and bloody-minded a scoundrel as ever lived, he departed from California just ahead of a vigilance committee which earnestly desired to confer upon him a hempen necktie for his crimes. Taking refuge in Chihuahua, he gathered about him a set of rogues and outlaws as bad as himself.

In an effort to make this dangerous element useful, General Carrasco, governor of Chihuahua, employed them to hunt Apaches. Glanton and his merry men went to work with a will and no scalp hunters brought in more scalps than they. Judging from the harvest of grisly trophies for which they were paid bounties, the Apache tribes should have been decimated. The reports of Apache raids continued and even grew in numbers and bloodiness. Friendly Indians and Mexicans were slaughtered and scalped sometimes in the very midst of settlements.

The suspicions of the Mexicans were aroused, and presently Glanton and his men were discovered in the act of taking the scalps of some Mexican citizens they had just murdered. Now the growing number of 'Apache raids' was explained. Glanton and his scalp hunters had been murdering and scalping the very people they were supposed to be defending – and collecting money from the Mexican government for those scalps.

With his men, Glanton barely escaped north into what – by that time – had become part of the United States. That his hegira might not be unprofitable, his men took along a herd of two thousand sheep they had appropriated, eventually arriving at the confluence of the Gila and the Colorado, where the present city of Yuma stands.

At that place was a ferry, operated by a Dr. Langdon. The Yuma Indians previously had derived some profit by ferrying immigrants across the Colorado with crude rafts and a scow. But Langdon ran the better ferry. He built a stockade on the California side, which he named Fort Defiance, and got most of the business. Still, the Indians continued to operate their scow, getting a little custom here and there, which prevented Langdon from charging as high a fare as he would have liked.

When Glanton and his outlaws arrived at the ferry, they first contented themselves with robbing immigrants and committing other outrages, which they blamed on the Yumas, a peaceful and rather law abiding people. The Yumas did not relish being scapegoats, but they endured it silently.

Then Glanton became associated with Dr. Langdon – probably through the method later known, by modern racketeers, as 'muscling in.' As soon as he had interest in the ferry, which was the chief means of crossing for the great tide of immigrants to California, Glanton decided to eliminate competition. Result : the Yuma who operated the rival scow was murdered. The Langdon-Glanton ferry had the field to itself and prices for crossing immediately became extortionate.

But the Yumas were now very weary of Glanton and his doings. Their chief, Caballo en Pelo (Naked Horse), arranged to dispose of the unwelcome intruders. Sometime in 1851 he and his warriors, with great professions of friendship, wandered as if aimlessly and casually from different directions into the desperado camp at Fort Defiance. There was a signal, Yuma weapons came out, Yuma yells resounded, and it is a pleasure to record that only three of the Glanton gang escaped their just deserts; all the rest, including the arch-criminal Glanton, were slaughtered.

After this wholesome elimination the Yumas appropriated the money which the outlaws had accumulated, reported as from $15,000 to $30,000 in gold, and used it in purchasing trinkets, luxuries and supplies from the immigrants. Not knowing money values, they frequently gave four or five doubloons for a worn-out blanket, or a gold eagle for a tattered shirt. They also resumed the ferry traffic, but did not enjoy it long, because it was too profitable. L. J. Ieger, with a party of men from San Diego, California, built a new ferryboat and pre-empted the business.

The Glanton episode is ahead of our story, but it belongs in a chapter about scalp hunters, since it illustrates the atrocities committed, which had deadly repercussions for half a century in the desert.

Prior to the bloody work of Johnson, Glanton and their ilk, the Apaches had shown surprisingly little hostility toward Americans, considering the Mexicans their real enemies. But after the scalp hunters began to operate, from 1837 on, Fangus Colorado, the greatest chief in the history of the Apache people, made the Southwest all but untenable for Americans and Mexicans alike. No Mexican dared enter Apacheria. Gold and silver mines which had been operated were abandoned and lost, many of them forever, and the great copper workings at Santa Rita crumbled in idleness.

CHAPTER THREE

Texans Can Also Be Treacherous

IN the sorry story of the treatment of Indians, Texas was about as bad as New Mexico. Sam Houston's first term as president ended in 1838, and he was succeeded by Mirabeau Buonaparte Lamar, the buck private he had promoted to colonel on the field of San Jacinto – who belonged to the Burnet party and devoted himself to the destruction of Houston's policies.

Houston, an adopted member of the Cherokee nation, understood the Indian's side of the argument with the white man. He also desired annexation by the United States as the only safe future for Texas. In the latter policy he was, without much question, also carrying out the wishes of his old friend Andrew Jackson, now, after his second term as President, in retirement on his plantation, the Hermitage, near Nashville, Tennessee.

In his inaugural speech Lamar expressed opposition to annexation. He also proclaimed a war of extermination against the Indians which would 'admit no compromise, and have no termination except in their total extinction or total expulsion'.

It was a politician's agreement with the demands of the land grabbers. Following San Jacinto a flood of immigration poured into Texas. New towns were established, new lands opened up, and promoters and land speculators, greedy for anything on which they could get their hands, appeared like the proverbial clouds of voracious grasshoppers. Indians and Mexican dwellers were victims of ceaseless fraud, pressure and outright violence, as their lands were taken from them. To cloak their own knavery, the land grabbers continually raised an outcry that the Mexicans were fomenting rebellion and the Indians were their allies. Very naturally there was resentment among the Mexicans at their treatment, but except for one futile, bloodless uprising, known as the Nacogdoches Rebellion, they actually made no great trouble.

The Indians were another matter. In the upper valleys of the Angelina, Neches and Trinity rivers dwelt a division of the Cherokees, a civilized, farming people, on land assigned to them by the Mexican government in 1824, long before the independence of Texas. Had Houston been president the Cherokees, who had stood good friends to the Texans, even fighting their Indian enemies for them, would never have suffered the treatment they received in 1839. Houston, in his administration, had gone to the length of making a treaty with these Cherokees, confirming their rights to their lands. But the treaty was repudiated by the Texas Congress in the Lamar administration.

No sooner was Lamar president than he notified the

Cherokees that they were to be removed, adding, 'Whether it be done by friendly negotiations or by violence of war, must depend on the Cherokees themselves'. In his message he made all the usual charges that the Cherokees had committed murders and robberies and had conspired with Mexican irreconcilables – charges in many cases without foundation.

Following this he sent Colonel Edward Burleson and General Thomas J. Rusk with a thousand men – as a threat – and a commission, consisting of David G. Burnet (now vice-president), Rusk, J. W. Burton, James S. Mayfield and General Albert Sidney Johnston, to confer with the Cherokee chiefs. It is interesting to note that Johnston, later one of the great Confederate leaders and notably fair-minded, was appointed at the request of Diwa-li (The Bowl), chief of this division of the Cherokees.

The Bowl, a venerable patriarch eighty-four years old, was the son of a Scottish trader and a Cherokee mother, and had been in his younger days a notable warrior. But now, seeing the hopelessness of their situation, he advised his people to accept the best terms they could get and retire from their lands as demanded. The Cherokees, however, indignantly refused. Thereupon The Bowl told them that he would live or die with them and exhorted them to fight bravely.

With the failure, July 14, 1839, by the commissioners to achieve a peaceful abandonment of the Cherokee lands, the most shameful act in the history of Texas began – the murder and robbery of a people whose rights were equal to theirs, and who had been their steadfast friends in the past.

On July 15, Burleson and Rusk, with their thousand men, attacked the Cherokees, who numbered about eight hundred warriors – including young boys and old men – and who had retreated from their own settlement to a Delaware village on the Neches River, where they had a somewhat stronger position for defence.

Texans invariably fought well, even in a bad cause, and in two days' fighting the Cherokees, resisting bravely but outnumbered and outflanked, were driven from their defences, with a loss of a hundred in dead and wounded, to a small Texas loss of eight dead and thirty-five wounded.

In the second day's battle The Bowl, the aged chief, when he saw the fight was lost, gave the signal to retreat. But he himself remained. 'I am an old man,' he said. 'I die here.' When he was found his hand grasped a sword which had been given him by his one friend among the white men, Sam Houston.

The Cherokees retreated toward the Red River, and the Texans, pursuing them, 'destroyed their houses and cut down their corn. This devastating march was continued up to the twenty-fifth, until the entire Cherokee country had been traversed. . . . Houses were burnt and crops and improvements destroyed every day until none remained. All cattle and other stock were appropriated.'

No Texan can be very proud of this chapter in his state's history. The Cherokees, destitute and miserable, made their way north and took refuge among their kinsmen in the Indian Territory, while Texas landhogs took over their fields and the charred sites of their villages.

When Sam Houston, who was in Tennessee visiting Andrew Jackson, heard of the expulsion of the Cherokees, he returned to Texas, raging. At Nacogdoches he made a savage speech. The Bowl, he said, was a better man than his 'murderers.' For that outspoken declaration threats were made against his life; yet shortly after, when he ran for Congress from the Nacogdoches District, he was elected overwhelmingly. In Lamar's turbulent administration, Sam Houston became the constant and scornful opponent of the ex-private of San Jacinto.

Among other tribes included in Lamar's anti-Indian policy, the Comanches, always hostile and troublesome, were the most powerful. Presently they were further inflamed by one of the ugliest pieces of treachery in the history of the frontier, part of Lamar's 'policy of destruction' – the so-called Council House Fight in San Antonio, March 19, 1840.

On that day a party of Comanches, thirty-two warriors

and thirty-three women and children, arrived in San Antonio for the advertised purpose of making a treaty of peace. In inviting them, the Texas authorities had promised them safety but told them to bring all prisoners in their hands. When this band arrived they had with them only one captive, a young girl named Matilda Lockhart, who had been carried away during a raid along the Guadalupe River in October, 1838. Probably this prisoner was the only one in the hands of this particular band, and they came in good faith to deliver her. The Texans, however, had the habit of regarding the entire Comanche people, not as a loose confederation of wandering bands, each autonomous, but as a nation, with a government which had some sort of authority and could compel obedience.

All told, thirteen captives were believed to be held by the Comanches, and there was anger when the other twelve were not brought in. Furthermore, the condition and story of Matilda Lockhart excited indignation. The girl's body was covered with bruises and sores, her hair had been singed to the scalp and her nose burned to the bone, evidently some time before, as the wound had healed. She told of brutal treatment and the usual indignities to which female captives were subjected.

Conferring in the courthouse with Texas officials, the Indians said she was their only captive, but the girl said she had seen other prisoners a few days previously. The Texans charged that it was Comanche policy to bring in captives one at a time, thus exhorting larger ransoms. Perhaps this was true. It does not, however, excuse what took place.

In the midst of the Conference Colonel William S. Fisher marched two companies of soldiers into the room and notified the twelve chiefs there that they were under arrest, to be held as hostages for the return of other prisoners in the Comanche camp. It violated every promise, and a Comanche was like a catamount when his freedom was threatened.

A war whoop sounded, followed by rapid gunshots. Every one of the twelve chiefs was slaughtered, while one Texan was wounded – Captain Howard, who was stabbed by one of the Indians in a desperate lunge for the door. Quick as it was, the bloody work within the building was not completed when a company of soldiers came around the corner of the courthouse and opened fire on the Indians who were within the enclosure outside. The Comanches, fighting with bows and arrows against Texas rifles, retreated toward the river, but were pursued relentlessly and killed. Twenty-eight Indian women and children were lodged in jail as prisoners. Thirty-one chiefs and warriors and three women and two children were slain. One escaped – a renegade Mexican – who carried the report of the treachery back to the Comanches. The imprisoned women and children later were exchanged for white captives and this much good, at least, came out of the episode.

The Council House treachery had its natural outcome. Next August the Comanches made the greatest raid in Texas history. A huge war party, estimated at a thousand warriors by some Texas writers of the period, swept across Texas from San Marcos to Lavaca Bay and the coast, burning and looting Victoria and Linville, then turned back by way of the Colorado River Valley toward Austin.

But the alarm had spread and armed men began to swarm on the trail of the marauders. General Felix Huston – no relative and no friend of Sam Houston – who was commander of the Texas army, intercepted the raiders on Plum Creek, near present-day Lockhart. There the Comanches were defeated by the Texans, who were led by such renowned fighters as Ben McCulloch, 'Paint' Caldwell, 'Old Gotch' Hardeman, John H. Moore, Edward Burleson and others, under the command of Huston.

The Texans recaptured more than two hundred head of stolen horses and mules, but of the prisoners – several kidnapped women and children – only one was recovered alive. This was Mrs. Watts, bride of Captain H. O. Watts, collector of customs at Lavaca, one of the men killed in the raid. The young woman was shot by an arrow in her body and left for dead, but she was found and eventually recovered. Among the prisoners killed was Mrs. Crosby, a granddaughter of Daniel Boone, who with her child and its nurse were speared to death.

Huston reported that 'upwards of forty Indians were killed', and a squaw and a child captured. His loss was two dead and six wounded. Instead of a thousand, as some writers said, Huston estimated the Comanche strength as 'upwards of 400', which is nearer the probabilities, allowing still for a little Texas exaggeration.

The Comanches retreated into their wilderness. They had been defeated but they also had inflicted great damage, killed twenty-two settlers, and carried off some captives. Texans charged that this raid was planned by Mexicans, including General Canalizo, commandant at Matamoros. The Comanches expected Mexican troops to join them at the sea coast, which is why they raided that far. At the failure of the Mexicans to appear the Indians were bitterly resentful, and the following October, in retaliation, made a very bloody raid into Mexico itself. More than four hundred Indians penetrated four hundred miles into Neuva León and Coahuila. 'Their track could be traced for miles by burning ranches and villages. They carried off a great many female captives, and thousands of horses and mules, escaping safely to their strongholds in their mountains with their booty.'

The Texans were not content with merely repelling the Comanches. That October – probably while most of the warriors were absent on the great raid into Mexico – Colonel John H. Moore, with ninety Texans and seventeen Lipan scouts, surprised a Comanche village on the Red Fork of the Colorado, at daybreak of the twenty-fourth. Unprepared to fight, the Indians fled in every direction. Many were killed in the village and others were shot or drowned as they tried to ford the stream toward which they stampeded.

Moore did very well in carrying out Lamar's 'policy of destruction'. All told, he killed 128 Comanches, including many women and children. Thirty-four prisoners were taken, but of these seven escaped when Moore's horses were stampeded in the night, and three others were abandoned, probably because they were too badly wounded to travel. The village was burned. Two Mexican boys, captives of the Indians, were rescued.

These defeats, however, rather than diminishing Comanche hostilities, seemed to increase them. In the years following, the hair sat light on a man's head on the Texas frontier, and there was an oversufficiency of death and excitement, especially when the moon was full in September – the time the Comanches usually made their greatest forays called by Texans *Comanche moon*.

CHAPTER FOUR

Treasons, Stratagems and Spoils

IT was Lamar who made Austin the capital of Texas. Founded as a frontier village in 1838, it was named for the Father of Texas and became the seat of government in 1839, when it was a mere collection of log huts, with a stockaded building used for sittings of Congress when that body was in session, and as a defence from Indians at other times.

Admittedly, Lamar's purpose was to push the Indians westward as far as possible by shoving the tide of settlement forward. Austin was much exposed and as an administrative site was strenuously criticized by those opposed to Lamar's government. As one early writer said, 'The nearest settlement on the west was San Antonio, about eighty miles away. To Lavaca bay, 150 miles distant, the only settlements were Gonzales and Victoria. To Houston, a distance of nearly 200 miles, the only settlements were about Washington. To the settlements on the Red River, nearly 400 miles distant, was a region unoccupied save by roving and murderous bands of Indians.'

Yet to this outpost President Lamar and his cabinet moved by October 1, 1839. 'The Court of King Witumpka,' which was the derisive title given by Sam Houston to the Lamar entourage, was finding the going more and more difficult. An invasion by the Mexicans, during the Lamar administration, was averted only by a curious uprising, in which Federalists of Mexico attempted to establish a 'Republic of the Rio Grande' in the northeastern states of that nation by driving the Centrists out. This abortive revolution was joined by some adventurous Texans, including Colonel Reuben Moss, S. W. Jordan and William S. Fisher.

One of the strangest, treachery-ridden campaigns in history followed. After one battle, in which the valour of the Texans gave victory to the Federalists at Alcantro, Mexican officers of the Federalist army conspired to deliver their Texas allies to their own enemies, the Centrists. A pair of colonels named Lopez and Molano were chief figures in the projected treachery, and General Antonio Canales, if he did not help form the plot, at least lent himself to it.

Colonel Jordan, commanding the Texas forces, successively captured Laredo, Guerrero, Mier and Camargo. From the last-named place, June 26, 1840, he marched for Saltillo, guided by Lopez and Molano. Since the Texans did not know the route, this pair actually conducted them toward San Luis Potisí, where large Centrist forces were waiting to overwhelm them.

Through an honourable Mexican, Captain Pena, who revealed the direction in which they were going, Jordan discovered the plot and changed the route of march. But much time was wasted in the counter-marching and when, October 22, the Texans reached a hacienda one day's journey from Saltillo, Jordon received a message from a friend in Victoria, confirming Captain Pena's revelations and stating that for 'a sum of money' the Mexican leaders had agreed to place the Texans in a position where they could be destroyed.

Profoundly worried, Jordan nevertheless continued his march for Saltillo. Next day the Mexican Centrist army, under General Arista, was discovered entrenched on a hill three miles south of the city. Against this force 1,000 strong, with two nine-pounder guns, Jordan had only 110 Texans,

150 mounted Mexican *rancheros* and 75 Mexican infantry, a total of 335 men, the loyalty of the Mexican allies dangerously questionable.

Fairly certain that his Mexican soldiers were only awaiting the chance to desert him, Jordan placed his Texans in an old hacienda building about a hundred and fifty yards from the enemy position. True to his misgivings, when he ordered his Mexican infantry to occupy a stone house near the hacienda, they turned and marched without hesitation over to the enemy lines, where they were received with cheers. A moment later the Centrists opened fire with their two cannon and at the first shot Lopez, Molano and 150 *rancheros* rode over to the Centrists, taking with them most of the ammunition.

In a desperate position, confronting now an enemy force of 1,225 men against their 110 – more than ten to one – and with artillery where they had none, the Texans, far from being cowed by the desertion of their allies, were only sternly angered by it.

Since they had so little gunpowder that they could afford to risk only sure shots, they lay grimly silent behind the old walls into which crashed the enemy cannon balls. At four o'clock in the afternoon, thinking that after the long bombardment the few Texans had little resistance left in them, Arista ordered his men to charge.

Not a shot came from the old hacienda until the advancing Mexicans were within thirty feet of the walls. Then, with their peculiar high-pitched yell, the Texans rose and blasted out a volley so devastating that hardly a bullet missed its mark. The Mexican ranks broke and fled.

But the fight was by no means ended. Many of the inhabitants of Saltillo, having been told that victory was certain for Arista's force and wishing to see the destruction of the *Americanos,* had gathered on the heights to see the battle. Encouraged by the shouts of these spectators, column after column charged the old hacienda, only to be met by the same withering fire and retreat. The final repulse so disorganized the Centrists that there was general panic. In full rout,

Arista's army stampeded to Saltillo – accompanied by the spectators, who now frantically feared they would be the next targets of the Texas rifles. The retreat came hardly a moment too soon. The ammunition of the defenders of the hacienda was almost all gone and they might not have been able to stop another determined assault.

In this singular engagement the Mexicans lost 408 killed and wounded, their two guns, and a great quantity of small arms and ammunition. The Texas loss was five killed and seven wounded.

With both Centrists and Federalists now against him, Jordan began a retirement to the Rio Grande. Once he was attacked by four hundred Mexican cavalry, but again the Texas rifles dispersed their foes. The heroic little band completed its successful anabasis of a hundred and fifty miles through hostile territory and without further loss crossed the Rio Grande to safety.

Jordan's fight was brilliant and his retreat masterly. The 'revolution' ceased as soon as the Texans withdrew from it; the 'Republic of the Rio Grande' disappeared as if in vapour; and nothing was accomplished save such another convincing demonstration of the deadliness of Texas riflery that Mexican leaders who may have been planning any invasion of Texas abandoned the idea, at least for the time being.

Except for this *émeute,* in which he had no part but which saved him from embarrassment, Lamar failed as an executive. His policy intensified Indians wars on the frontier; his financial practices made four times greater the national debt, while reducing the national credit to zero; and exports were ruinously on the debit side – in his administration the balance of trade showed $4,625,843.98 imports, against $687,242.24 exports, or a trade balance against Texas of $3,948,600 in round figures.

In this critical situation Lamar decided on one last gamble. The bold traders of the Missouri frontier in the United States had broken down Mexican official opposition to their commerce with New Mexico. Santa Fe, the capital, was rich in silver, wool and mules, but lacked the simplest manufactured

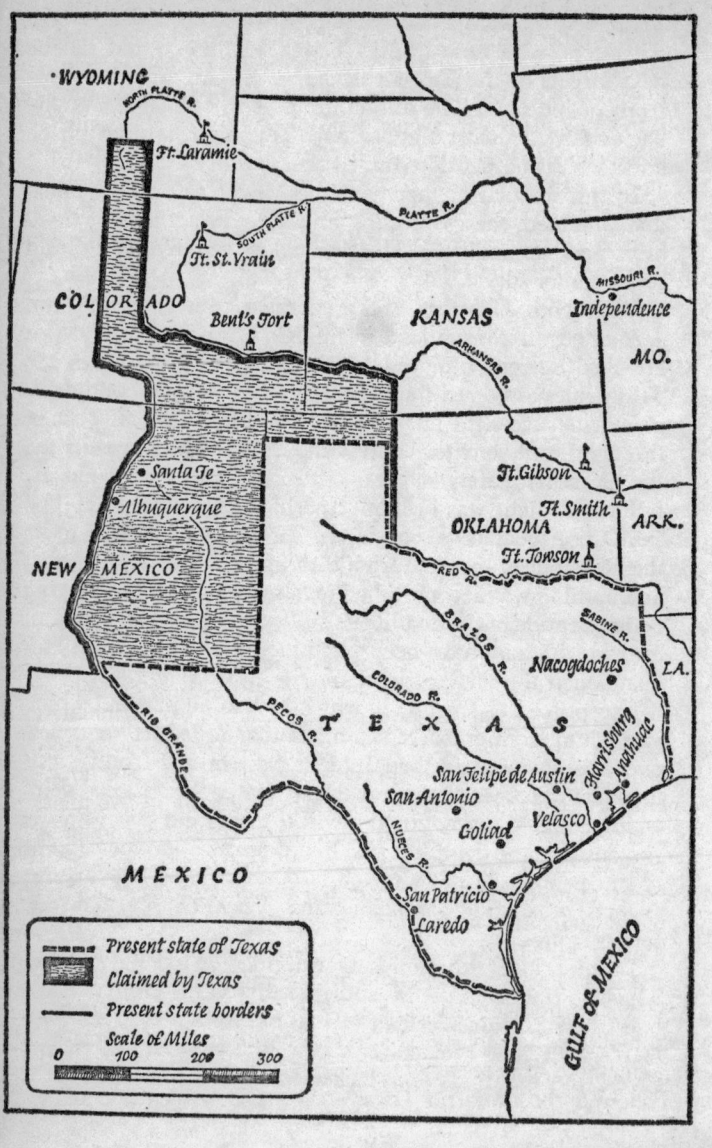

articles; and the Santa Fe trail had been pioneered in 1821 by William Becknell, of Arrow Rock, Missouri, who, hearing that Mexico had gained independence from Spain, reached Santa Fe with a mule pack train November 6 of that year and sold his goods at ten to twenty times their prices in St Louis.

Becknell's route started from the steamboat landing of Franklin, Missouri (near the present site of Kansas City), followed the prairie divide between the tributaries of the Kansas and Arkansas rivers to the great bend of the Arkansas, then pursued the latter river upstream almost to the mountains before turning south to New Mexico. There were later mutations of this route, but in general it was the Santa Fe trail.

On his second journey, in 1822, Becknell carried part of his merchandise in wagons. The feasibility of rolling stock having thus been proved, wagons thereafter were generally employed in the Santa Fe trade. In spite of Indian attacks and other dangers, trade grew continually, until in 1843 Josiah Gregg reported in his *Commerce of the Prairies* that $450,000 worth of goods at St. Louis prices – much higher in Santa Fe – had been transported over the trail that year, this lucrative business being monopolized by American traders.

Lamar believed that if he could capture the Santa Fe trade for Texas he could do much to mend the republic's financial fortunes. But he also had a larger scheme in mind.

When Texas won its independence it set forth claims not only to its territories lying within the present state but to all of New Mexico to the Rio Grande, the parts of Oklahoma and Texas lying south of the Arkansas River and west of the present north-south border of the Texas Panhandle, and a liberal segment of Colorado, extending to the headwaters of the North Platte in southern Wyoming. It was a very large claim, including the cities of Santa Fe and Taos and other New Mexican towns along the Rio Grande; and it could not be maintained legally, but Lamar was willing to use extralegal methods, if necessary.

Followed the fantastic Texas – Santa Fe expedition of

1841. The president first tried to gain for it government financing, but the Texas Congress, faced with an already disastrous national debt, rejected this in both houses. Lamar, thereupon, organized it on a non-official basis, its recruits to furnish their own weapons, horses and outfits, although the government 'sequestered' to them some supplies, including wagons and beef cattle. In spite of this self-financing aspect, Lamar's call for 'volunteers to meet at Brushy Creek for an expedition to New Mexico' brought adventurers not only from Texas but from all over the United States, England, France and other foreign countries.

Among these was George Wilkins Kendall, an editor of the New Orleans *Picayune,* who left a spirited and minute account of the misadventures of the expedition in his *Narrative of the Texan Santa Fé Expedition*. The commander was General Hugh McLeod; and with it went three 'commissioners', William G. Cooke, Dr. R. F. Brenham and J. A. Navarro, whom Lamar instructed to offer to the people of New Mexico the priceless privileges of having 'the laws [of Texas] extended over that territory; but in case the people were averse to changing their allegiance, then . . . to establish friendly commercial relations with New Mexico.'

The expedition was military in character, with five companies of 'mounted infantry' and òne artillery company with a brass six-pounder – in all 270 men. Yet it was repeatedly proclaimed that the objective was entirely pacific and the troops were only for protection against Indians who might be encountered on the way. Some fifty other persons – traders, teamsters and adventurers – made up the full total of about 320 men in all who set out from the Brushy Creek camp ground, about twenty miles from Austin, June 20, 1841.

A skylarking spirit was abroad, with hunting and merriment; expectations were high and the adventurers looked for excitement and perhaps danger and welcomed them; the traders believed they would reap rich profits on the goods they were conveying; and the emissaries of Lamar had every anticipation of winning enthusiastic approval for their proposal to have Texas annex New Mexico's eastern areas.

Except for the danger and adventure, not one of these hopes was to be fulfilled.

From the outset the expedition suffered the consequences of its amateur organization and leadership. Wagons were overloaded, guides ill-acquainted with the route, distances far under-estimated, and the actual hardships and difficulties of the journey little understood. Evidence of their lack of knowledge was the lateness of the state. Although it gave President Lamar opportunity to make a fine oratorical address when he reviewed the men on Brushy Creek, it was so far along in the season that rainfall was sure to be lacking, water hard to find, and grass scarce for the animals.

The expedition blundered along, got lost, mistook the Quitaque River for the upper waters of the Red, and was baffled by the escarpment of the Staked Plains, which seemed to defy being surmounted by wagons. Kiowa Indians, the fierce allies of the Comanches, cut off a party of five scouts, including young Lieutenant Hull, the only son of Major General Trevor Hull of the British army, killing and scalping all five.

The disaster convinced the leaders of the grave necessity of getting on with their journey and somehow climbing the escarpment, with its caprock, to the plains above. A horse party of ninety-nine men under Captain Lewis, the artillery officer, was sent ahead to find the settlements; while General McLeod followed with the wagons.

Kendall, historian of the expedition, wrote, 'However impolitic it may be considered to divide a command, in this instance such a course could not be avoided. We were completely lost, and without power of moving forward; our provisions, which for weeks had been scanty, were now almost entirely exhausted.'

Across the Staked Plains, Lewis led his men, preceded by three 'envoys', Howland, Baker and Rosenberry, who were to sound out the disposition of the New Mexicans and obtain, if possible, provisions for the starving expedition. When the three reached San Miguel, however, they were immediately arrested and transported to Santa Fe as invaders. Escaping, they were overtaken, Rosenberry killed when they resisted, and Howland and Baker executed later.

Governor of New Mexico at this time was General Manuel Armijo, one of the typical tyrants that have risen periodically to rule despotically in Spanish-Indian countries. Cruel, corrupt and pompous, he was assuredly the last man to consent to have his power taken from him.

Proclaiming that the Texans were coming to 'loot and destroy', he marched against them with a strong force of soldiers. As the two Texas columns appeared, one after another, starved, ragged, continually harassed by the Indians, and forced to abandon almost all their baggage, including their wagons, they were, to quote Kendall again, 'so reduced in both body and spirit that surrender was inevitable.' Captain Lewis, now a prisoner of the Mexicans, induced his comrades to lay down their arms on a promise that they would receive good treatment.

The promise was not kept. At Armijo's orders the prisoners were plundered, tied together in groups of four, six or eight – depending on the different lengths of the lariats which bound them – and prodded on a cruel, two-thousand mile march all the way to the City of Mexico. No complete record ever was made of the fate of these men. Some few escaped; some were executed; and some died on the journey, or in the prisons where they lay for months and even years, in Puebla, Perote and the City of Mexico. Those who were citizens of the United States or of European countries were the most fortunate, for the diplomatic forces of their various nations laboured for their release.

And here the ineffable Santa Anna played a part once more. When he returned to Mexico from the United States after the Texas revolution, he was ignominiously defeated in a presidential election by his old rival Bustamente, and retired to his estate at Manga de Clavo in eclipse. That would have ended most careers. But Santa Anna had the regenerative powers of a phoenix. Within less than a year opportunity came in a strange guise, enabling the extraordinary opportunist to become once again the idol of his people.

Late in 1838 a French squadron anchored off Vera Cruz to demand reparation for damages sustained by French subjects in one of the sacks of the City of Mexico. One item included the loss suffered by a French baker, whose shop was destroyed during Guerrero's occupation in 1828, whence the affair has been called the Pastry War.

The French squadron bombarded and occupied Vera Cruz. Now Santa Anna came from retirement and accepted command of the Mexican army which was to oppose the French. The commander of the fleet, having accomplished his purpose, withdrew from the city, but the Napoleon of the West, wanting it to appear that he was driving this foe from the sacred soil of Mexico, advanced with a small army to the outskirts of Vera Cruz.

Some shooting occurred. Santa Anna, approaching closer to the firing line than he intended, was struck in the knee by a French bullet. It was necessary to amputate the leg below the knee. Loss of such a member would have been deemed a calamity by most men, but to Santa Anna it was like a benison from heaven.

First, he pretended to be at death's door, issuing a pathetic 'farewell' to the Mexican people, containing among other things this sentence : 'My dying request is that my country permit my body to be buried in these sand dunes that my companions in arms may know that this is the line of battle I have marked for them.'

He thereupon rapidly recovered.

But the amputated leg had not recovered. Santa Anna considered that it was a part of his sacred person, and it had died for his country. It must receive proper honours.

When he was once more back in power – which was quite soon – the martyred extremity was tenderly exhumed from the ground where it had been inconsiderately buried by the surgeons who removed it, carried to the City of Mexico, and there interred with impressive ceremonies of both church and state, with Santa Anna, as chief mourner, dropping a pensive tear over it. The Mexicans were touched by this evidence of tender sentiment on the part of *El Presidente*. Santa Anna became stronger with only one leg than he had even been with two.

It was he who was head of the state when the Texas prisoners were brought in, and on June 13, 1842 – his birthday – he released 113 of them, who could prove citizenship other than Texan, to return to their countries. Of the remainder of the 320 who started the journey from Brushy Creek, few ever reached Texas again.

Meantime, in Texas, no word had been heard from the Santa Fe expedition and an election was due. Santa Anna, once more dictator, was adopting a threatening attitude and in this crisis, complicated by the fall of Texas currency to as low as three cents on the dollar, Sam Houston was overwhelmingly elected to his second term as president.

Four weeks after he took office, Houston announced sadly that the Santa Fe expedition had been captured and was being marched, with excessive brutality, to the City of Mexico. Texas was infuriated. A resolution was adopted by the Congress 'annexing' New Mexico, upper and lower California, and four other Mexican provinces. Houston vetoed the measure, remarking that it was a poor time for a 'legislative jest'. Congress repassed it over the veto. It was never implemented. Texas soon had so many troubles that such ambitions were forgotten.

In March, 1842, a Mexican force under General Rafael Vasques invaded Texas, occupied San Antonio, Goliad and Refugio for a few days and then retired. It was intended as an iteration of Mexican claims that independence had never legally been granted Texas and it set all the young republic aflame.

An unauthorized communication sent to Santa Anna by James E. Hamilton, who with Bernard E. Bee was in Mexico seeking to obtain good treatment for the Texas-Santa Fe expedition prisoners, further complicated matters. Hamilton suggested that Mexico recognize the independence of Texas – already recognized by the United States, Britain and France – and receive as compensation $5,000,000 together with '$200,000 to the secret agents of the Mexican government.' This last not very adroit attempt to bribe *El Presidente* became public knowledge, thus losing any effectiveness it may have had.

Santa Anna, of course, chose to be affronted. He called the offer 'an insult and infamy unworthy of a gentleman,' and sent to Houston a message proclaiming that Mexico would not vary her hostile attitude until she had 'planted her eagle standard on the banks of the Sabine.'

Houston could write a magniloquent letter himself. He now penned it, ending as follows, 'Ere the banner of Mexico shall triumphantly float on the banks of the Sabine, the Texan standard of the single star, borne by the Anglo-Saxon race, shall display its bright folds in liberty's triumph on the Isthmus of Darien.'

With this exchange of presidential courtesies both sides might have rested on their laurels, such as they were, but in September General Woll, with a thousand Mexican troops, again occupied San Antonio. He fought three engagements with hurriedly assembled bodies of Texans, each far fewer in number than his force, was defeated in the most important of the three, and fell back across the Rio Grande, pursued by the Texans under Colonel Matthew (Old Paint) Caldwell, who had been a Texas-Santa Fe expedition prisoner but had escaped.

Texas demanded retaliation. Brigadier-General A. Somerville, with 750 men, marched from San Antonio, November 18. The personnel was inferior, 'a rabble of adventurers and self-willed individuals assembled in the hope of participating in any excitement but with little expectation of subordinating their impetuous desires to the general good.'

They plundered Laredo and, when Somerville returned the plunder to the *alcalde* of the town, 200 of them marched back home. Somerville occupied Guerrero, across the Rio Grande, but soon returned to the Texas side. His men were so critical of this movement that he resigned his command and returned to Gonzales. With him went about 250 more of the best officers and men, including Major Jack Hays and Ben McCulloch, both famous later with the Texas Rangers.

That left 300 men on the Rio Grande. They elected Colonel William S. Fisher commander, and marched to Mier, a desolate adobe town a few miles south of the Rio Grande. The town was occupied by a Mexican force under Generals Ampudia and Canales when the Texans approached, December 23.

Desperate fighting followed, the Texans seeking to force their way into Mier, from building to building. Colonel Fisher was wounded and Captain Berry killed. The Texans led by Captain Ewen Cameron, a powerful Scot, were gaining headway when reinforcements arrived for the Mexicans.

Confronted and practically surrounded by 1,700 enemies, against whom he had only 261 men, and with his ammunition running low, Fisher, sick from his wound, surrendered. The Texans lost sixteen killed or mortally wounded, seventeen severely wounded and many more slightly wounded. The Mexican loss was never announced, but Bancroft a rather reliable investigator, suggests that it may have been at least 600 in killed and wounded.

A desperate effort was made by 193 of the Texans to escape from their guards at Rinconada, January 11, 1843. Led by Cameron, they broke out of their prison and tried to reach Texas. All were recaptured, except ten who died in the desert mountains and four who got back to the Rio Grande.

They were imprisoned once more at the Hacienda del Salado and Santa Anna sent orders to decimate them. What followed was the celebrated 'black bean' episode. On March 22 the prisoners were lined up before an earthen jar in which were 159 white beans and 17 black ones, representing 176 prisoners, the sick not being included. Each was to draw out a bean, those receiving the black one to be executed.

Cameron, the leader in the escape, was made to draw first. He 'dipped deep' and came up with a white bean. Three fourths of the beans in the fatal urn were drawn before the last black one came up.

The seventeen men condemned by this deathly lottery were blindfolded, seated on a log, and shot.

Thereafter the survivors were marched on foot to the City of Mexico, several dying on the way. At Huehuetoca, about six leagues from the capital, Captain Cameron, although he had drawn a white bean, was executed on special orders from Santa Anna.

Of 245 prisoners taken at Mier, 68 were executed or died, 25 escaped, and 121 subsequently were released. The 31 not accounted for in those figures probably perished.

So ended another piece of foolishness.

Yet the Santa Fe and Mier expeditions, disastrous as they were, had a far-reaching effect. Together, they hastened the annexation of Texas by the United States, both by arousing sympathy in the United States and by quelling opposition in Texas. Hence they also helped bring on the Mexican War, by which the entire Southwest and California came into the domain of the Union.

CHAPTER FIVE

"Manifest Destiny"

ANDREW JACKSON finished his second term as President in 1837 and retired to the Hermitage. He was not, however, out of reckoning in the government.

Martin Van Buren, who succeeded him, proved less than satisfactory as an Executive and inherited also a panic, wherefore the Whigs swept into power in 1840, electing as President General William Henry Harrison, the hero of Tippecanoe; and John Tyler of Virginia, as Vice-President.

Jackson, as the moving spirit in the Democratic party, seemed in eclipse, but fortune again favoured the old tiger of Tennessee. One month after his inauguration, Harrison died; and Tyler, who succeeded him, became so involved in disputes with the Whigs of whom Daniel Webster was the leader, that his entire cabinet resigned and he was a man without a party. He therefore threw the weight of his influence into the scales for the annexation of Texas, which though opposed by the Whigs was desired by most Virginians.

The Texas Congress, in 1836, had voted almost unanimously in favour of annexation to the United States, but Van Buren refused to consider it. The matter came up again in 1842, prompted by fears of British designs on Texas – fostered, incidentally, by crafty Sam Houston in his correspondence.

The underlying reason for the laggard tactics in the Texas annexation was not fear of war with Mexico (although Mexico was making belligerent gestures and threatening hostilities if the annexation took place) but the struggle for power between the free states of the North and the slave states of the South. If Texas entered the Union, it would be as a slave state, and Northern senators bitterly opposed it.

When Tyler, turning against the Whigs and joining his old foe, John C. Calhoun, submitted to the Senate, in April, 1844, a treaty of annexation for Texas, it was rejected; but by now the movement had gained resistless power.

That fall, the grey and ailing master of the Hermitage reached out his hand and placed before the Democratic presidential convention James Polk. 'Who is Polk?' many in the nation asked. It developed that he was a veteran of nine terms in Congress, one of Andrew Jackson's right-hand men, an da Tennesseean, part of that remarkable political force built up about the personality of Old Hickory, which included another Tennesseean, Sam Houston of Texas.

Polk ran as a dark horse, was nominated over Van Buren and Tyler by the convention, and in the election defeated Henry Clay, the Whig candidate, on a platform which boldly pledged the annexation of Texas. His election was a mandate from the people who were in sympathy with Texas and in no mood for political juggling by the Senate – so much so that the opposition of the North weakened, especially in view of sudden diplomatic activity in Mexico and Texas by Britain.

Santa Anna sent a trumpeting warning to the United

States that annexation of Texas would be a signal for immediate hostilities.

Houston, playing a game so obscure that he was accused of everything, including being in the pay of both Britain and Mexico, feigned indifference and blandly suggested to General Murphy, *chargé d'Affairs* of the United States, that there were numerous 'advantages' which might accrue to Texas if annexation did not occur. Should negotiations fail, he said, 'the glory of the United States has already culminated. A rival power [Texas] will be built up.'

He went on to outline a possible future division of the continent. The slave states of the South, including the 'border states' of Virginia, Tennessee, Arkansas and what is now Oklahoma, would join with Texas and extend their domain to the Pacific, as far north as the border of the Louisiana Purchase – including Oregon, upper and lower California, Chihuahua, Sonora and the present states of Nevada, Utah, Arizona, New Mexico, half of Colorado, most of Idaho and part of Wyoming.

History was to show that this conjecture was not chimerical. Houston foresaw almost exactly the division of the nation which took place in the Civil War; and he envisaged the certain westward thrust which would carry the borders of the United States to the Pacific, over-estimating the latter only in the matter of the northern Mexican states which did not become part of the Union.

It caused some worried speculation in Washington and it alarmed Andrew Jackson, now not long for this world, who wrote pleadingly to Houston, beseeching him to 'act & that with promptness & secrecy' in the annexation of which Jackson had always dreamed.

Houston replied with assurances of his affection and prayers for his old chief's health and happiness, and then laid before Jackson in his letter the cold situation : 'Now, my venerated friend, you will perceive that Texas is presented to the United States, as a bride adorned for her espousal. But if, so confident of the union, she should be rejected, her mortification would be indescribable. She has been sought by the United States, and this is the third time she has consented.'

Were she now spurned, he added, it would forever terminate the possibility of annexation.

Having read the letter, Jackson roused himself from his sickbed to dispatch what amounted to orders to Washington. The resolution of annexation was passed by the two-thirds majority required, Tyler signed it March 1, 1845, just three days before his term expired, and Polk was left to carry through its momentous provisions.

Houston concluded his second term as president of Texas and Anson Jones succeeded to what was to be a forty-day term of office. After a little manoeuvring the Texas Congress accepted the annexation resolution.

Already Houston, with his wife and son, were hurrying with all the speed the conveyances of the time could muster to pay his final respects and lay Texas in the hand of his old leader, to whom, for all his devious strategy, he had wavered never once in loyalty. A letter sent by special courier outspeeded his coach. Jackson received it June 6, 1845, as he lay on his deathbed.

It announced that the long fight was won. The old general rallied and spoke with joy and a sense of great fulfilment of this achievement of his hopes for his country.

'All is safe at last,' he said. 'I knew British gold could not buy Sam Houston.'

But he could no longer wait. 'My lamp is nearly burned out, and the last glimmer has come,' he said. For two days he fought, to see 'his old friend and comrade in arms,' but when Houston at last reached the Hermitage, his coach driving through the gate at a gallop, Jackson had been dead three hours.

War between the United States and Mexico was now a certainty. Santa Anna, twice dictator of that country, had again been overthrown, in spite of his martyred leg, and exiled in May, 1845, to Cuba, where he devoted himself to continual intrigue and graft. As a curious side note of the coming conflict, President Polk attempted – and almost succeeded – to conspire with this untrustworthy man to gain a bloodless victory over Mexico. Colonel Atocha, as 'unofficial envoy' from the exiled man, visited Polk and suggested certain sums of money – $30,000,000 to the nation and, say, $500,000 – 'to meet present purposes' for a certain personage for whom he could speak, who would, if he returned to power, conclude a peace at a show of force by the United States, ceding Texas and certain lands to the west of Texas.

Unfortunately the agent selected to arrange the negotiations, Captain A. Slidell Mackenzie of the United States Navy, lacked discretion. He arrived at Havana with pomp and in full uniform, giving such publicity to the matter that, though Santa Anna was allowed to pass unmolested through the American naval cordon to Mexico – under the impression, apparently, that he would co-operate in the scheme he himself had instigated – he repudiated the matter in tones of such virtuous indignation that it served to reinstate him in the favour of the Mexican people. In December, 1846, Santa Anna was once more elected *El Presidente*, announcing that he would 'punish the foreigners.'

In the United States, meantime, a new slogan had been coined. Writing in the *United States Magazine and Democratic Review* for July-August, 1845, John L. O'Sullivan spoke of 'our manifest destiny to overspread the continent alloted by Providence for the free development of our yearly multiplying millions.'

Manifest destiny! It became a watchword, the expression of the devotees of expansion. What a fine, large sound it had! And who would cavil at *destiny*, especially when *manifest* – and so enticing?

After some preliminary manœuvres, including an unsuccessful effort made through John Slidell to purchase New Mexico, Arizona and California for $30,000,000, General Zachary Taylor, who had landed with a force of United States troops at Corpus Christi, Texas, was ordered by President Polk to proceed to the Rio Grande.

Mexico recalled her minister from Washington and

handed the American minister his passports. General Ampudia advanced toward the Rio Grande from the south, and sent a note to Taylor, politely inviting him to evacuate to Texas. General Taylor, equally polite, declined the invitation, saying he was in United States territory. When Ampudia displayed some hesitation as to what to do next, he was replaced by General Arista, with orders to fight.

Learning that two vessels with supplies for the Mexican army were about to enter the Rio Grande, Taylor ordered the river blockaded. Arista pronounced this an act of war and prepared to attack a newly built American fort, across the river from Matamoros, called Fort Taylor but later renamed Fort Brown (this was the beginning of Brownsville, Texas).

Mexican troops were thrown across the Rio Grande by Arista to cut communications between Taylor and his base of supplies at Point Isabel. On April 24, 1846, Captain Thornton and a company of dragoons who were reconnoitering this movement fell into an ambush by a superior force. After a loss of sixteen men killed and wounded, the whole company was captured save for Thornton himself, who escaped by a tremendous leap of his horse over a high hedge, in a storm of bullets.

First blood had been shed – and on Texas soil.

'Old Rough and Ready' Taylor knew he was heavily outnumbered and in a perilous position but he was never unwilling to fight. Leaving Major Jacob Brown to defend the new fort with a hundred men, he marched first to Point Isabel to secure his supplies. Interpreting this as a retreat, the exultant Mexicans attacked the fort, in the defence of which Major Brown was killed.

But Taylor, picking up reinforcements of Texas volunteers and United States marines from the fleet, hurried back to relieve the fort at the head of two thousand men. Arista still had heavier battalions. With six thousand men he posted himself in a strong position at Palo Alto, about nine miles north of the beleaguered fort, where Taylor found him. Old Rough and Ready did not hesitate.

Wrote historian Bernard de Voto, 'What did he [Taylor]

have? A sound principle : attack. A less valuable one which was to serve him just as well in this war : never retreat. Total ignorance of the art of war. And an instinct, if not for command, at least for leadership.'

The Battle of Palo Alto was significant as the first major engagement of the Mexican War, and also the first demonstration of artillery fire power. American artillery outranged the Mexican guns and American small arms outshot Mexican muskets.

As always the Mexican soldiers were handsomely uniformed, with buckles, plumes, epaulettes, sashes and all the glittering panoply which their Latin hearts loved. But they had a deplorable tendency to shut both eyes at the moment they pulled the trigger, which made for very bad marksmanship. After a time they perceived that pretty costumes were a poor substitute for execution in the enemy's ranks and went away from there in a body – and at a speed that made pursuit hardly practicable. In the battle the Mexicans lost close to 600 killed and wounded; the Americans 53 killed and wounded.

Among the young West Point officers who took part in this day were Lieutenants Ulysses Simpson Grant and James Longstreet, who would win lasting fame in a greater war, when they would fight on opposite sides.

Next day Taylor moved forward and discovered that Arista had rallied his army and formed it in a heavily wooded ravine. The Americans went forward to engage the Mexicans, who were well concealed in the dense chaparral. It was hide and seek, almost a series of single combats in the thorny brush, with commanders unable to see the enemy or even their own men, the fighting so close that the smoke of gunfire of both sides seemed to rise from the same places in the choked jungle.

Once the Mexicans charged the American artillery and almost captured it. That annoyed Old Rough and Ready. He called to him Captain Charles A. May, son of a member of the Boston Tea Party and commander of a company – the word 'troop' was not used in cavalry after the Civil War –

of eighty dragoons. In an army filled with spectacular personalities, May was the most spectacular. Six feet four inches he stood without boots, and he wore his beard full and his unshorn hair falling in dark brown locks down his back. A superb horseman and impatient of restraint, he had been in difficulty with the law once or twice in the East, for riding his horse up and down the steps of local hotels and public buildings.

Taylor indicated that he desired the capture of the Mexican artillery. May undertook to comply. Away he went, beard and long hair streaming, his eighty dragoons hell-bent after him, their horses clearing the bushes and rocks at a dead run. They leaped the parapet and began sabreing the gunners. The guns were captured and with them General La Vega. A surge from the Americans bore back a Mexican flank and the battle was over, the better-costumed army again in full and frantic flight.

This battle – called Resaca de la Palma because it was there that Taylor later write his report of it – cost the Mexicans (an estimated) 1,000 men, against an American loss of 100. It cleared the Mexicans out of Texas, and the reports of the newspaper correspondents not only filled the United States with excitement and enthusiasm but set off the boom which carried Old Rough and Ready Taylor to the White House.

Taylor relieved the fort and renamed it Fort Brown after its slain commander. Then he moved across the river and occupied Matamoros. There he kept his army idle while he awaited reinforcements, conferred with political friends, and gave his 'consent' to their opening his campaign for the presidency. Having so done, he moved lumberingly – American transport and logistics were incredibly bad – to Monterrey.

Ahead of his army rode a body of Texas Rangers under Ben McCulloch and Jack Hays. 'In outlandish dress with huge beards, looking almost like savages,' they threw a chill into the Mexicans wherever they appeared, and with some reason. When Mexican lancers – Santa Anna's favourite cavalry – tried conclusions with them, the Texans simply sat their saddles and, after one blast from their rifles, drew their Colt's five-shooters – the first really practical repeating weapons – and continued cutting down their enemies who carried those foolish spears. The lancers – what was left of them – quickly lost enthusiasm for the combat and went elsewhere.

Encircling Monterrey, Taylor captured it in some sharp street-to-street fighting, from September 21 to 24. The Rangers, spearheading this combat, signalized it with the yell already well known to Texans, and later to be famous as the Rebel Yell, when the Texas troops introduced it to the Confederate Army. A combination Indian war whoop and cattle call, 'it started with a low bass rumble and rose in a crescendo to a frenzied treble shriek which suggested a sort of berserk mania of blood lust,' as one writer described it. Blood-chilling it was, and quite effective, as Union troops in the Civil War later agreed.

By the time American detachments occupied most of the cities of northeastern New Mexico, Taylor received orders depriving him of some of his best men, particularly cavalry, which were sent by ship to reinforce General Winfield Scott, who was advancing on the Mexican capital by way of Vera Cruz. He was left with about forty-five hundred men, but when his scouts reported that Santa Anna, who had learned of his weakened army, was advancing against him in person with twenty thousand troops, Old Rough and Ready did not quail.

At Buena Vista, February 22, 1847, he met the full power of Santa Anna's attack. The enemy was overwhelmingly superior in numbers, but Taylor, inept as a general but courageous and cool as a man, sat his horse in the midst of all the fury of the battle, letting his subordinate officers run the battle. It raged for two days. Once an Indiana regiment, through a mistaken order, gave way and it appeared that the American array was in peril. But Mississippian and Kentuckians, led by Colonel Jefferson Davis, threw themselves into the breach and the line was maintained. The young colonel who thus distinguished himself later became United States secretary of war and president of the Confederate States of America.

On the second day Taylor thought he saw signs of wavering in the Mexican front. Near him was a battery of artillery commanded by youthful Captain Braxton Bragg – who would one day be famed as a Confederate general.

'Give 'em a little more grape, Captain,' said Old Rough and Ready.

It was his only direct contribution to the orders of battle.

Captain Bragg did as ordered. The signs of wavering became more apparent and presently the Mexicans broke and fled. Taylor had won the bloodiest battle of the war and ensured himself residence in the White House.

Santa Anna lost (an estimated) 2,000 dead and wounded in the battle, the American casualties being 746. Northeast Mexico was conquered and Zachary Taylor returned shortly to the United States to oversee personally his campaign for the presidency.

Scott's campaign from Vera Cruz to the City of Mexico was out of the periphery of the American Southwest, but the Texas Rangers, under Hays and McCulloch, who were sent by Taylor to Scott, played a brilliant part in the series of manœuvres and battles and in the occupation of the capital. They became acquainted also with another young officer who later won considerable renown. He was Captain Robert E. Lee, who by a brilliant and audacious reconnaissance enabled Scott to win the Battle of Cerro Gordo. Later, General Robert E. Lee of the Confederate Army would greatly value the Texas troops during the Civil War.

CHAPTER SIX

Los Goddammies

OTHER parts of the Southwest had meantime been witnessing equally interesting activities from other American forces.

Polk, now that the war with Mexico had begun, 'wanted the whole hog, not just the trotters.' Particularly he wanted California. He had tried to buy it and failed. He hoped to get it by revolution, for the *Californios* cared little for Mexican rule. When war came, he intended to get it by conquest.

Captain John C. Frémont, the self-styled 'Pathfinder,' was in Oregon with what appear to have been secret instructions to create an 'incident' in California if war occurred. He did so and the so-called Bear Flag Revolt followed, a rather ludicrous affair, in which some horses were stolen and a hamlet and an abandoned fort were 'captured.'

Meanwhile, back in Missouri, something more important was getting under way. Colonel Stephen Kearny, ordered to organize an 'Army of the West,' gathered what assuredly was one of the most heterogeneous forces in history for a descent on New Mexico.

Kearny had 300 regulars of his own regiment, the First Dragoons. Governor Edwards of Missouri issued a call for volunteers and enlisted a regiment known as the First Missouri Mounted Volunteers. It numbered 856 men, divided (roughly) into eight companies, and its elected commander was Alexander Doniphan, a thirty-eight-year-old lawyer, whose entire military experience had been during the so-called 'Mormon War,' in which members of that sect were expelled from Jackson County, Missouri. Doniphan's chief contribution to that disorder was his refusal to obey the command of Governor Lillburn W. Boggs to execute Joseph Smith, the Mormon 'prophet'. This insubordination saved Smith's life – thus giving him time to receive the celebrated 'revelation' whereby polygamy became a popular feature of Mormon life, until it was abandoned in 1890. Doniphan did not know he was pushing back time for this purpose, but his act won him the regard of all Mormons. And though his military training was hardly impressive, he turned out to be a good soldier in a backwards sort of way; as well as an orator and a humorist.

Besides these units, Kearny had two companies of light artillery and two battalions of volunteers, making a total of 1,658 men and sixteen cannon, which he mobilized at Fort Leavenworth.

The start for New Mexico was in June, 1846. Kearny was to be followed by another Missouri regiment, commanded by Colonel Sterling Price, and a unit even more remarkable – the Mormon Battalion, enlisted among the whiskery followers of that sect living in Iowa and in a good many cases accompanied by their families, a total of 540 persons of both sexes and all ages, shepherded rather than commanded, after it reached Santa Fe, by a much-harried but excellent officer, Colonel Philip St. George Cooke. The Mormon Battalion did no fighting, but made its way by the extreme southern route along the Mexican border to San Diego, California.

Preceding it, Kearny and Doniphan and the 'Army of the West,' marched some six hundred and fifty miles, accompanied by four hundred wagons of the annual Santa Fe trading expedition from the Missouri river towns, and camped, early in August, at Bent's Fort, where the Mormon Battalion caught up with them.

From Bent's Fort Kearny sent Cooke with twelve picked men, nominally as an 'ambassador' to treat with Governor Armijo of New Mexico, but actually to escort James Magoffin, a Kentucky Irishman, much liked in Santa Fe as a trader for his bluff and jovial ways. Magoffin had been in conference some weeks before with President Polk in Washington, and had a secret mission – in which money was a large factor. With this advance party Kearny sent a proclamation, announcing the annexation to the United States of all New Mexico east of the Rio Grande – those shadowy claims of Texas again, which now had been espoused by the Union.

Exactly what happened in Santa Fe is not known to this day, but later on Congress appropriated $25,000 to Mr. Magoffin for 'expenses and money expended by him' in this enterprise.

Perhaps Armijo's actions furnish some clue to those expenditures. The general, who was portly, and a scourge to the poor and helpless of his own province, was no fighter and held his title by courtesy. But he announced that he was going to 'exterminate the invader' and marched with four thousand men and a couple of cannon. The men – mostly Indian or peon levies – were poorly armed. Half had muskets of ancient vintage and the other half carried pikes or spears, even bows and arrows. They proceeded to Apache Canyon to defend that strong point.

Kearny, by now at Las Vegas, New Mexico, issued a new proclamation 'absolving' the people of New Mexico from allegiance to Mexico, and announcing himself as governor. But he still had to reach Santa Fe and the way led through Apache Canyon, where Armijo, even with ill-armed troops, might have made a strong resistance. But here Armijo's actions became passing strange.

Whether or not Magoffin's money was involved the governor suddenly declared that all was lost and ordered a retreat. When some of his officers demurred, he threatened them with his cannon. The New Mexican army immediately retired, led by its showy commander, who paused in Santa Fe only long enough to gather up his valuables and continued the 'retirement' all the way to Mexico. Among his valuables he did not include his wife, whom he left behind in his hurry.

Lieutenant George Frederick Ruxton, a British Army officer with a taste for adventure and sport, who was travelling north to the buffalo plains and Indian country, encountered Armijo in Chihuahua and described him as 'a mountain of fat.' When Armijo asked what people were saying about his doings in Santa Fe, the bluff Britisher replied that there was but one opinion, expressed everywhere – that Armijo and the New Mexicans 'were a pack of arrant cowards.'

To this Armijo replied, *'Adiós!* They don't know that I had but seventy-five men to fight three thousand. What could I do?' And with that he continued his retirement, followed by a long line of wagons carrying his goods, which he disposed of at considerable profit in Durango. Later Ruxton saw the general's wife in Santa Fe, where her spouse had abandoned her. 'I had a good view of the lady, who was once celebrated as the belle of New Orleans,' he wrote. 'She is now a fat, comely dame of forty, with the remains of considerable beauty, but quite *passé.'*

After Armijo's retreat, Kearny marched through the dangerous canyon; entered Santa Fe without bloodshed; raised the flag of the United States over the governor's palace; appointed Charles Bent, a partner in the fur-trading firm of Bent & St. Vrain, governor of the new territory; began the construction of Fort Marcy; gave Doniphan orders to draw up a set of laws and then march south to join General Wool at Chihuahua City; and, having done all these things, hurried on westward with all his army except the First Mounted Missouri Volunteers.

His objective was California and his haste was occasioned by the fact that he encountered Kit Carson, riding east with dispatches telling of the 'conquest' of California by Frémont and Commodore Stockton of the United States Navy. He persuaded Carson to turn around and guide him on the journey west; made the trip successfully, his cannon being the first wheeled vehicles to cross this part of America; and not only put down the real resistance which was engendered by Frémont's 'Bear Flag' *émeute,* but court-martialled that vainglorious officer for insubordination, in spite of all the powers of nepotism as exemplified by Senator Thomas Hart Benton, Frémont's father-in-law.

In Santa Fe, Alexander Doniphan solved the necessities of law-making by declaring the statutes of the state of Missouri legal and binding, with a few exceptions covering *acequias,* land grants and other such matters, peculiar to New Mexico.

His men, meanwhile, quickly perceived that there were many ways of enjoying themselves. They also, from their constant use of certain favourite words, which they uttered on all occasions, whether happy or angry, labouring or at play, fighting or frolicking, gained for themselves a name by which they continued to be known.

They were called 'Los Goddammies.'

The New Mexicans had been led by Armijo to expect the worst at the hands of the Americans, and were pleasantly surprised when they found themselves treated as well as could be expected under martial law. The pretty women of Santa Fe began smiling upon the sons of the North and some interesting amours followed. The men, on the other hand, were almost obsequiously polite. Some of the wealthier families, which had fled from the city in terror of the 'lewd and licentious soldiery,' gradually returned – the more quickly since they discovered that, rather than seizing supplies, the American army was paying for them at a good round price.

A little over-indulgence naturally took place. The Missouri volunteers were mostly backwoods boys seeing the world for the first time – both Doniphan's regiment and more particularly Sterling Price's Second Missouri Regiment, which presently arrived to take over the garrisoning while Doniphan went south. 'Among the volunteers of both regiments,' wrote Hubert Howe Bancroft, 'there was much sickness, caused to a considerable extent by indulgence in the various dissipations of the New Mexican metropolis. Some 300 of the Missourians are said to have been buried at Santa Fe.' Which was a rather high price, however you look at it, for New Mexican love and liquor.

It was time for Doniphan's boys to end their vacation. The lawyer-colonel, having provided New Mexico with a set of statutes, now had a more difficult problem. Since Kearny had undertaken, for the American army, to protect New Mexican citizens, it devolved upon the Missouri Volunteers to make good on the promise.

Los Goddammies were equal to the job. The First Missouri

Mounted Volunteers set out on far-flung expeditions into the desert and mountains, led by Fischer, Gilpin, Jackson, Parsons, Reid and other officers on the company commander level. They rode into the heart of the Indian country, rounded up chiefs, and talked turkey with them. So impressed were the Navajos by the cold-blooded audacity of the Missourians that they made and kept a rendezvous with Doniphan at Bear Springs, and promised not to raid the New Mexicans again – a promise they actually kept for a few months.

Now Doniphan felt free to leave Santa Fe to Sterling Price and march southward, invade Mexico proper, and make a juncture with the army of General Wool, which was supposed (erroneously) to be marching from the east to meet him.

Down the Rio Grande Valley straggled Los Goddammies. That is the only way it can be described, since to call it a march indicates some sort of military precision. Lieutenant Ruxton encountering them on his northward trek, left the shocked impressions of a professional soldier of a European army concerning this amateur aggregation of frontiersmen :

'From appearances no one would have imagined this to be a military encampment. The tents were in line but there all uniformity ceased. . . . The camp was strewed with the bones of the cattle slaughtered for its supply, and not the slightest attention was paid to keeping it clear from other accumulations of filth. The men, unwashed and unshaven, were ragged and dirty, without uniforms, and dressed as, and how they pleased. . . . The most total lack of discipline was apparent in everything. These very men, however, were as full of fight as gamecocks, and shortly after defeated four times their number of Mexicans, at Sacramento, near Chihuahua. . . . Of drill and manœuvring the volunteers have little or no idea. "Every man on his own hook" is their system in action; and trusting to, and confident in, their undeniable bravery, they "go ahead" and overcome all obstacles.'

Lieutenant Ruxton was a little hard on the Missourians, because they did show some discipline, or at least regard for the commands of their officers, a little later when, approaching El Paso, they encountered a Mexican army led by General Ponce de León. It was the afternoon of Christmas Day, and the boys were just making camp at Brazito, on the east bank of the Rio Grande at the foot of the Organ Mountains.

It is recorded that when scouts brought word of the approaching enemy Colonel Doniphan and several of his officers and buck privates – no distinction being accorded to rank on such occasions – were playing 'three trick loo' to decide who would own a fine horse captured that morning by the advance guard. When Doniphan saw he was in the face of the Mexican army, he 'sprang to his feet, threw down his cards, grasped his saber, and observed, "Boys, I held an invincible hand, but I'll be damned if I don't have to play it out in steel now" '.

The Missourians were widely scattered, fetching wood and water and caring for their animals, but they rallied around the nearest flag in sight, regardless of units, each loading and looking to his gun. In an incredibly short time, by this primitive and unmilitary method, Los Goddammies were in line of battle.

'León's battle line far outflanked the Americans, pinning them against the river. He had 514 regular dragoons, 800 infantry, and four pieces of artillery, with their companies, in all more than 1,400 men. As usual they were gorgeously uniformed. Whatever failings Santa Anna had, he always costumed his soldiers picturesquely, and the dragoon in particular were eye-filling in tall caps plated in front with brass and plumed with horsehair, green coats trimmed with scarlet, and white pantaloons. Against this combination of numbers and sartorial splendour Doniphan could at the moment oppose only about 500 ragged and be-whiskered men, the rest of his command not yet having come up, because of the habit of straggling for which the First Missouri was notorious.'

Yet nobody on the American side doubted they would win; while the Mexicans, seeing the ill-disciplined and shabby force before them, were equally confident of victory.

A mounted officer, bearing a black flag on which were

painted two skullsand crossbones, and the motto *Libertad o Muerte* – which, given in the Mexican code, was a notification that no quarter would be given – galloped forward. Colonel D. H. Mitchell rode out to meet him. The Mexican ultimatum was surrender 'at discretion'. The Missouri answer was, 'Go to hell, and bring on your forces!'

The Mexican officer rode back to his lines waving his black flag, a bugle sounded, and the Vera Cruz Dragoons charged the American left. They encountered a fire so withering that they fell back quickly, harried by Captain Reid and a squad of sixteen mounted men – the rest of the army fighting dismounted, horses to the rear. One company of dragoons, outflanking the Missourians, got in as far as the baggage train. But the muleskinners and packers carried shootin' irons too, and the rash dragoons, with losses, extricated themselves from that hot position with celerity.

Now the Chihuahua infantry moved forward. Advancing to within gunshot, they took cover in the chaparral, from which they fired three volleys at the Americans. Since they could see nothing to shoot at, the Missourians did not return the fire, but threw themselves flat on their faces, according to the frontier instinct to present as small a target as possible. High overhead the Mexican bullets sang without harm.

In the misguided belief that they had all but wiped out their enemies, since only a few Americans remained standing, the Mexicans rushed forward. They were treated to a most unhappy surprise. As soon as the Mexicans broke from the brush, Los Goddammies rose as one man, and the long, rippling fusillade of the rifles echoed from the mountains. Down went Chihuahuans by scores. There were yells of terror and the gaily uniformed lines reeled, then retreated in confusion.

Only one of León's four cannon had been brought into action – a six-pounder howitzer. James Peacock, who was in the centre, facing the gun, related afterward that when it was fired two or three times, its balls sailing harmlessly overhead, one of the Missourians, who had never seen a field-piece fired, asked, 'What the hell do you reckon that is?'

'A cannon, I believe,' said another.

'Let's go get it!' several cried.

A handful of Howard's company ran right into the Mexican lines, putting to flight the artillerymen. Los Goddammies had captured the cannon. Lieutenant Kribben was sent up to take charge of it, but before he could get it into action the whole Mexican array was gone – he had no target for his captured gun.

That ended the only battle of the Mexican War on New Mexican soil. Doniphan, who commanded with the greatest coolness, humorously belittled his own part in it. At a welcoming banquet given himself and his men when they returned to Missouri after the war, he described the Battle of Brazito in the following words:

'I remained behind, on the hill overlooking the battle, as any prudent commander would. I soon found the Mexicans were overshooting the boys who were below me. Their shot were falling thick all around me. I put spurs to my horse, charged to the front, hallowed, "Come on boys".... The boys thought I was brave as hell, but they did not know what drove me there.'

The Mexican loss was 43 killed. About 150 were wounded, including General León. The Missourians had 7 wounded, all of whom recovered. They captured the Mexican baggage, ammunition and supplies, including 'gourds of delicious wines of El Paso'. That night they had a Christmas banquet on the captured delicacies and a frolic thereafter.

General León retreated all the way to Chihuahua, where he was arrested for cowardice. When he was shown the fortifications there, he is reported to have said, 'Yes, those are all right; but those *Americanos* will roll over them like hogs; they do not fight as we do.'

An uncomplimentary simile, but a correct prediction.

Doniphan occupied El Paso and remained there forty-two days, awaiting the arrival of artillery under Major Clark. The battery of six pieces arrived February 1, 1847, and the whole population of the city, together with all the Missourians, gathered to watch its entrance.

All at once a soldier suggested that a salute should be fired from the brass cannon captured at Brazito. Men hurried to carry out this inspirational notion. Into the gun they poured powder, but wadding of some kind was needed to make it a blank shot, and nothing could be found. Rising to the emergency, one of the men pulled off his socks and rammed them down on the powder.

So great was the hurry – and perhaps the men had taken a pull or two at El Paso *aguardiente* – that they paid little attention to the direction the gun pointed. When it was fired, the socks hit one of the incoming artillerymen in the face. He raised a loud outcry, after it was found he was not in the least injured.

Asked why he kept bemoaning the matter he replied that 'he would rather have been shot with a solid ball than with a pair of socks worn from Fort Leavenworth to El Paso, without a change for eight months'.

On such a note of incongruity ended the campaign of Los Goddamies through New Mexico, and perhaps it was fitting considering the general humorous informality of the whole affair.

To sum up briefly the later career of Doniphan's Missourians : they marched down to Chihuahua; defeated with sheer exuberance and reckless courage an army of 4,200 men commanded by General José A. Heredia; and occupied Chihuahua and found that General Wool, who was supposed to meet them there, was still lingering at Saltillo. Thereupon Doniphan marched his men from Chihuahua to Saltillo, all Mexican resistance being broken in his area. Wool, the regular, was scandalized when he reviewed Los Goddammies, 'some dressed like Mexicans and some like Comanches.'

Nevertheless they made a great marching and fighting record. Their one-year enlistments having expired, they rode jubilantly to the mouth of the Rio Grande, embarked to New Orleans, and thence went up the river to be received with barbecues and barn dances at home. They had covered thirty-six hundred miles by land and two thousand by water, won two battles against superior enemy forces, captured two provinces, and enjoyed an exuberant good time. Perhaps they were not soldiers, in the conventional sense, when they started, or even when they arrived home after their memorable campaign. But man for man they were as formidable fighters as then walked the earth.

The Mexican War came to an end with the Treaty of Guadalupe Hidalgo, February 2, 1848, whereby the United States gained undisputed possession of not only Texas but the territory covered by the present states of New Mexico, Arizona, Nevada, Utah and California, on the payment of $15,000,000.

CHAPTER SEVEN

The Last War of the Pueblos

ALREADY the new order of things was in effect to all appearances in New Mexico. Trade went on, young people made love, households took up the old familiar routine, and everything seemed peaceful.

Yet there were some who resented the American occupation. When Armijo fled from New Mexico, his second in command, Colonel Diego Archuleta, remained. Ashamed of his chief's cowardice, or venality, or both, Archuleta presently, with Thomás Ortiz, began to conspire against the conquerors. And since the New Mexicans had little apparent interest in warlike activity, Archuleta and Ortiz conceived the notion of stirring up an insurrection among the Pueblo Indians.

To Sterling Price, commanding the military forces at Santa Fe, it never occurred that he should watch the pueblos. Not in generations had those Indians caused trouble. The pueblo at Taos was particularly well known to Americans, many of whom – including Charles Bent, the new governor, and such men as Kit Carson, JJuJdge Beaubien, Ceran St. Vrain and others – dwelt in the town nearby and were on familiar terms with the Indians.

Yet this very pueblo was chosen by Archuleta and Ortiz as the centre of a witches' brew of evil they were concocting. In their plot they were aided by some padres who preferred the government of Catholic Mexico to that of the Americans. Since the Taos Indians trusted the padres, the latter were able to aid the conspirators greatly by acting as intermediaries with the natives.

The Mexican promoters of the rebellion displayed their usual incompetence. Plans miscarried; delay followed delay. Eventually the plot was exposed by a mulatto woman, wife of one of Armijo's disbanded soldiers. Colonel Price, learning of it, arrested some of the ringleaders. Both Archuleta and Ortiz, however, escaped and followed Armijo to Mexico.

But the mischief was done; the powder train was laid. Even with the arch conspirators gone, the Taos Indians were so stirred up that an explosion only awaited some spark.

The inflaming act was supplied January 19, 1847, when three Taos Indians were arrested for theft. In a sullen crowd their fellow tribesmen gathered around the *calabozo* in the town of Taos and demanded their release. An angry dispute with the authorities followed.

All at once the Indians began to kill. Cornelio Vigil, the prefect, and Stephen Lee, the sheriff, were murdered first. Then the Indians spread through the town, looking for Americans who previously had been marked for slaughter by the conspirators.

Governor Charles Bent, a known friend of the Indians, was surrounded in his house by the blood-maddened mob. He refused to defend himself, saying when his wife brought him a pistol, 'I will not kill any of them, for your sake. At present, my death is all these people want.'

They broke into his room and riddled him with arrows and bullets. Tomasito, the Taos chief, scalped him. But because he made no resistance Mrs. Bent and the rest of his family were spared.

James W. Leal, the prosecuting attorney for the district, was tortured to death. Judge Beaubien was to have been a victim, but he had gone the day before on business to Santa Fe. Nevertheless, the Indians murdered his son, Narcisse, a promising youth who had just finished his education in the States. Only two Americans escaped death in the town. General Elliott Lee was saved by the intercession of a friendly priest, and Charles Towne rode out of Taos on a fast mule and carried the news of the uprising to Santa Fe. All other male Americans were killed.

Now fully launched, the insurrection spread over the country. On the road to Mora, Taos Indians and New Mexicans murdered eight Americans, and others here and there, the list of victims mounting hourly. At Turley's Mill, on the Arroyo Hondo – a place rather widely celebrated for the distilling of a brand of whiskey known as 'Taios Lightning', were the owner, Simeon Turley, and eight mountain men who were his guests. The Indians surrounded the place and called on Turley to surrender.

But they were encountering here some gentlemen who were averse to having their scalps lifted without a contest. Nine men defended themselves in the mills against perhaps two hundred Indians. Before the building was at last set afire, the mountain men had already sent more than their own number of assailants 'shouting home to glory', as the expression was. The fire forced the defenders to make a rush for safety after dark. Two broke through the cordon alive, one being Turley. He was betrayed by a Mexican who found him hiding, and killed. John Albert, a trapper, hid in the darkness and later made his way north. He encountered the peripatetic Britisher, Ruxton, camping near the present site of Pueblo, Colorado, and in his book, *Wild Life in the Rocky Mountains,* Ruxton preserved a spirited account of the fight at Turley's Mill, as told by Albert. Those who died were Turley, Albert Tarbush, Bill Hatfield, Louis Tolque, Pete Roberts, Joe Marshall, Bill Austin and one other, not named. The Indians lost twenty warriors.

There were other murders and much looting. Then came retribution.

Charles Towne, who escaped from Taos, brought the report of the tragedy to Price next day, January 20. The colonel immediately began concentrating his forces and within three days was marching for Taos. A second detachment, under Captain Isaac R. Hendley, started from Las Vegas at about the same time. It was driven back from Mora in a sharp fight in which Hendley was killed. Captain Morin revenged him February 1 when he captured Mora and destroyed everything in it.

With 354 infantry, four howitzers and a company of 'cavalry' – 65 mountain men on horseback, led by the redoubtable Ceran St. Vrain, close friend of the murdered Charles Bent – Price marched up the Rio Grande Valley, brushed aside disorganized forces at La Cañada and Embudo, and reached Taos the afternoon of February 3.

The Taos Indians, deserted now by their Mexican allies, had retired to their pueblo. Then, as now, Taos consisted of two large structures, several storeys high, flanked by a church and some lesser buildings. Between the two main edifices gurgled Taos Creek. It was in the larger, northern pueblo, and in the church, that the Indians made their stand.

At sight of Price's forces, the Taos warriors swarmed on the *azoteas,* yelling defiance. Price looked the place over, had his howitzers fire a few exploratory shots at the church, then fell back on the town to camp for the night. This movement was believed by the Indians to be retreat, and loud were taunts and jeers they sent after the Americans. With morning, however, they saw the soldiers returning.

This time Price – later a Confederate general – made his dispositions in a businesslike manner. St. Vrain and his mountain men were ranged on the eastern side, to cut off escape toward the mountains. Two of the howitzers, with Burgwin's dragoons, were stationed on the west, facing the church and corrals; and the infantry, with the two remaining guns, formed on the north, directly confronting the pueblo.

For two hours the heavy booming of the artillery echoed

from the mountains. The church was the chief target but its thick spongy walls of adobe simply swallowed the cannon balls and refused to breach.

At eleven o'clock Price ordered a charge. Under a heavy fire the infantry swept forward from the north, while Burgwin and his dragoons made a rush from the west. Several men were killed in this attack, including Captain Burgwin.

But presently the soldiers broke into the church and its defenders fled in some cases to the pueblo and in others toward the mountains. The last was a fatal election, because on that side were the mountain men. Jesús Tafoya, one of the chief conspirators was killed by St. Vrain himself. He was wearing the coat of the murdered Charles Bent and this circumstance did not make St. Vrain any more merciful to him. Of fifty-four fugitives who attempted to escape to the mountains, fifty-one were ridden down and slain. The mountain men took no prisoners.

The day ended, and with darkness the firing ceased, but this time Price kept his men about the pueblo. At dawn next day the Taos Indians, bearing white flags and crucifixes, came out and begged for mercy. Inasmuch as, of 650 persons in the pueblo, 150 were dead and many wounded, Price considered that they had perhaps been chastised sufficiently. He granted the plea for mercy, specifying that they should surrender their war captain, Tomasito, and others who were leaders in the massacre.

These were tried, and before Judge Beaubien, whose son had been murdered. Tomasito was shot while trying to escape and the others were hanged as murderers in Taos, February 9. It was the last flicker of resistance by the pueblo people.

But a more lingering and deadlier Indian war was shortly to begin. When Kearny's army marched across the deserts toward California, every foot of the way was paralleled by Apache scouts. The Americans stopped briefly at the Santa Rita copper mines and there Kearny was visited by the giant chief of the Mimbreños, Mangus Colorado.

Mangus highly approved of the war on Mexico and offered

to furnish guides. One of his subchiefs addressed Kearny through an interpreter along the following lines :

'You have taken Santa Fe; go on and capture Chilhuahua and Sonora; we will go with you! You fight for honour; we fight for plunder. So we agree perfectly. Let us punish the Mexicans as they deserve!'

The Apaches could not understand why Kearny would not join them in a war of extermination, yet it is an historic fact that, though Apaches were encountered along the way thereafter, this warlike people made no attacks on Kearny. In a perfect truce, almost the only one in the whole experience of the Southwest, he and also the Mormon Battalion marched to California and the first American invasion of Apacheria ended bloodlessly.

The truce did not last long. About to move west was the great tide of empire. On January 24, 1848, James W. Marshall, overseer of Sutters lumber mill on the American River in California, found a glittering stone in the millrace. It was a gold nugget. Though he and John A. Sutter, the Swiss owner of the mill, tried to hush the matter, to keep such news from spreading was impossible. By May, all America knew that gold in fabulous quantities had been found in California.

Followed that strange, hysterical stampede known as the California Gold Rush. Cold, heat, hunger and every imaginable peril failed to stop it. Trampling their way westward, the gold seekers thrust out of their way, or slaughtered, the Indians who lived in the country. Almost overnight life changed for the aborigines, caught in the road of a crazed typhoon of humanity which charged deliriously west, deaf to every consideration except the desire to reach the coast – and dig gold.

War with the Indians was an inevitability. On the northern plains the Sioux were the white man's chief foes. In the deserts of the south the Apaches bloodily merited their name – Enemies.

Book Three

WAR BETWEEN THE STATES

CHAPTER ONE

Raiders and Traders

It was some time after the Treaty of Guadalupe Hidalgo before New Mexico, which still included Arizona, was anything but a passive and none too happy appanage of the United States. The bulk of the people were Mexicans or Pueblo Indians, and after the brief Taos revolt they relapsed into subserviency made the more imperative by martial law under which the territory was ruled for the next four years.

Accustomed to tyranny, the peons did not complain over-much at brusque military methods, and as a matter of fact their condition was somewhat improved. American soldiers might be a little hard-fisted, but systematic looting of the populace ceased, and a man's life and a woman's honour were safer than they had ever been before. Nevertheless, it was not until the complexion of the population was greatly changed by the infusion of newcomers from the States that New Mexico became thoroughly Americanized.

Texas, on the other hand, was American from the first – aggressive, self-confident and somewhat robustious. It believed in claiming everything in sight, and the more far-fetched were these claims, the more loudly Texas upheld them. Right after the Mexican War, Texas re-asserted its contention that it owned all of New Mexico to the Rio Grande. In March, 1848, the Texas legislature created the 'County of Santa Fe' – all of eastern New Mexico – and conferred on this 'county' the privilege of sending one representative to the Texas legislature, passing ordinances relating to militia, establishing a judicial circuit, and paying taxes — to Texas.

New Mexico denied every Texas claim, and citizens (chiefly Americans) held indignation meetings to denounce the Texas assumptions. Texas was a slave state, in full sympathy with the South. New Mexico's still scanty American population was largely from free state areas.

What followed was a minor crisis, not without its ridiculous aspects. Early in 1850, Texas sent Robert S. Neighbors into New Mexico as 'commissioner', to divide the territory east of the Rio Grande into several counties and hold elections in them for county officers. Judge Beard also was sent to hold district court.

But New Mexico was under martial law; and the military rulers simply refused to pay attention to Texas pretensions. Although Neighbors issued a proclamation fixing time and places for an election, nobody went to the polls. The military courts continued to try cases and Judge Beard appeared to be without jurisdiction. To cap all this, Colonel Munroe, commandant of New Mexico, ordered an election of a *territorial delegate* to the United States Congress.

This was a flat denial of Texas claims and erected New Mexico into an independent territory. Considerable heat developed in Texas and Governor George T. Wood made a ringing demand that his legislature put the whole military establishment of the state under his control so that he might *enforce* the sacred claims of Texas to New Mexico.

But from Washington, presently, came a terse warning that if the Texans attempted to take forcible possession of the neighbouring territory they would be 'treated as intruders'. Texas contemplated the exact meaning of those words, and armed intervention did not take place. Wood was defeated for re-election; and under his successor, P. Hansborough Bell, the vexing boundary questions were settled, the government paying Texas $10,000,000 to relinquish all claims outside of its present limits. The terms were not popular with many Texans. One of the factors in the settlement was the circumstance that Texas still possessed a 'national debt' of some millions of dollars. The creditors, seeing a chance to recover their money, formed lobbies, both in Congress and in the Texas legislature, which had much to do with gaining the compromise – and the cash.

In Texas the population swelled. Where there were but 20,000 Anglo-American settlers at the time of the Texas revolution, a census in 1847 showed 100,508 persons of white blood, including European immigrants from England, Ireland and Germany. It was a motley combination of many racial, political and religious complexions, yet as Bancroft wrote :

'In their intercourse with each other and with strangers, they exhibited a freedom, and a want of the tinsel of politeness – so often the cloak of insincerity – which might not always have pleased the transient traveller; but if he possessed ordinary common sense, he soon discovered the virtues of frankness, truthfulness, and hospitality in the Texas settler.'

The Texans were perhaps 'frank, truthful, and hospitable' to one another, and to strangers (if white), but they showed less amenity toward the 4,000 Mexican people living among them; and thorough enmity and ferocity – repaid, it must be admitted, in kind – toward the Indian tribes on their plains.

One of the important effects of the Treaty of Guadalupe Hidalgo was that it brought within the limits of the United States an estimated 120,000 additional Indians, some of them very savage and warlike. Of those on the Texas borders, the Comanches and their inveterate allies the Kiowas were the most actively hostile. To their hatred of the white man was added a profit motive – impelling even among savages – for continuous warfare and raiding on the Texas frontier.

That motive was supplied by a strange, shifty, yet colourful people known as *Comancheros* (those dealing with the Comanches). They were chiefly Mexican, though unscrupulous white men and even some semi-civilized Indians took part in their transactions. New Mexican by origin, their activities may have been inspired somewhat by detestation of the Texans, which they felt before and after the American occupation.

At first they had gone out on the plains from the New Mexican settlements as *ciboleros* (buffalo hunters), selling the dried meat of the bison as *carne seca,* an important article of commerce in the early days. Camping along the streams under the cap rock of the Staked Plains, they met the nomadic tribes and a small trade sprang up. Gradually this trade grew more important, until the original object, buffalo hunting, was forgotten, and the former *ciboleros,* now called *Comancheros,* went forth each year with caravans of pack burros and loaded *carretas* for the sole purpose of trading with the Indians.

Rendezvous were established and there were even camps or villages of a more or less permanent nature in strategic places, where the Indians came to barter. At first, in the 1820's, such trading was mostly for furs and meat; but by 1832 it had taken on a more sinister character, the most valuable commodities the Indians offered being loot from the Texas settlements, chiefly horses and cattle.

That year, 1832, Albert Pike crossed the Staked Plains with a party of traders, noted the trails over which the Mexicans journeyed, and himself had commerce with the Comanches. Josiah Gregg, in 1839, wrote of the 'rude indigent' residents of some New Mexico villages, who traded with the Plains Indians. Kendall told of encountering some of these traders on the ill-fated Texas-Santa Fe expedition of 1841, and Captain R. B. Marcy, in his Red River expedition of 1849, saw camp sites along the Canadian River and cart trails leading west.

Between 1850 and 1870, Comanche raids for loot and livestock to trade to the *Comancheros* grew in magnitude and terror. In those twenty years an estimated hundred thousand cattle and horses were driven across the Staked Plains from Texas to New Mexico. Texans angrily charged that white persons, including officials and even army officers in New Mexico, were financing the traders in this nefarious practice.

It was profitable, for the Indians sold cheap – for liquor, gunpowder, red calico, knives, guns, lead, beads and gaudy decorations.

Nobody ever tried to total up the human lives taken, but in addition to the sale of livestock there grew up a traffic in prisoners. Captive white women and children sometimes were 'ransomed' by the *Comancheros* – who expected a wide profit on their 'investment' before they returned them to their relatives. Mexican women and children also were taken, and the *Comancheros* often bought these captives of their own race and kept them as slaves, the women and girls sometimes for immoral purposes, and with no more compunction than if they had been dumb brutes.

Some interesting place names were left in the western Texas plains through *Comanchero* activities. For example, Canyon Rescate means 'Canyon of Ransom'; Las Tecovas Springs got its name from the *tecovas*, or buffalo-hide sacks in which dried meat was stored; Valle de las Lágrimas – 'Valley of Tears' – was where the Comanches, returning from their raids, separated weeping captive mothers from their children; Rio de las Lenguas, or Tongue River, was an important rendezvous where the Comanches, Kiowas and other Indians, together with Mexicans and renegade whites, gathered to barter, with a resultant babel of languages.

While the Comanches made a hell of the Texas frontier, the Apaches and Navajos were busy in northern Mexico, also finding a market for stolen livestock and captives among the unscrupulous traders of New Mexico. Over the long years the Apaches had come to regard their raids for murder and plunder into Sonora and Chihuahua as a legitimate occupation; and the Navajos had grown rich, by Indian standards, with livestock carried off from southern *ranchos*.

After the Mexican War, in 1851, J. R. Bartlett, at the head of the American Surveying Commission, with a military escort, began the survey of the Gadsden Purchase, territory bought at a price of $10,000,000 paid to Mexico, to straighten out the southern border of New Mexico and Arizona and obtain a feasible railroad route.

When he arrived at the ruins of the village of Santa Rita del Cobre and camped near there, he was visited by a considerable personage, Mangus Colorado. Bartlett assured the giant chief that the Americans were there only temporarily and Mangus departed with promises of friendship.

Shortly thereafter three Mexican traders came to the camp, bringing with them a Mexican girl about fifteen years old, named Inez Gonzáles. She had been kidnapped by Pinal Apaches, who sold her to the traders, who in turn, with the callousness of their breed, were conveying her to Santa Fe, to sell her or make a prostitute of her. Bartlett intervened and released her, under the provisions of the treaty whereby the United States agreed to free such captives and suppress traffic in them. Parenthetically, the subsequent career of the fair Inez, as recorded by J. P. Dunn, is of some interest.

'Inez was returned to her parents by the commissioner when he arrived in Santa Cruz [Mexico]. She subsequently became the mistress of Captain Gomez, who commanded the troops in northern Sonora. He married her on the death of his wife, and after his death, Inez married the *alcalde* of Santa Cruz, her social standing not having been at all affected by her romantic adventures.'

The case of Inez was not unique. Since their system of peonage amounted to life servitude in most cases, Mexicans could never see any great evil in slavery – of their own variety – and there was no particular sentiment against devoting women to debauchery.

In his report of 1850, John C. Calhoun, the first Indian agent in New Mexico, had this to say: 'The trading in captives has so long been tolerated in this Territory that it has ceased to be regarded as a wrong; and purchasers are not prepared willingly to release captives without an adequate ransom. . . . Unless the Mexicans are paid for such captives as they have purchased and now have in possession, very few of them will be released.'

In the New Mexico market, female slaves were more sought after than male. 'A likely girl, in her teens, often brings three or four hundred dollars. The men are valued less.' The reason is self-evident.

Without emotion the Apaches observed the release of the girl. But a few days later this policy came home to them. Two Mexican boys, Savero Aredia, thirteen years old, and José Trinfan, eleven, darted into Captain John C. Cremony's tent, begging protection. He took them to Bartlett.

Shortly a delegation of Apache chiefs appeared, headed by Mangus Colorado, to demand the return of their property, the boys having been captives in their camp. Mangus, as the spokesman, said in part :

'You came into our country. You were well received. Your lives, your property, your animals were safe. . . . We were friends – we were brothers! Believing this, we came among you and brought our captives, relying on it that we were brothers and that you would feel as we feel. . . . We believed your assurances of friendship, and we trusted them. *Why did you take our captives from us?*'

Bartlett's position was awkward, for at the very moment there were millions of Negro slaves in the American South. But the treaty was binding. After a long argument, he prevailed on the Indians to take about $200 worth of trade goods for the boys. The Apaches departed sullenly.

Still they kept their peace. Then, July 6, Jesús Lopez, a Mexican labourer employed by the commission, shot an Apache during a petty argument. At once the chiefs came, demanding the murderer's life. But Bartlett could not summarily execute Lopez, guilty as he was. He could only promise a fair trial and execution in Santa Fe, if the man was found guilty.

This by no means coincided with Apache ideas. 'Apaches will not be satified to *hear* that the murderer has been punished in Santa Fe,' said Ponce, one of the chiefs. 'They want to *see* him punished here, at the copper mines . . . where all Apaches may see him put to death.'

Bartlett suggested that he would keep the prisoner in chains, make him work, and give the money he earned to the family of the slain man.

'Money will not satisfy an Apache for the blood of a brave,' said the chiefs with scorn.

Bound by American law, Bartlett was forced to refuse their demands. The Apaches left his camp scowling. Shortly thereafter, horses and mules began to disappear from the expedition's herd, until within a month nearly two hundred were gone – taken by the Mimbreños. Bartlett attempted no retaliation. Greatly handicapped by the loss of so many riding and pack animals, the commission moved on about its business. The Apaches believed they had driven the white men away.

Unfortunately for everyone concerned, some white men remained in the country. While the boundary commission was at Santa Rita, gold was discovered at Pinos Altos, not far away. When Bartlett moved on there were 140 miners at the diggings and they stayed. Their presence was a source of deep anxiety to the Apaches. After a time, Mangus Colorado went to their camp and gave the miners to understand that he could show them much more *oro* (gold) elsewhere than could be scratched out at this place. Quite probably the chief was making an honest offer. There was considerable gold in the country and it would not be strange if he knew where some of it was. He explained that he only wanted them to leave his hunting grounds and go to the land of the Mexicans, where he would show them the better gold.

But the miners could only think of treachery. To 'teach the big buck a lesson' they overpowered him, tied him to a tree, and cut his back to ribbons with a blacksnake whip. Then they released him and jeered him as he staggered out of camp.

They could not have made a greater mistake. Mangus Colorado never forgot that whipping, the greatest humiliation an Indian could suffer. How many white lives paid for each stroke of the lash on his bare back can never be known, but the number was not scant.

CHAPTER TWO

Secession and Sam Houston

A TALL gangling lawyer named Abraham Lincoln was stumping Illinois in 1858, and holding a series of debates with Stephen A. Douglas, whose admirers called him the 'Little Giant'. The tall man lost the election, but he put his opponent in such a dilemma on certain aspects of the slavery issue that, though Douglas went to the Senate, he was finished as a presidential prospect, while Lincoln emerged as the sign and symbol of a new party, opposed to secession and slavery.

There were rumblings in the South and dark clouds of war brooded over the nation. In this time of crisis Texas called back to public service Sam Houston, electing him governor once more, in 1859.

Now sixty-six years old and looking even older because of the strenuous life he had lived, Houston took over the government at the most difficult times. Texas was secessionist, bound by ties of blood and ideas to the South. But a strong minority in Texas opposed withdrawal from the Union which was being openly advocated. Chief of these was the veteran governor, who remained true to his principles learned under Andrew Jackson, that passionate believer in a united and powerful America. His victory at the polls was believed by some to be a victory for Unionism, but in reality it probably was a tribute to his personal popularity.

Shortly after Houston assumed office, John Brown raided Harper's Ferry and was captured and hanged. The always inflammable South Carolina passed startling resolutions in both branches of its legislature, affirming the right to secede, charging that the rights of Southern states were being threatened, and calling on all slave states to meet and adopt united action.

Sam Houston, on receipt of these resolutions, sent a well-reasoned message to the Texas legislature in January, 1860, opposing secession. One paragraph of the message contains much of the gist of his belief :

'The union was intended as a perpetuity. In accepting the conditions imposed prior to becoming a part of the confederacy, the states became part of the nation. What they conceded comprises the power of the federal government; but over that which they did not concede, their sovereignty is as perfect as that of the union in its appropriate sphere.'

The legislature debated and resolutions were adopted, but in the main the majority were in harmony with Houston's views for the time being.

To complicate Houston's problems, Texas was undergoing at this time various excitements not connected with the national issues. The Comanches had increased their attacks so that on March 20, 1860, Houston reported that in four months fifty-four persons had been murdered and as many more wounded or carried away as prisoners, the raiders hardly ever being punished, so rapid was their escape.

And clear across Texas, in the lower Rio Grande Valley opposite the Comanche plains, life was at the same time being enlivened by the so-called 'Cortinas War'.

Juan Nepomuceño Cortinas, commonly called Ceño, was a Mexican criminal who had murdered an American named Somerville in 1847, stolen his mules, sold them to the government on the American side, and escaped into Mexico before his crime was discovered. For some years he lived as a bandit in Tamaulipas, stealing cattle and horses, robbing travellers, frequently crossing over into Texas – where his mother owned the Rancho del Carmen, about nine miles above Brownsville – to raid with his following of outlaws.

Then, July 13, 1859, occurred an incident which suddenly changed Cortinas' status from that of a shabby desperado into a cactus country Robin Hood – in the opinion, at least, of many Mexicans. Cortinas and some of his men were in

Brownsville when one of his followers was arrested for disturbing the peace by Adolph Glaevecke, the city marshal. Cortinas interfered, shot Glaevecke through the shoulder and carried his follower triumphantly out of Brownsville, mounted behind him on his horse, followed by his whooping, sky-shooting *compadres*.

Such a feat of derring-do made Cortinas a hero among Mexicans on both sides of the river. He received ovations, gifts and 'enlistments' for his outlaw band. Encouraged by all this, he rode boldly into Brownsville with his mounted banditti, the morning of September 28, killed three Americans and two Mexicans, and terrorised the town before he withdrew upriver to the Rancho del Carmen, which he turned into a 'military camp'.

There he issued his first 'proclamation', announcing that he was the defender of his persecuted people', the chastiser of their enemies and the righter of their 'wrongs'. The proclamation was worded in just the kind of lofty and glittering phrases that appealed to the peons and *vaqueros* and aroused among the semi-outlaw Mexican population a prideful enthusiasm.

American authorities did not share this enthusiasm. Neither did Mexican authorities south of the Rio Grande, for that matter. The commandant at Matamoros, in fact, sent a detachment of soldiers across the river to protect Brownsville from further 'chastisement' and kept them there for some days.

About October 12 a sheriff's posse rode for the Rancho del Carmen. Cortinas and most of his men hurriedly departed and recrossed the Rio Grande. A man named Thomas Cabrera, said to be Cortinas' lieutenant, was not quite fast enough and the posse scooped him up. At once Cortinas sent a message to Brownsville, saying he would 'lay it in ashes' unless the prisoner was released. But Captain Tobin's company of Texas Rangers arrived in the city and the citizens, encouraged by this circumstance, took Cabrera out of jail and quietly lynched him.

With a roar Cortinas rode back into Texas, where his

forces were augmented by scores of Mexicans from the American side. He defeated two posses sent against him and issued a second 'proclamation' in which he announced that a secret society had been organized for 'the extermination of the tyrants'. Captain Tobin and his Rangers and a crowd of volunteers from Brownsville attempted to oust Cortinas from the Rancho del Carmen, November 24, but the 'Protector' was well intrenched, had cannon which he had captured, and Tobin was forced to fall back.

This series of 'victories' boosted Cortinas' stock to the sky. He now had between four and five hundred followers, from both sides of the border, including a number of dangerous criminals who escaped from the Mexican prison at Victoria.

But his triumph was near an end. On December 5, Major S. P. Heintzelman – later a Union general – arrived in Brownsville with 165 officers and men of the regular army. With these and Tobin's Rangers, he attacked Cortinas and the rancho was captured with expedition. The 'Protector' retreated up the Rio Grande Valley, devastating the country as he went. But, on December 27, Heintzelman caught up with him, soundly whipped him in a fight outside Rio Grande City, and chased him across the river.

In his report Heintzelman said : 'The whole country from Brownsville to Rio Grande City, 120 miles, and back to the arroyo Colorado, has been laid waste. There is not an American, or any property that could be destroyed, in this large tract of country. Business as far as Laredo, 240 miles, has been interrupted or suspended for five months. . . . There have been fifteen Americans and eighteen friendly Mexicans killed. Cortinas has lost 151 men killed; of the wounded I have no account.'

To follow Cortinas' career a little further : So strange are the turnings of events that this bandit, hunted alike by Mexican and American authorities, joined the revolution of Juárez, became a general in the Mexican army and at last governor of Tamaulipas.

Elsewhere in Texas affairs grew progressively hotter. Lincoln was nominated for the presidency of the Republican party at Chicago and the campaign created unexampled bitterness.

Some of the more extreme secessionists determined to push matters to a crisis. To do so they revived a curious secret organization, the Knights of the Golden Circle. Formed years before, its original purpose was almost ridiculously visionary : the formation of an 'empire', including all the lands within a great circle, the centre of which would be Havana, Cuba, and which would include everything between the Isthmus of Panama on the south and the Pennsylvania line on the north – taking in the West Indies and islands of the Caribbean Sea, a large part of Mexico and Central America, the northern tip of South America, all Texas and the South, and even generous portions of some Northern states. The foundation of this eccentric realm, enclosed arbitrarily in a circle without regard to geographic, ethnic, political or other considerations, was to rest on the institution of slavery. Its impracticability is evident, yet all the filibustering movements from 1850 to 1857, including the expeditions of the gasconading William Walker, were associated with it.

With its main purpose defeated, the order was in danger of being entirely forgotten, until the secession movement gave it a new motive for action. It began to grow wonderfully, rapidly forming 'castles' (lodges), in every important town and city of Texas. It provided 'vigilance committees', flogged and terrorized unionists, burned property of free state advocates, and committed some lynchings. Very definitely its activities created a shift in sentiment in Texas, the secessionists becoming emboldened, the anti-secessionists afraid to speak their opinions.

In the midst of this turmoil Abraham Lincoln was elected President, November 6, 1860, and his victory inflamed the South. Heavy pressures were exerted on Houston to call a special session of the legislature and he at last unwillingly did so, setting the opening of the session for January 21, 1861. The Knights of the Golden Circle, to which many if not most of the legislators belonged, had the upper hand, called a highly informal state convention, voted it lawfully constituted over the protests of Houston, who declared it illegal, and when he vetoed it, overruled his veto.

This convention, only about half of its members duly elected, on January 28 passed the ordinance of secession by a vote of 167 to 7, subject to the ratification of the people at an election to be held February 23.

Before that, however, the Knights of the Golden Circle, numbering three hundred or more men, led by Ben McCulloch – who was destined to die a Confederate general at the Battle of Pea Ridge – took possession of the Alamo, and the main square of San Antonio. The manœuvre was to provide General David E. Twiggs – a Southern sympathizer who was in command of the national troops in Texas – the excuse of 'a show of force,' upon which he surrendered the troops, forts and military supplies in the state to the Confederates. Thus twenty-two hundred soldiers wearing the uniform of the United States became on February 18, 1861, the first prisoners of the Confederacy, which was not yet actually organized. Twiggs was dismissed from the United States Army but was given high rank in the Confederate Army in the war that followed.

One soldier who did not surrender at Twiggs's command was the grey-bearded colonel of the Second Cavalry, the former commander of the Department of Texas, who quietly took a stage to Indianola, where he boarded a ship for New Orleans, and thence travelled to Washington for an interview with his commander-in-chief, General Winfield Scott. The Texas uprising did not comport with his notions of honour and, though he was threatened with arrest, he rejected Texas demands that he declare for the Confederacy. In Washington, however, face to face with his superior and in the seat of government, he felt free to tender his resignation and go to his own state, where shortly he began to play a rather important role. He was Robert E. Lee of Virginia.

A few days before the popular vote on the ordinance of secession was taken, February 23, old Sam Houston made a grave and ominous speech from the balcony of the Tremont

178

House in Galveston, warning his people of the consequences of secession. His friends tried to prevent him from doing so, fearing that in the excited state of public opinion violence might be done to him. But Sam Houston never stood back because of a threat of danger to himself.

In prophetic language he pictured the dark future, the loss of life, the destruction of property, the sacrifice of treasure and the small chance of winning Southern independence even after all this.

'I tell you,' he said gloomily as a latter-day Jeremiah, 'that while I believe with you in the doctrine of states' rights, the North is determined to preserve this union. They are not a fiery and impulsive people as you are, for they live in cooler climates. But when they begin to move in a given direction, where great interests are involved, such as the present issues before the country, they move with the steady momentum and perseverance of a mighty avalanche, and what I fear is that they will overwhelm the South in ignoble defeat.'

His address had little effect. At the polls Texas voted 53,256 to 13,841 for secession. Houston refused to take the oath of allegiance to the Confederate government and was deposed from office March 18, retiring to private life. Followed Lincoln's decision to send an expedition to relieve Fort Sunter, the firing upon the flag of the Union, April 12, 1861, and the cataclysm of civil strife, the bloodiest and most destructive of wars.

Before the Civil War ended, every warning Houston gave his people was proved true and all the tragic consequences he foresaw were being suffered by the South. But Sam Houston did not live to see the end. Even his own family was divided. His son, Sam, Jr., was a Confederate soldier, wounded and in a Northern prison, which embittered his last days. On July 26, 1863, the steadfast old patriot, architect of Texas independence and guide of its crucial years, died at his home in Huntsville, Texas.

CHAPTER THREE

Texas Invades New Mexico

THE great War between the States overshadowed all lesser events. Vast eruptions of blood and fire, such as the battles of Bull Run, the Seven Days, Fredericksburg, Chancellorsville, Antietam, Gettysburg and the Wilderness Campaign in the East; conflicts of equal ferocity, such as Shiloh, Vicksburg, Chickamauga, Chattanooga and Atlanta in the West; Sherman's 'scorched earth' march to the sea; and Lee's final defeat and surrender to Grant at Appomattox, made anything that happened west of the Mississippi seem unimportant by comparison.

Yet the Southwest was not entirely devoid of excitement. Texas did not suffer in the same sense that the rest of the Confederacy suffered. There were a few battles along her coast, of secondary importance, and chiefly of a naval-landing party nature; her ports were blockaded; and Galveston was captured by a federal fleet and later recaptured for the Confederacy by General Magruder. Otherwise Texas soldiers fought chiefly on other ground than their own.

Under General John B. Hood, the Texas Division made an everlasting reputation for hard and heroic fighting in Lee's Army of Northern Virginia – and, incidentally, introduced to the world the shrill Texas war cry which became celebrated as the Rebel Yell. Texans were a redoubtable part, also, of the Confederate Army of the Tennessee, and took an important part in the western operations of the war.

And as a state Texas came to the long-delayed grapple with its neighbour, New Mexico. Ever since the first days of Texas independence it had been building up. The cruelties toward the Texas-Santa Fe expedition, the evil activities of the *Comancheros,* the claims to territory made by Houston and his successors and rejected by New Mexico, all caused Texans to regard with considerable animosity the territory just on the other side of the Staked Plains.

This was given point by plans of wider strategy made by the Confederate high command. At the outbreak of the war the capture of all the Southwest was envisaged, chiefly for the purpose of reaching and taking possession of California, with its gold fields, which would greatly aid the financing of the Confederate cause. There was supposed to be strong Southern sentiment in California, but it did not importantly materialize. Union supporters dominated the state, in point of fact, and sent military aid eastward as the sequel will show.

In this scheme of things Arizona had no especial value, except that through it lay the route to California; and New Mexico hardly more, save that besides lying across the California road it might also serve for a flanking movement against Union forces along the Missouri River.

New Mexico itself, except for its comparatively small American population, had a *'Quién sabe?'* attitude toward the issues which had riven the nation. Although a census showed fewer than one hundred Negro slaves held in the territory, the institution of peonage existed and Indian captives were held as slaves, so that New Mexicans found themselves unable to work up much excitement over the controversy that inflamed both North and South. Since many Americans in the territory had Southern backgrounds and traditions, it was supposed that when Confederate troops came the people might support them. But nothing like that occurred.

These were *Texans* who were invading! The old fear and hatred, arising out of the Mexican War and the territorial claims of the Lone Star State, reasserted themselves. New Mexicans did not even remain neutral – they enlisted in droves, furnishing between five and six thousand Union volunteers. To be sure, some of them were a trifle volatile, and had a tendency to go elsewhere when needed, so that Colonel E. R. S. Canby cautioned his subordinate officers, 'Place no reliance on the New Mexican troops except for partisan operations, and then only when the main operations will not be affected by the result.' But at least they showed their loyalty and provided a friendly country for the operation of Union forces, and furnished supplies (at wartime prices). They didn't like Texans.

Handicapped by the Confederate misjudgment of the temper of New Mexico, Lieutenant Colonel John R. Baylor crossed the state line from El Paso, July 25, 1861, and occupied Mesilla. Major Isaac Lynde, commanding the Union forces in that part of New Mexico, advanced on Mesilla with seven hundred men.

There is a fairly well substantiated story that Lynde's warlike followers on the way to Mesilla, by a brilliant manoeuvre, 'captured' a saloon and 'confiscated' its whiskey supply, so that many of them were more convivial than bellicose when they encountered Baylor's Texans. A brief skirmish took place, with few casualties, although 'dead soldiers' (empty bottles) lay thick upon the field. Major Lynde surrendered his men. They were at once paroled and sent marching back to Albuquerque by the Texans, who seemed to fear that they might assail the visible whiskey supply of Mesilla if they remained there. Lynde was later dismissed from the United States Army for lack of zeal in fighting the enemies of his country.

Having achieved this notable victory, the Confederates prepared to further their plan of occupation of New Mexico, Arizona and California. General H. H. Sibley, an officer who had fought in the Seminole and other Indian wars, was sent to take command of the forces of occupation.

Sibley was opposed by an old comrade-in-arms of the Seminole campaigns, Colonel E. R. S. Canby, who later became a general in the Union Army and was murdered by Modoc Indians in 1873. Finding matters badly disorganized in New Mexico, Canby worked feverishly to prepare the territory for defence. His persuasions, with those of Governor Henry Connelly, swelled his forces to about four thousand men, some of whom, however, were not worth much as fighters.

Against him Sibley marched up the Rio Grande with 1,750 men, including some hard-bitten Texas Rangers, accustomed to Indian warfare and hard campaigning. At the same time Sibley dispatched a small force westward, under Captain Hunter. This detachment occupied Tucson, where it remained until the California Brigade began its march eastward from Yuma, two months later, at which time Captain Hunter retired to New Mexico and thence to Texas.

Canby concentrated his forces at Fort Craig, on the west bank of the Rio Grande, just north of the Jornada del Muerto, a severe desert stretch which Sibley must cross. The post was situated opposite a basaltic mesa which created steep banks forty to eighty feet high, down which there were only one or two bridle paths, and nowhere a place suitable for fording the river or even watering an army's horses and mules. This stretch of inaccessible bank reached from the Pandero crossing, seven miles below the fort, to the Valverde crossing two or three miles above it. Fort Craig was supposed to cover both these fords; and since Sibley was east of the river, Canby believed his foe would attempt to cross at this point.

He was right. With considerable sweating and swearing, Sibley's command at last dragged its way across the Jornada del Muerto by mid-February. After a feint at the Pandero ford, where a picket skirmish was fought the morning of February 16, the Confederate commander moved north toward the Valverde crossing, which was better suited for getting his army, and particularly his supply train and artillery across the river.

Canby guessed the manoeuvre and Major Benjamin S. Roberts, with a strong force, was guarding the ford. On the afternoon of February 20 the advance guard of Texans appeared and camped across the river after a brief engagement in which Roberts withdrew to his own side of the stream.

Warfare in the Southwest was bound to be informal. In Canby's little army was Captain James Graydon, better known as Paddy Graydon, who commanded an independent company of scouts. Graydon, among various quaint traits, had an ingenious method of keeping his ranks filled. Whenever he lost a man, by death, capture or desertion, he would ride up to the next simple peon he saw, accost him by the missing trooper's name, and promptly put him in the ranks, in spite of the despairing and often tearful protests of the man thus 'enlisted'. As a result, when his company was mustered out it had a full complement; and judging by its roster, the same identical men who originally enlisted in it.

The night of the twentieth Paddy Graydon was the hero of one of the more bizarre episodes of a campaign filled with the bizarre. Looking across the Rio Grande at the Confederate campfires, he suggested to Major Roberts a night attack which was, to say the least, ingenious and original in plan. Permission was granted.

Taking two old mules unfit for service, Graydon had them loaded with explosives, to which were attached fuses, and led them as near as he could with safety, to the Confederate camp. When he thought he was close enough he lit the fuses and drove the animated land torpedoes toward the hostile lines. Thereupon, he and the men with him began to withdrawing to a safe distance to await the expected explosion.

But horrors! The two old mules were accustomed to Paddy Graydon and his men. They would have nothing to do with those Confederates, who were total strangers to them. No sooner did they see Graydon and his men fall back than they also turned and sought to rejoin their masters.

Graydon's men quickened their withdrawal. The devoted mules broke into a trot, then a gallop, to overtake them. The fuses were burning short and now Graydon and his command were in a panic.

Whip and spur were frantically applied, but the too faithful mules, with a burst of speed of which nobody could have suspected them, appeared about to overtake the stampeding scouts.

Just as they reached the Rio Grande and plunged their horses headlong into its waters – not an instant too soon – two giant explosions lit up the night and deafened everyone near. The mules were obliterated. Fortunately Paddy Graydon and his men had been able to keep a sufficient interval between themselves and the animals so that nobody was actually hurt. Of course the Confederate camp was fully aroused and no surprise was possible for the rest of the night. 'Graydon's charge' (for the river, with two mules pursuing) became a topic for many a delighted quip among Canby's soldiers.

Next morning Roberts crossed the river, attacked the Confederate advance party, and drove it back. Toward noon Sibley's main force came up, and about the same time Canby appeared with reinforcements and took charge of the Union operations. Sibley was sick, so that he could not sit his saddle and the direction of the Texas forces was relinquished by him to Colonel Thomas Green.

At once the engagement became general, the Texans having the greater incentive – they were mighty thirsty and wanted to reach that water. On Canby's left, Hall's battery hammered the grey lines, and on his right McRea's battery was equally busy with grape and shell. The two battle lines took such protection as they could behind sand hills and lava beds, and in groves of trees that dotted the field.

A feinting charge by the Texans on the Union left drew off troops from the right. Then, suddenly, from behind sand hills and a thick bosque, the Texas cavalry burst out and thundered down upon McRea's guns.

'The charge was most desperate,' wrote A. A. Hayes, a member of Canby's force, 'the men [Confederates] relying principally on revolvers and bowie knives, and being maddened by thirst.'

The guns were taken, the captain being killed with many of his men. Some of the New Mexico militia stampeded. Colonel Kit Carson, the old frontiersman, who commanded a regiment he had himself raised, held firm in the centre; but Canby was forced to withdraw across the river and retreat to Fort Craig.

The Texans had won the ford, and a victory. They drank muddy Rio Grande water until all the wrinkles were smoothed out of their bellies. Canby reported his casualties as 68 dead, 160 wounded, and 35 missing, a total of 263. Green gave the Confederate loss as 36 killed, 150 wounded, and 1 missing, a total of 187.

Not bothering to reduce Fort Craig or further deal with Canby, Sibley marched on up the Rio Grande Valley. Without much opposition Albuquerque and Santa Fe were occupied. But Sibley's real objective was farther along.

At Fort Union, about thirty miles north of Las Vegas, was an important concentration of military stores. Since the post was not heavily garrisoned, no real trouble was expected in taking it, and Sibley dispatched a force of about a thousand men, under Colonel W. R. Scurry, to seize all that luscious matériel. To reach the fort, Scurry must pass through Apache Canyon, the gateway through the Sangre de Cristo Mountains. The Texans reached the mouth of the canyon March 10.

At Fort Union there was something like despair. Major Gabriel R. Paul, sure that he could not defend the post, mined it, prepared to blow it up and destroy the military supplies, and retreat north. But at the last moment help arrived.

Down from Colorado was marching a force of volunteers, composed chiefly of hard-rock miners from the Pikes Peak region, the toughest kind of fighting men, not taking too kindly to restraints or discipline, but eager when the bullets began to fly. At times whole companies of these miner-soldiers were under arrest for mutiny, but when word was passed that they soon would be going into battle they behaved well, as if this was what they had been waiting for.

Colonel J. P. Slough was their commander, but the man who was forever connected with the name, for good or ill, was a robustious, fanatical, fearless, Bible-pounding, presiding elder of the Methodist Church, Lieutenant-Colonel J. M. Chivington. It was this same Chivington who two years later directed the massacre of peaceful Cheyennes at Sand Creek, for which history has never forgiven him; and who coined the bloodthirsty slogan, 'Kill and scalp all [Indians], big and little; nits make lice.'

He had been one of Jim Lane's bushwhacking Jayhawkers in the border troubles of Kansas and Missouri during the John Brown days, alternately preaching brimstone-and-damnation and cutting throats. When the Colorado volunteers were mustered he was in Denver, and he spoke to them with such fire-eating eloquence that he was offered the chaplaincy of the regiment. He refused. 'If I go with the soldiers, I am going to fight,' he said. Governor Gilpin of Colorado gave him a major's commission, and eventually he became colonel of the regiment. War – whether against Hell, the Missourians of the Kansas border, Indians, or the Texas invaders of New Mexico – gave his extraordinarily belligerent nature the strife it enjoyed.

The Colorado troops descended to the foot of Raton Pass in northeastern New Mexico, March 7. A message reached them March 12 from Fort Union calling for help. In the next twenty-four hours they made a march of sixty-four miles, arriving at the fort March 13, when the Confederates were preparing to ascend Apache Canyon to Glorieta Pass.

Colonel Slough had a total force of 1,342 men, including his hard-rock Pike Peakers, 300 regular infantry and two batteries of artillery. With these he plunged into the eastern end of Apache Canyon to stop the invaders.

The first brush occurred March 26, near the summit of Glorieta Pass, at the ranch of a Frenchman named Alex Valle, a colourful character who bore the nickname of Pigeon because of his enthusiasm in 'cutting the pigeon's wing' – one of the more violent manoeuvres in frontier dances, in which the dancer leaped in the air and cracked his heels together. His ranch was called Pigeon's ranch and the engagement fought on it often is given that name.

The headlong Chivington was in command of the advance guard which encountered the Confederate van. At the appearance of the Union troops two Confederate fieldpieces began to boom, sending grapeshot and shells screaming down the defile but not causing much damage. Chivington acted at once.

Deploying his infantry across the canyon and posting about a hundred cavalry behind a spur of the cliffs, he attacked. It was the first battle for the Colorado soldiers, but their deportment was far from that of ordinary green troops. With muskets rattling and the big guns creating thunderous echoes in the defile, they began a forward movement so businesslike, and a fire so deadly, that presently the Confederate commander limbered up his guns and prepared to fall back.

At that Chivington sent an order to his concealed cavalry. Out from their canyon pocket swept the horsemen, and down on the enemy's flank with yells and a flashing of sabres, 'running over and trampling them under their horses' feet.'

The Confederates retreated in full flight down the canyon, having lost 32 killed, 43 wounded, and 71 taken prisoner. Chivington, with a loss of only 5 killed and 14 wounded, did not pursue.

'It now being sundown, and we not knowing how near the enemy's reinforcements might be, and having no cannon to oppose theirs, hastened to gather up our dead and wounded and several of the enemy's, and then fell back to Pigeon's ranch and encamped for the night,' he reported in a rather involved sentence, which nevertheless made sense.

All the honours of the brisk little skirmish rested with Chivington and his Colorado hard-rock men. A Texan, writing to his wife, described them : 'Instead of Mexicans and regulars, they were regular demons, that iron and lead had no effect on them, in the shape of Pikes Peakers from the Denver gold mines.'

Said Alex Valle, the ebullient, heel-cracking Frenchman, 'Zat Chivington, he poot 'is 'ead down, and fought loike mahd bull !'

Next day Slough, with the main Union force, came up and joined Chivington at Pigeon's ranch. Scouts reported the approach along the canyon of considerable numbers of Confederates. It was the main Texas force under Colonel Scurry and the hour had come for a conclusive engagement.

The night of March 27, Slough detached Chivington with 440 men to make a steep and dangerous detour through the mountains and if possible fall on the Confederate rear. The following morning Slough moved forward and encountered the enemy in force just beyond Pigeon's ranch. It appears to have been something of a surprise to the Federals, and Slough later reported, 'Having met the enemy where he was not expected, the action was defensive from its beginning to its end.' As a matter of fact, the action became a rather hasty retreat, with the Texans driving the Union troops a considerable distance along the canyon in this contest for Glorieta Pass.

It was, as Colonel Scurry asserted in his report, a Confederate victory. Yet just when he should have made another, and perhaps decisive, attack, a flag of truce instead was sent forward, asking an armistice for the burial of the dead. This was agreed to by the Federal commander. The following day, at the expiration of the armistice period, the grey-clad forces were in full retreat from the canyon.

Why this surprising withdrawal, after the Federals had been whipped and driven? The activities of the bellicose parson, Chivington, provided the answer to that question. Guided by Lieutenant-Colonel Manuel Chavez, who was a native of the country and knew the remote trails, he led his 320 Colorado volunteers and 120 regulars over treacherous paths across the rugged mountains.

About noon he reached a point where, from the heights of precipitous cliffs, he could look down on Johnson's ranch, at which were assembled the supply trains, ammunition wagons, one piece of reserve artillery and the transport livestock of the enemy, under a guard of about two hundred men.

Chavez indicated the steep and dangerous path down. Chivington nodded. In single file, horses sometimes sliding, sometimes almost toppling over as they fought to keep their footing, the whole command began the descent. All reached the bottom safely.

The appearance of Federals almost literally from the clouds took by complete surprise the Confederate rear guard, which did not imagine a blue uniform within miles. Chivington led the charge. The Confederates were briskly swept back, finally routed.

Chivington proceeded systematically to destroy everything of military value. All ammunition, supplies, rations, even surgical stores were demolished. He later reported that his men bayoneted eleven hundred mules and burned sixty-four wagons with their contents, besides spiking the gun they captured.

It was a messenger from his defeated rear guard, flying to Scurry with this news, who caused the Confederate colonel to ask for an armistice and retreat. Chivington, meantime, climbed up the mountains, retraced his path of the night before, and joined the Union Army where it was camped on the pass.

The fight at Glorieta Pass was the high-water mark of Confederate advance in the Southwest. What began as an invasion turned into a retreat. His ammunition gone, Scurry and his Texans fell back on Santa Fe. Colonel Slough wished to pursue him, but received orders to remain and protect Fort Union at all hazards. In disgust he resigned and Chivington became colonel of the regiment. It was a rank he certainly had earned, for that little side operation of his was the decisive blow of the entire New Mexico campaign.

His army defeated, its supplies gone, Sibley retreated from Santa Fe, harried every step of the way by the Colorado soldiers and by Canby, until early in May they were out of New Mexico. So ended the Texas invasion of New Mexico, threatened since the days of Santa Anna. Of the force sent out to capture the territory, more than half were left behind in killed, wounded or captured.

In his general report, written May 4, Sibley made clear his feelings :

'I cannot speak encouragingly of the future, my troops having manifested a dogged, irreconcilable detestation of the country and its people.'

The 'dogged, irreconcilable detestation,' he might have added, was contributed to, in no small degree, by the Colorado hard-rock men.

CHAPTER FOUR

Reaping the Whirlwind

ALTHOUGH Mangus Colorado had long been on the warpath against the white men, Cochise, chief of the Chiricahua Apaches, while always ready to raid against the Mexicans, held back from fighting the Americans.

The Chiricahua Mountains of Arizona, which were the camping and hunting grounds of Cochise's people, are pierced by the steep-sided and narrow Apache Pass – not to be confused with the Apache Canyon of New Mexico – the only natural highway through the great barrier and therefore the route of the Butterfield mail stagecoaches. About half-way through the pass stood a stone stage station, the keeper of which, a man named Wallace, gained the friendship of the Chiricahuas and contracted with them to furnish wood for his station. So loyal was Cochise to this agreement that the stage line operated without molestation through the very heart of his country.

Some time previously a comely Mexican woman had been captured by the Apaches and kept by them for a year or two before she was ransomed or rescued. During this period she gave birth to a child, of which one of the Apache warriors was the father. The lady retained her comeliness; and after her return to her people, Johnny Ward, a bachelor, took her to his ranch shack on the Sonoita River, where she lived with him and her small son in evident content.

But in October, 1860, a band of Apaches raided the ranch, burned Ward's house, ran off with his cattle, and carried away the child. This child, incidentally grew up among the

Apaches and is believed to have been Mickey Free, who gained some renown in later years, during the Geronimo days, as a scout and interpreter for the United States Army.

When report of the raid reached Fort Buchanan, Lieutenant George N. Bascom set out with sixty men to recover the boy and livestock. Bascom was just out of West Point and knew a lot about spit and polish but less than nothing about handling Indians.

Told that there was an Indian camp in Apache Pass near the stage station – where Cochise and his band lived for convenience in supplying the station with wood – Bascom led his men directly there, without bothering to ascertain whether or not those particular Indians were guilty of making the raid. At his summons, Cochise and several of his leading warriors came to the stage station. Bascom began by demanding that they return the missing cattle and the child to him, and ended by peremptorily ordering the arrest of Cochise.

At first the Apache chief could not believe the officer was serious, since he himself had been noted for his peaceful policy toward the white man. But when he saw Bascom's men advancing to arrest him, he led a dash for freedom in which, though wounded, he escaped, with all his warriors except five, who were captured and held.

From that moment began the hostility of one of the deadliest Apache leaders. Firing broke out along the canyon sides, to which the soldiers in the bottom replied as well as they could, inasmuch as they could see nothing of their enemy, concealed in the trees above. Bascom lost several men. In the midst of this the five captured warriors tried to escape. Two were killed and the other three overpowered.

That night a stagecoach reached the station. It was the last to traverse Apache Pass in many long months. It had been attacked, but the driver cut loose a horse shot down in its traces and managed to get to the shelter of the stone station.

On the third day Captain B. J. D. Irwin – later a general – arrived with fifteen men to reinforce the soldiers in the canyon and take command. Irwin had captured three

Apaches on his way up, so now there were six prisoners. The troops at the stone station were suffering from thirst and there were wounded to be attended.

Next night a wagon train, unaware of the suddenly created hostility of the Chiricahuas was cut off and eight persons killed, while three were carried away as captives. Matters were becoming desperate. At last Wallace, who knew the Indians, said he would try to talk with Cochise and see if he could get a peaceful settlement. With two of the stage employees he went up in the woods. They did not return. So hostile had the Indians become that they seized their former friends, the stage people, and held them.

Next day Cochise brought his six captives into view of the soldiers and offered to exchange them for his six warriors. Irwin and Bascom feared treachery and would not make the exchange.

That night Cochise tortured his six prisoners to death.

The providential arrival of two companies of cavalry from Fort Buchanan saved the survivors in Apache Pass. As they retreated down the gorge they found the bodies of the six white men who had been put to death. In reprisal they hung the six Apache warriors and left them for Cochise to cut down.

A blundering West Point shavetail had started something greater and more terrible than he could have imagined – a general Apache war. From this time forth Cochise gave full co-operation to Mangus Colorado, and for the next twenty-five years the Apaches as a people never really ceased fighting.

In Western Texas the Mescalero Apaches, under their chiefs Cadete and Nicolás, kept Fort Davis, occupied by the Confederates in the Big Bend country, in a state of siege. They wiped out the settlements along the Rio Bonita, ambushed and destroyed a column of Confederate cavalry under Lieutenant May, and depopulated the entire area.

In New Mexico, Mangus Colorado attacked his old enemies of the Pinos Altos mines and cut off a wagon train, but was forced to draw away by the timely arrival of the highly informal Arizona Rangers. The chief was not, however, through with the mining settlement. Balked of direct attack, he began the same sort of siege he had formerly thrown about Santa Rita del Cobre – a silent, unseen watch, warriors prowling in concealment, keeping all supplies from reaching it, and cutting off any who ventured out from it, except in strong parties. Slowly Pinos Altos starved.

Elsewhere in the country the Apaches were supreme, so that Colonel Baylor, appointed Confederate military governor of New Mexico and Arizona during the brief months of Sibley's campaign up the Rio Grande, recommended that every Apache man, wherever found, be killed on sight, and the women and children sold into slavery. President Jefferson Davis promptly rejected the policy and demanded an explanation. To justify himself, Baylor wrote to General Magruder, commanding in Texas, including a ghastly exhibit, the scalp of a Miss Jackson, which had been taken by the Indians, with a request that it be forwarded to Davis. His letter said :

Arizona has been kept in poverty by Indian depredations . . . and the general belief among the people is that extermination of the grown Indians and making slaves of the children is the only remedy. This system has been practiced in New Mexico. There is not a family of wealth in that country but has Indian slaves derived from that source. In fact so popular is this system of civilizing the Indian that there have been several efforts to pass a law in the New Mexico legislature, making all Indians slaves for life.

Davis, far from agreeing with Baylor's 'civilizing' method, removed him as governor. But shortly after, the Confederates ceased to be a factor as Chivington and Canby drove them out of the territory.

Early in April, California, having settled within its own borders the question of loyalty to the Union, sent eastward a little army of about fourteen hundred men under the command of General J. H. Carleton.

Mangus Colorado and Cochise had due notice of their coming. In fact Carleton himself supplied the warning. He sent three express riders with dispatches for Canby from Tucson, June 15. The men were Sergeant Wheeling, Private John Jones and a Mexican guide named Chavez. In a running fight the Apaches killed Wheeling and Chavez, and though Jones, 'almost by a miracle' – to use the words of Carleton's report – succeeded in escaping to the Rio Grande, he was captured by the Confederates.

Realizing from the incident of the three dispatch bearers that something was happening toward the west, the Apaches scouted in that direction, discovered Carleton's force advancing from Tucson, and prepared to resist it in Apache Pass.

On June 12, Carleton forwarded another set of dispatches to Canby, this time by Lieutenant-Colonel E. E. Eyre and an escort of 140 men. The size of the escort is sufficient evidence of the gravity of the Apache peril. While camping near the abandoned stage station in Apache Pass, Eyre had a parley with the chief of a band of about seventy-five warriors – undoubtedly Cochise. The Apache leader asked for tobacco and food, and departed after viewing Eyre's detachment, which was too strong for his immediate force of warriors. As he went, however, he cut off three men and killed them. Eyre ordered a pursuit but the Indians easily outdistanced it. Later the same day they did some sniping from the top of the canyon wall, wounding Surgeon Kittredge and killing a horse. The Apaches were not yet ready for a full-dress battle, and Cochise did not molest Eyre further as the latter went and joined Canby. Probably at this time Cochise was awaiting the arrival of Mangus Colorado and his Mimbreños.

By the time Carleton's main army neared Apache Pass the Indians were ready. As the advance guard of three hundred men, under Captain Thomas Roberts, started up the gorge toward the stage station and its springs, the Apache yell was suddenly raised, and bullets and arrows came whizzing down from the canyon walls where, according to Roberts, several hundred Indians were concealed.

Although he lost only two killed and two wounded in the

first fire, Roberts fell back from his position, which was untenable. But he had to reach the water and he had the answer
to an Indian ambush. Bringing up two howitzers, he began
shelling the heights. To the Apaches the experience was novel
and terrifying, since they never before had encountered the
'wagon guns that shoot twice' – a reference to the shells,
which exploded after being fired. In astonishment and some
panic they retreated far enough up the canyon so that
Roberts could reach the springs on which the army depended
for water.

A messenger, escorted by a small detachment of cavalry,
was sent back to Carleton, requesting reinforcements, and
Roberts prepared for the next day's fighting, which he
supposed would be a real and perhaps costly battle. But when
morning came the Apaches had disappeared. The whole
army marched on through the pass without seeing another
Indian.

Two miles beyond the pass they found what was left of
nine men from the Pinos Altos mines. Carleton's report said,
'One of them had been burned at the stake; we saw the
charred bones and the burnt ends of the rope by which he
had been tied.' It was another of Mangus Colorado's little
attentions to Pinos Altos. His back still smarted from that
flogging.

But what happened to create such a different situation in
Apache Pass? Why did what appeared to be a formidable
fight turn out to be no more than a preliminary skirmish?
The resolute behaviour of one man, and a stroke of luck,
brought about the surprising change.

When Roberts sent his message back to Carleton, Indians
on horseback tried to cut off the small escort. In the running
chase they killed the horse of Private John Teal. His comrades could only ride for their lives with the message, which
was imperatively important, leaving him to his fate.

Teal prepared to die gamely, crouching with his carbine
behind his dead horse. At a fairly long range about him
galloped the Apaches, preparing for the scurrying charge by
which they would close with him. The trooper noticed that

their leader was an exceptionally large man, but did not dream that this was the famous Mangus Colorado himself. He aimed at the giant with great care and pulled the trigger. The huge warrior tumbled out of his saddle.

To Teal's amazement, the Apaches at once seemed to lose all interest in him. They gathered about their fallen leader and bore him away, their voices 'growing fainter in the distance'. After a time, it having grew dark, Teal rose and walked unmolested to camp, carrying his saddle with him.

It was the wounding of Mangus Colorado that ended the Apache Pass fight. From their positions in the heights the Indians withdrew, leaving the way open. Southward to Janos, a Mexican town, they carried their chief, and occupied the streets while the inhabitants cowered in their homes. A Mexican doctor was confronted by the warriors bearing the wounded Mangus Colorado.

'Make Indian well,' said the spokesman curtly. 'He die, everybody in Janos die. He no die, everybody live.'

No physician ever exerted more prayerful care, perhaps, than this one as he treated his savage patient. Fortunately the rawhide constitution of the sufferer was in his favour. The bullet was extracted, the wound bound up, and Mangus lived. The people of Janos watched thankfully as the unwelcome visitors departed without any new scalps. But the chief, who was growing old, never fully recovered from his wound.

Meantime, Carleton and the California column, safely through the Chiricahua Mountains, reached New Mexico, where Carleton took over the command from Canby.

One of his acts was to send a strong detachment under Lieutenant E. D. Shirland to convey food to the people at Pinos Altos, who were starving under the Mangus Colorado's siege. The rescue force reached the mining settlement August 6, with five beeves, six hundred pounds of pemmican, three thousand pounds of flour and fifteen hundred pounds of *panocha* (Mexican sugar), and found the people in terrible destitution. Shirland reported there were 'about thirty Americans, French, Germans, &c; two of the Germans with families; all the rest were Mexicans . . . received . . . little assistance before our arrival, before which time they had been living on purslane and roots, and several had become insane from hunger.'

Mangus Colorado's dealings with those he hated were not light.

With New Mexico secure from the Confederates, Carleton, who was no lover of Indians, turned his full attention to the Apaches. The Mescaleros in west Texas and southeast New Mexico were the objectives of three columns sent against them, all with identical orders : 'The men are to be slain whenever and wherever they can be found. The woman may be taken prisoners, but, of course they are not to be killed.'

Captain McCleave with two companies of Californians encountered the Mescaleros in Canyon del Perro, shot it out with them, and routed them. The Indians knew when they had enough. They also knew better than to surrender to the Californians. Instead they fled to Kit Carson, who was in their country with five companies, and surrendered to him.

Cadete, whose Indian name was Gian-na-tah (Always Read), made a short speech to Carson, which is preserved and is reminiscent of the famous 'From where the sun now stands' utterance of Chief Joseph of the Nez Percés on a similar occasion : 'You are stronger than we. We have fought you as long as we had rifles and powder; but your weapons are better than ours. Give us like weapons and turn us loose, we will fight you again; but we are worn out; we have no more heart; we have no provisions, and no means to live; your troops are everywhere; you have driven us from our last and best stronghold and we have no more heart. Do with us as may seem good to you, but do not forget that we are men and braves.'

Carson, the old frontiersman, understood the Indians. He took the liberty of disobeying Carleton's extermination orders. Instead he sent the Mescaleros to the Bosque Redondo reservation.

Carleton with equal assiduity devoted himself also to the western Apaches – the Mimbreños, Chiricahuas and other bands. Results against those desert sidewinders were at first disappointing. But, in January 1863, came a windfall for the white man.

Prospectors were encouraged by Carleton to go in strong parties into the Indian country, looking for gold or silver, because this gave him an excuse to ask for more troops to hunt down the Indians for the 'protection' of the gold seekers. One such party, under Captain Joseph Walker, camping near Fort McLean, learned that old Mangus Colorado was in the vicinity with some of his Mimbreños. That day E. D. Shirland, the rescuer of Pinos Altos, now a captain, visited the prospectors with a detachment of soldiers. Walker conferred with him and suggested to him a plan to 'eliminate' the Apache chief which would have made a Judas blush. Shirland, however, was no Judas. He agreed promptly, and without blushing.

Under a promise that peace would be made between the white men and his people, Mangus Colorado, sick and ageing, was induced to come alone into the camp. Once they had him among them, the soldiers and prospectors disarmed him and made him understand that he was a prisoner.

When word of this reached Colonel J. R. West, commanding at Fort McLean, he rode over to the prospectors' camp with an escort. Arriving after dark, he surveyed the great-limbed Indian captive by the light of a campfire, where he was being guarded by Shirland's soldiers, and gave instructions to two of the guards, Privates James Collyer and George Mead.

'Men,' he said, 'that old murderer has got away from every soldier command, and has left a trail of blood for five hundred miles on the old stage line. I want him dead or alive tomorrow morning. Do you understand? *I want him dead.*'

That night, according to a witness, D. E. Conner, one of the prospectors, the soldiers heated their bayonets in the fire and burned the feet and legs of the sleeping prisoner. When Mangus Colorado rose on his left elbow in pain and angry protest, they shot him to death. Colonel West reported that the prisoner was 'killed while attempting to escape'.

So treachery ended the life of the Apache who could not be conquered by honest force of arms. Mangus Colorado had made a vast contribution to the history of his race. Captain John C. Cremony, who knew him and his people well, wrote of him, 'He was the greatest and most talented Apache of the Nineteenth Century. . . . His sagacious counsels partook more of the character of wide and enlightened statesmanship than those of any other Indian of modern times. . . . He found means to collect and keep together, for weeks at a time, large bodies of savages, such as none of his predecessors could assemble and feed . . . and taught them to comprehend the value of unity and collective strength. . . . Take him all in all, he exercised influence never equalled by any savage of our time.'

Later Apaches, such as Cochise and Geronimo – who waged war on the whites when the writing of sensational Western literature became popular – received more publicity than Mangus Colorado. But Geronimo never was more than a minor outlaw raider; and Cochise never did a tithe of the warlike damage to white interlopers that Mangus Colorado did. Cochise was present and unhurt when Mangus was wounded at Apache Pass; yet so much greater did Mangus Colorado loom in the minds of the Apaches that they desisted from the battle and bore him away. He was the rimrock Apache, the greatest figure of his race.

A disgusting detail of the murder of the old chief was that the head was severed from the body by a surgeon and the brain taken out and weighed. The head measured larger than that of Daniel Webster and the brain was of corresponding weight. For a time the skull ornamented the phrenological museum of Professor O. S. Fowler. It is said now to be in the Smithsonian Institution, in Washington, D.C.

The final comment on him by J. P. Dunn was: 'It was time for him to die. He was about seventy years old, and had secured all the revenge to which one man is entitled.'

After the death of Mangus Colorado, the Apaches took to their hiding places and there was a cessation of raids on the border. But the extermination policy continued. One of its ugliest episodes was the so-called 'Pinal Treaty', January 24, 1864. Colonel King S. Woolsey, with thirty Americans and fourteen Pima and Maricopa Indians, encountered a band of Pinal Apaches, led by a chief named Par-a-muck-a. When he invited them to come in and make peace, thirty-five of them did so. Woolsey seated them, and announced with a vicious sort of irony – which escaped them – that he would 'give them certificates of good conduct such that no white man would ever molest them'. The Indians remained seated while Woolsey's followers gathered about them, making ready for the 'treaty'. When his men were posted, 'Woolsey drew his revolver and gave Par-a-muck-a the Arizona certificate of a "good Indian" at the first shot. His men signed on the bodies of the others. Only one Indian – a lame man who could not run away – affixed his signature. He did it with his lance, on the person of Mr Cyrus Lennon.'

The Apaches were for the moment relatively inactive, but the Navajos frisked wild and fancy-free in northern New Mexico and Arizona. They made numerous 'peace treaties', beginning with Doniphan, but found it inexpedient to keep any of them. The Navajos warred on the Mexicans, and the Mexicans on the Navajos, 'the common opinion being that the Navajos captured the greater number of sheep, and the Mexicans the greater number of slaves.'

Navajo slaves were in demand, 'on account of their tractable nature, intelligence, light skins, and the voluptuousness of the females'. One writer, Dr Louis Kennon, said between five and six thousand Navajos were held as slaves at this period. 'I know of no family which can raise $150 but what purchases a Navajo slave,' he recorded, 'and many families own four or five – the trade in them being as regular as the trade in pigs or sheep.'

Kit Carson was the man most conversant with Indian ways, and at last Carleton called on him to solve the Navajo problem. During the winter of 1863-64 the Navajos retreated as usual to their stronghold, the Canyon de Chelly. The canyon is one of America's natural wonders, rivalling in some respects even the Grand Canyon in spectacular features. Its sheer walls of red sandstone reach a height of nearly fifteen hundred feet in places, and it is so narrow at certain points that a stone can almost be thrown from one precipice lip to the other. In only a few places can it be entered by men, and in even fewer by animals. The bottom of this great chasm is flat and sandy, with the waters of Chelly Creek flowing through it.

Before the Navajos occupied the canyon the Cliff Dwellers lived there, and their deserted habitations may still be seen in niches high on the canyon walls. On the floor of the gorge the Navajos had their little orchards of peach trees and herded their sheep, while there and above, on the level desert, were their *hogans*, the distinctive moundlike dwellings of logs and earth which they build. In Canyon de Chelly the Navajos believed themselves safe for the winter, as they always had been.

But Kit Carson had another notion. He knew where the canyon was, and though neither he nor any other officer had much knowledge of its topography or the difficulties which confronted an expedition to it, he decided that winter was the time to strike the Navajos there.

With 390 officers and men he left Fort Canby, January 6, 1864. It was a season of bad weather and snows which exhausted animals and men, and would have appalled anyone except the old Indian fighter. Even he had to abandon part of his supply train, but he pushed on, reaching Canyon de Chelly January 12.

That day his scouts, under Sergeant Andrés Herrera, jumped a party of Indians, killed eleven, and captured two women and two children. Carson next day divided his command in three divisions, one on each rim of the canyon, the other on its bottom. They moved the entire length of the great fissure in the earth, fought two or three skirmishes and, as Carson reported, killed 23 Navajos, captured 234, seized two hundred sheep, and destroyed about three thousand peach trees in the canyon.

In despair over this destruction, the Navajos asked how they could have peace. Carson told them to go to the Bosque

Redondo, a reservation on the Pecos River. It was named from a round grove of trees and was said to have been visited by both Coronado and Espejo in early explorations. Later it was a trading post. In 1862, Fort Sumner was erected there and the Mescaleros established on a reservation near it, Captain Cremony becoming agent for them.

Kit Carson's 'long walk' – as the Navajos still call it – had a most salutary effect. The Indians began coming into the Bosque Redondo in such numbers that Carleton's resources were heavily taxed to support them. By the following July more than seven thousand of them had surrendered and were living off the government. They stayed at the Bosque Redondo until 1878, when they were removed to their present reservation. Exit the Navajos from history as enemies of the white man.

But the Apaches were of different stuff. They refused to surrender even though the Indian hunt went on throughout the dreadful sixties. The number of encounters which took place with them is illustrated by the fact that six pages of fine type were required to enumerate them in the General Orders of 1865. By that time official reports showed 363 Indians killed and 140 wounded; 7 soldiers killed and 25 wounded; 18 civilians killed and 13 wounded.

In spite of this progress along the road toward extermination, however, the Apaches still bushwhacked and ambushed, made it almost impossible to maintain the stage routes, scalped and raided and escaped. While the Apaches were on the loose, settlement in southern Arizona was virtually impossible.

Book Four

EPIC OF THE HORN-SPIKED HERDS

CHAPTER ONE

In Spite of Hell and High Water.

ON April 9, 1865, General Robert E. Lee, after an incomparable defence for four years against great odds, surrendered what was left of the Confederate Army of Northern Virginia to General Ulysses S. Grant, whose hammer blows at last had crushed him. It was the end of the Civil War, although other Confederate armies made their surrenders later.

The last shot fired in hostility between North and South was an engagement in Texas, at Palmito, near the scene of Zachary Taylor's Mexican War victory of Palo Alto, May 12, 1865. It might, incidentally, be called a Confederate victory, since the Union force under Colonel Theodore H. Barrett was forced to retreat. If there was any consolation to the Southern cause that it won the final battle, that was about the only grain of saisfaction remaining. The South was completely beaten and prostrate.

In Texas, with the coming of peace, came also those years of bitterness, misrule, strife and readjustment known as the Reconstruction. For five years Texas drained the bitter cup of Carpetbagger rule to the dregs. Then, in 1870, having complied with the statutory requirements, the state was re-admitted to the Union. The Amnesty Act, signed by President Grant in 1872, re-enfranchised all in the South except for a few who had been especially prominent as leaders in the Confederacy; and even these gradually were readmitted to citizenship by special acts, and at last by the general Amnesty Law of 1898.

Aside from Texas, the Southwest was little affected by the Reconstruction and other postwar problems. One aftermath of some importance in New Mexico was the abolishment of peonage, or debt service, by Congress March 2, 1867 – a tardy reform, brought about by the emancipation of Negro slaves, of an abuse which had continued in one form or another since the first Spanish occupation of the territory.

Meanwhile something else was taking place; something having nothing to do with laws or lawmakers, elections or race problems, but which intimately affected the whole Southwest, starting with Texas and extending to New Mexico and Arizona – which had become separate territories in 1863 – spreading eventually over the entire West. In its way it had greater influence on history than the gold rushes and its effect was infinitely more permanent. It brought about indirectly the subjugation at last of the warlike Indian tribes, the arrival of civilization in the farthest confines of the nation, and put the stamp of the Southwest on a full half of the continental United States.

It was the sudden, strange extension, amounting almost to an explosion, of the cattle range in America.

From the very first arrival of the white man, cattle were part of the authentic Southwest scene. That visionary explorer, Coronado, when he made his long and disappointing march through the pueblo country and on up into the high plains, had large herds of slaughter animals, including sheep, hogs and cattle, driven at the rear of his army. Such of his cattle as survived the journey up through New Spain, and the necessity of the mess kettles, were the first to cross the present borders of the United States.

It has been theorized that some of Coronado's horses and cattle escaped and lived to perpetuate their breeds, thus being the ancestors of the wild herds of mustangs and longhorns which later were so typical and colourful a part of the wilderness. This speculation, unfortunately for romance, is hardly acceptable. Coronado's soldiers were Spaniards, and the Spaniard had a preference for stallions as steeds. The padres rode mules, when they did not walk 'in the apostolic manner'. Arthur H. Aiton, who made a study of the Coronado muster rolls, discovered that there was an accurate count of horses, with a distinction between *caballos* (stallions) and *yeguas* (mares). Only two mares were listed, wherefore, as he pointed out, 'the possibility, biologically considered, that stray horses from Coronado's expedition stocked the plains is slight.' As to cattle, when the expedition, disillusioned and bitter at its failure to find the cities of gold, returned to New Spain in 1542, the record says 'no slaughter animals were left'.

But if Coronado did not bring cattle and horses permanently to the American West, others soon did. In New Spain cattle *ranchos* spread rapidly from the time of the final conquest of the Aztec Empire, the nature of the country and people being favourable to them.

Indian slaves were the first herdsmen and became the forerunners of the *vaquero*, and hence of the cowboy. And here arises an interesting speculation. When the Spaniards at last wearied of slaughter, in the bloody conquest of Tenochtitlán, they took thousands of captives. These Cortés caused to be branded on the cheek with a G, for *Guerra* (War), and sold as slaves. That was in 1519. The first tiny seed herd of cattle was brought to New Spain by Gregorio de Villalobos two years later. It can be surmised almost with certainty that Villalobos had a herdsman to care for his cattle who wore an angry red G scarred on his brown cheek. If so, by a curious twist, the first 'cowboy' in this hemisphere bore a brand before the first cow.

In the beginning the Spaniards made it unlawful for a native to ride a horse, and the first herdsmen worked on foot. But after a time this prejudice was erased, the advantage of the horse in handling cattle being so obvious, and gradually certain characteristics were developed by the *vaqueros*, through generation after generation, which became part of the cattle tradition. Loyalty to the outfit, reckless disregard of personal danger, wonderful skill and dexterity with the lariat, a prejudice against walking when one could ride even a short distance, pride in the ability to mount and stay on anything with four legs and hair – these grew up in the cattle country of New Spain. Some principles also were established. Water rights, for one thing, whereby possession of water was tantamount to possession of the range surrounding it. Also the sacredness of the brand.

The *vaquero* provided also a distinctive argot for the range. Spanish-Mexican influence is seen in words like corral, tapaderas, remuda, segundo, bronco, jinete (bronco buster), orejano (unbranded steer), frijoles, hombre, loco, arroyo, and morral which are almost pure Spanish. Other words were more or less twisted in transition to the American tongue. There is little difference between *lazo* and lasso, *la reata* and lariat, *rodear* and rodeo, *adobe* and doby, *pinta* and pinto, or *rancho* and ranch. But there were further distortions. The cowboyism 'cavvy yard', for instance, is from the chaste Spanish *caballado*. *Vaquero* was turned into buckaroo. *Mesteño* became mustang. The Mexican word *cocinero* (cook) wound up as coosie. The Spanish *jáquima* was corrupted into hackamore. *Chaparreras* was shortened to chaps. There are many others, among which one of the strangest is the mutation of the name for the act of wrapping the lariat two or three times around the saddle horn when roping an animal, in order to throw it. The Spanish phrase for this was *de la vuelta* (a turn). On the tongue of the American cowboy this degenerated into an approximation in sound if not in written appearance – dolly welter, or simply dolly.

Oñate brought the first permanent cattle herd of record across the line in 1598. Thereafter cattle spread quite rapidly. A vital part was played by the missions, which encouraged livestock culture. Every mission outpost had its herd and its native *vaqueros*.

By the time Austin's first Anglo-American colonists settled along the Brazos in 1821, lower Texas swarmed with cattle. Most of the first settlers became cattle owners for a good reason. Mexican land grants had this peculiarity: if a married colonist declared his intention to farm only, he received one *labor* (177 acres) of land. If, on the other hand, the same man declared his intention to raise livestock as well as farm, he was granted one *sitio* or square league (4,438 acres) of grazing land, besides the *labor* of tillage land – adding up to 4,615 acres. These grants were modified as time passed, but the distinction, which was based on a consideration of what land a farmer could till to crops, as contrasted with what a rancher could utilize, gave impetus and character to the whole economic life of Texas.

Taxes were paid in Texas on the following numbers of cattle, not including 'wild cattle', in the years indicated:

1848	382,873
1855	1,363,688
1860	3,786,443

During the Civil War, ranches, unable to sell their increase, saw their herds grow to such an extent that when the ranchmen returned from the Confederate Army they found the cattle roaming wild in vast numbers, and so valueless that rounding up and branding them was almost a waste of time and labour.

It was a period of intense gloom and discontent in Texas. 'Cattle poor' was the phrase of the day. Thousands of head were slaughtered for their hides and tallow, the carcasses being left to rot or be consumed by the buzzards, coyotes and other carrion eaters. Small packeries which rendered tallow, salt-cured hides, and pickled a little beef, were known as 'hide and tallow factories'. But they offered a market so small that the surface of the supply was hardly touched.

Yet through these clouds of darkness for the ranchers was coming a ray of light and hope. In the North, during the war, an industrial revolution had taken place. Military orders, greatly stimulating manufacturing, brought tens of thousands of people, who otherwise would have been raising food on the farms, to industrial cities. At the same time the nation became transportation-conscious. In the military campaigns railroads had played a part so vital that their importance was dramatically emphasized. It became apparent that the Pacific coast and the East must be linked, and in 1862 Congress passed the Union Pacific Act, offering government assistance to the proposed railroad which was to be built across the continent.

The war prevented construction of more than a few miles of this line, but after the war Congress passed other laws, whereby ten sections of public lands and a loan of $16,000 per mile of construction in United States bonds were offered as a stimulus to railroad building. By 1866 a construction race was under way, two great rival rail interests fighting for the government bounty by seeking to outdistance each other in ground covered, as they hammered their way toward a common meeting place. Gangs of Irish immigrants pushed the steel westward from the Missouri and gangs of Chinese coolies pushed it eastward from the Pacific. The railheads met in Utah, at Promontory Point, and with the driving of a golden spike the continent was joined from coast to coast by rail.

That golden spike symbolized an event of far-reaching consequence to the West. In the postwar era of inflated prosperity the country was seized by a railroad-building mania, so that within a decade the nation's map was criss-crossed by the greatest web of rails anywhere on the globe; and as vast distances shrank because of regular and faster transportation, the United States became closely knit instead of widely scattered and provincial. One of the westward-pushing railroads was the Kansas Pacific, and Texas was the first of the Western states to profit greatly from the transportation it offered.

Long before the war some Texas cowmen had tried the experiment of trail-driving cattle to distant markets. As early as 1842 a rancher took a herd all the way to New Orleans. Shreveport became something of a market. And there is one strange story, shrouded in complete absence of details, and contained in a newspaper item quoted by the United States Department of Agriculture in 1855, which mentions that a drove of several hundred cattle from Texas was passing through Indiana County, Pennsylvania, on the way to New

York City. Who were the adventurers who made that epic journey? What difficulties and perils did they meet? And what, in the end, became of their cattle? History is silent.

After 1849 a few daring Texas cattlemen, attracted by the market created by the gold stampede to California, trailed herds westward across the desert country, fighting Indians and hunting water as they went. Most went by the 'northern route' – following the Rio Grande north to the mountains, crossing the continental divide in southern Colorado, angling again north to the California Overland Trail in northern Utah, and following that southwest across the Nevada flats and over the high Sierra passes, to San Francisco. It took two years for a trail herd to make that march, which was a lot of time, but on the northern route you avoided the Apaches.

There was a 'southern route', too, by way of Albuquerque, across Arizona, and to the Mother Lode country of California by way of Walker's Pass over the Sierras. It was shorter by months than the northern route, but such unpleasant personages as Mangus Colorado, Cuchillo Negro, Delgadito and their various Apache bands might be encountered while travelling it, and the scalp of a man with the temerity to go that way sat uncomfortably loose on his skull.

Yet some Texans had the nerve to try it. One was Jack Cureton, a Ranger captain who took an outfit and a herd across the Indian-infested desert to California's lush pastures. He paid $10 a head for cattle in Texas, and sold them for $30 a head in California, which left him a neat profit even after deducting strays and deaths. But most men with a lingering prejudice in favour of living to a reasonable old age eschewed the Apache country. All in all, those first blind drives had little effect on the mounting numbers of cattle in Texas.

With the Civil War came one of those industrial miracles wars sometimes bring. P. D. Armour, a square-set, side-whiskered man, who bet on Grant and the Union Army by selling pork short during the last stages of the conflict, cleaned up $1,500,000 and with his partner, John Plankinton, decided to establish a beef-packing business at Chicago, where the Union Stockyards, greatest of all livestock delivering and holding points, were completed Christmas Day, 1865.

The war had cleaned most of the cattle out of the East, while at the same time increasing the per capita demand for meat. Soldiers had discovered that beef was both satisfying and strengthening as food. Armour concluded that the West was the source to which the nation must look for its beef supply and acted accordingly. Others decided similarly, notably G. F. Swift. Competition grew up among them, so keen that they went to incredible lengths to utilize every bit of a carcass, and at the same time cut prices to a point where their actual profit came from the by-products, the meat of the carcass little more than paying expenses. Refrigeration was introduced. Freight costs were studied and the westward march began. In 1869, to be still nearer the supply, Armour established the first packing plant in Kansas City. The American factory hand and clerk found that they could afford to eat meat, and with the middle years of the 1860's the packing companies had not only evolved cheaper meat for their customers but created a vastly increased demand for the steers of the cattleman – and a great industry, to go hand in hand with the spreading ranges of the West, was born.

Word of this trickled down into Texas, where war-worn Confederate veterans were wondering what to do with their enormous and apparently worthless herds.

Texas cattle were mostly true longhorns, products of climate, soil and surroundings, as well as of mixed bloods, and evolved by Nature to fit their environment and the conditions confronting them. They were not ideal for butcherings, being bony, long-legged and tough. In colour they ranged from brown, dun, red, black, occasional yellow, even white, to curious combinations of all colours. It was their horns, outrageous and unbelievable, that gave them their names. These grew to lengths and shapes that tax the credulity. Sometimes they corkscrewed. At others they made prodigious sweeps. At still others they extended almost straight out from the sides of the head. The longhorn steer reached his full growth when he was about ten years old, but not so his horns.

They continued to lengthen and spread as long as the animal lived. Old steers often carried horns seven feet from tip to tip. There is a reliable record of seven feet, nine inches, by 'pole measurement' – straight across the tips of one pair of horns – and about nine feet following the curves of that particular pair. J. Frank Dobie, the greatest authority on the longhorns, believes the most magnificent pair of horns was worn by a steer named Champion. No measurement was attested by affidavit, but the steer was exhibited in the East and Midwest, and Chicago papers published an account of him, stating that his horn spread was nine feet, seven inches. 'A steer hitched to a pair of horns' was a saying for the longhorn. Yet these cattle, turned loose to shift for themselves, developed the endurance and the ability to survive which alone fitted them for the trail drives that were to begin.

In the spring of 1866 many stockmen simultaneously decided to drive cattle north to the markets then centring in Chicago. There also were venturesome speculators from the North who went into Texas and by purchase made up herds for the drive.

The shocking state of cattle prices that year was shown by Joseph G. McCoy in his *Historic Sketches of the Cattle Trade*. A buyer looked over a herd of 3,500 Texas steers and struck the following bargain : he would purchase 600 head of his choice at $6.00 a head, and a second 600 at $3.00 a head. He thus took the 1,200 choicest cattle from a herd of 3,500, at an average of $4.50 a head, or about 40 cents a hundredweight, gross.

Between 225,000 and 260,000 Texas cattle crossed the Red River and strung out on their way north to a hoped-for market in the early months of 1866. They were guided and guarded by bronzed riders, many of whom had just exchanged the cavalry saddle for the stock saddle, and wore their holstered six-shooters – and sometimes used them – with practiced ease.

But that drive of 1866, with a few exceptions, proved to be a vast failure and disappointment. The herds were preyed upon and stampeded by Indians in the Indian Territory. At the border of Kansas and Missouri they were stopped by 'committees' of grangers, who feared the 'Spanish fever' – later identified as being caused by blood ticks – which the Texas cattle would transmit to domestic stock.

To the legitimate opposition of the farmers was added guerrilla work by bands of outlaws, the product of the war, known as Jayhawkers. These sometimes extorted bribes before they would permit cattle to pass; sometimes stampeded herds so that they could make off with part of the scattered animals; and abused, flogged, and even murdered trail drivers who would not accede to their demands.

South of the Kansas border the herds piled up, ate off all the grass, and countless cattle died of starvation. Others were disposed of by their despairing owners for little or nothing, and even these owners were sometimes defrauded by glib-tongued strangers who gave them bogus cheques or drafts. Of more than a quarter of a million Texas longhorns which were driven north with infinite labour and peril that year, very few were sold at anything approaching a profit.

One trail driver of 1866 kept a diary – the only one, so far as is known. He was George C. Duffield, a young Iowan, and his journal was published in the *Annals of Iowa* in 1924. It gives a first hand picture of trail-driving conditions, and is worth glancing at.

It was on April 29, 1866, that he and his partner Harvey Ray, with a herd of cheap cattle bought in Texas and an outfit of Texas cowboys, began what was to be a hard and exasperating northward journey. Stampedes occurred May 1, May 6, and very frequently thereafter. By May 9 young Duffield was wishing fervently that he was through with his task, as his entry on that date shows : 'Still dark & Gloomy River up everything looks *Blue* to me.' Four days later, in a thunderstorm, another maddening stampede added to his gloom, although he recovered all but fifty of his steers : 'all tired Everything discouraging.'

When he reached the Brazos real trouble began. It took three days to cross his approximately one thousand cattle, and his camp outfit and remuda. The animals swam and the provisions and camp equipment were rafted over. Unhappily, most of the 'Kitchen furniture such as camp Kittles Coffee Pots Plates &c &c' were lost in the stream. After rounding up the cattle on the other side of the river, 'all Hands gave the Brazos one good harty dam,' and rode away, without joy.

Rain fell, the wind blew almost continuously, and some of the Texas herders grew sulky and quit. On May 20, Duffield wrote: 'Rain pourd down for two hours Ground flooded Creeks up — Hands leaving Gloomey times as ever I saw.'

Most of their few remaining cooking utensils were lost crossing the Trinity, and the following night, May 23, 'Hard rain that night & cattle behaved very bad — ran all night — was on my Horse the whole night & it raining hard. Glad to see Morning come counted & found we had lost none for the first time — feel very bad.'

At the Red River three more days were required to put the herd across. And here a cowboy named Carr, caught in a whirlpool while working with the swimming herd, was drowned. To make matters worse, the perverse longhorns stampeded the night after the crossing. Duffield wrote: 'hard rain & wind Storm Beeves ran & had to be on Horse back all night. Awful night, wet all night clear bright morning. Men still lost quit the Beeves and go Hunting Men is the word — 4 p.m. Found our men with Indian guide & 195 Beeves 14 miles from camp, allmost starved not having had a bite to eat for 60 hours got to camp about 12 m *Tired.*'

For a few days things went a little better, although the country was boggy with heavy downpours and the rivers and creeks gave constant trouble. But on June 12 came the following entry: 'Hard Rain & Wind Big stampede & here we are among the Indians with 150 head of Cattle gone hunted all day & Rain pouring down with but poor success Dark days are these to me Nothing but Bread & Coffee Hands all Growling & Swearing.'

It was enough to make them swear, but their troubles were only beginning. On June 17 they reached the Arkansas where Duffield spent four days swimming the herd across that flooded river. 'Worked all day hard in the River trying to make the Beeves swim & did not get one over,' wrote the doleful chronicler at the end of the first day's effort. 'Had to go back to the Prairie Sick & discouraged. Have *not* got the *Blues* but am in *Hel of a fix*.'

Eventually the cattle were crossed and they reached the vicinity of Baxter Springs, Kansas, July 10. There Duffield found the cap of his misfortunes. The Jayhawkers were swarming on the border. Duffield encountered several cattle herds being held on the grass and heard from their drivers disquieting reports of the Jayhawker activities. One cowboy already had been killed and many cattle stolen. Anger and discouragement prevailed.

For several days Duffield tried to negotiate a way through the barrier. He faced an impossibility. But he had plenty of courage, for all his woeful feelings. On July 25 his entry was : 'We left the Beefe Road & started due west across the wide Prairie in the Indian Nation to try to go around Kansas & strike Iowa. I have 490 Beeves.'

His herd was reduced by more than half, but with pleasure one reads on that he made the western circuit around the settlements of eastern Kansas, reached the Missouri River early in September near Nebraska City, and ferried his herd across to the promised land in Iowa. Even with his losses he must have made a worth-while profit on the dolorous expedition.

CHAPTER TWO

Cattle Take Over the West

SOME Texans sought other outlets. One pair, as salty a team of cattlemen as ever forked saddles, was that of Charles Goodnight and Oliver Loving. Goodnight had been a freighter, bullwhacking out of Fort Worth, and during the Civil War served four years with the Texas Rangers, fighting

Indians, Mexican bandits, renegade cattle thieves and road agents. His partner, Loving, was one of the most experienced trail drivers in Texas. He was first to take a herd north through the Indian Territory to Quincy, Illinois, establishing the Sedalia route. Two years later, in 1860, he took a herd to Colorado, where a gold rush was on, and during the Civil War drove cattle for the Confederate armies – going broke when the Confederate currency in which he was paid became worthless.

Together these two, knowing there must be a government market which had suddenly been created by Kit Carson's gathering of several thousand Navajo and Apache Indians at the Bosque Redondo, decided to take a herd thither in 1866.

It was an ordeal sufficiently severe to have daunted most men. They had, first of all, to pass through the Comanche country. Then there was a deadly drive of ninety-six miles, from the middle Concho to the Horsehead crossing of the Pecos, without a drop of water on the entire route. The first chuckwagon in all history was designed by Goodnight for this journey, built of tough Osage orangewood and equipped with water barrels, covered with a canvas tilt, with a chuck box at the rear, containing dishes and cooking utensils, the lid provided with a folding leg so that when it was lowered it formed a table on which the cook could work. So excellent was the idea that it became universal in the range country.

Since the probabilities were strong that they might have to fight Indians, Confederate veterans were chosen exclusively for trail drivers – men who could handle shooting irons and weren't afraid of being shot at. The drive began in June. Fortunately, at that season the Comanches were elsewhere, and they escaped Indian trouble. But they had enough woes of other kinds to make up for it.

When they reached the head of the middle Concho River the cattle were rested for three days and encouraged to fill their hides with water for the dreaded ninety-six-mile dry leg of the drive which was about to begin. At last the herd was strung out and the brutal test began. All day the cattle and the drivers toiled across the plains. And again the next day, the men riding with neck handkerchiefs masking their faces to the eyes so that they could breathe, in the stifling dust. By the second night the beasts were suffering, restless and bellowing with thirst. Next morning the partners decided they would not dare to camp again.

On the third evening the outfit presented a pitiable spectacle. The men were haggard, with lips cracked and bloodshot eyes; the cattle so gaunt that their ribs stood out like basketwork, tongues lolling from their mouths, and a continual bawling and moaning sound coming from them in their misery of thirst. But they had to be kept moving, because if they ever lay down they would never rise again. So above the noise of the herd rose the yells and whistles of the cowboys as they urged on their charges.

On the fourth morning they entered Castle Gap, an opening through the Castle Mountains, and debouched down into the Pecos Valley, where they saw the river twelve miles away. Only the exhaustion of the cattle prevented a stampede at the smell of water. As it was, Goodnight later said, when they reached the river, 'They had no sense at all. They stampeded right into the stream, swam right across it, and then doubled back before they stopped to drink.'

Three hundred of the weaker cattle lay dead along that dreadful back trail, but the rest of the herd, which originally numbered two thousand, after being allowed to rest and graze for a time to put back some of the lost tallow, was driven on to Fort Sumner, where the seven thousand Indians of the Bosque Redondo, who were almost starving, greeted it with whole-souled yowls of rejoicing. Beef was so scarce in New Mexico that it was selling for sixteen cents a pound, dressed. The partners got eight cents a pound on the hoof – say $13,000 for their herd – a price unheard of for Texas cattle in that day.

They had made history, and having proved the Horsehead crossing possible, pioneered a flood of cattle which would make both New Mexico and Arizona cattle domain, and would vastly change the aspect and history not only of those territories but of Colorado and all the northern plains.

One other epic of trail driving.

Up in Montana the discovery of gold had caused a lurid, mushroom growth of population in the mountains which hitherto had been exclusively Indian hunting grounds. The fabulous strikes in Grasshopper Gulch and elsewhere created in rapid succession Bannack City, Virginia City, Helena and other booming mining camps. By the end of 1865 the successive gold excitements had brought into those areas a population so large that the problem of feeding it became acute.

Nelson Story a man of some prominence in Montana – having been a leader of the Vigilantes who broke up the Plummer gang of desperadoes by hanging twenty-two of its members on assorted trees and barn girders – conceived the idea of bringing beef from Texas all the way to Montana. After cleaning up $30,000 in a placer mine he rode south in the spring of 1866 and put part of his money in a cattle herd.

Hiring hard-bitten Texas trail drivers, he started the herd north, swimming turbulent rivers, dodging Indians who wanted to collect toll in the Indian Territory, evading thieves, heading off stampedes, and at last arrived at the Kansas border without losing a man – which was a wonder – and with very few of his cattle missing.

There he discovered, as had many others, that the Jayhawkers were swarming on the border. But Story merely swung his herd west. Ten thousand miners were in the Montana towns – and beef was mighty scarce there. His Texas cowboys were nothing loath. They hankered to see Montana anyhow. So out of the jam below Baxter Springs Story headed his steers around the settlements – making a side trip to purchase a wagon train loaded with groceries and supplies at Leavenworth – and then with his cattle and this train took the Oregon Trail along the Platte.

When the caravan reached Fort Laramie, Wyoming, army officers shook their heads and warned Story not to go any farther north. The Bozeman Trail, the only feasible route, was swarming with Sioux on the warpath, led by Red Cloud. They were besieging Fort Reno and Fort Phil Kearny – and so ferociously that the following December was to occur the disaster in which Captain William J. Fetterman's entire command was annihilated.

But Nelson Story didn't scare, and neither did his men. There were twenty-seven of them, and he armed them all with Remington breech-loaders, besides the Colt revolvers they already carried.

Northward they swung. Near Fort Reno Indians attacked them, wounded two cowpunchers with arrows, and drove away part of the herd. Story's ex-Confederates followed them, recovered the cattle, and 'dealt' with the Indians. One of the riders, John B. Catlin, described the operation years later.

'How many cattle did you lose?' he was asked.

'Not a single head. We just followed those Indians into the Bad Lands and got the cattle back.'

'Did they yield the steers willingly?'

'Well, you might say so. We surprised them in their camp and they weren't in shape to protest much against our taking the cattle.'

Story left his wounded men at Fort Reno and drove the herd on. When he reached Fort Phil Kearny, General H. B. Carrington ordered him to stop and proceed no further without permission, because of the danger of the Indians. Story obeyed just long enough to find that he risked destruction if he stayed where he was, because the fort could not protect him since he must graze his herd at some distance away. On the night of October 22 he slipped around the fort and was gone up into the Sioux country.

From then on every hour was filled with tension. Story trailed his herd only at night and herd-guarded them by day, gradually making his way through the rough country. Near Clark's Fork of the Yellowstone River the Indians killed a cowboy who was hunting about a mile away from the herd. But after scalping him the band of warriors rode away.

Story was lucky. Red Cloud and most of the Sioux, numbering thousands, were at this time considerably to the south, preparing for conclusions with Fort Phil Kearny, and except for an occasional flying band of young scalp-hunting braves – who developed discretion about tangling with the Remington-armed herd guards – they were unmolested.

On December 9 the entire herd and the trainload of groceries rolled into Virginia City, where Story was greeted by his young wife, whom he had left there, also by a whooping celebration by the whole bonanza town. It was a record-breaking drive. Not for four years would another trail herd make that trip. The Sioux made it look too much like suicide.

Individual trail-driving exploits like those of Duffield, Goodnight and Story were successes, but in the main the great effort of Texas cattlemen in 1866 was a failure. Nevertheless, the fact that even a few drovers made a profit lifted the spirits of Texas cowmen and in the spring of 1867 they were busy again, gathering herds for the great gamble, on the slim hope that somehow a market would open up for them to the north. For this and the next several years, gathering cattle and driving them up the trail was a major activity in the state.

And in that year, 1867, the man and the need met; and the range industry not only was saved but was given a tremendous impetus. In Springfield, Illinois, a young cattle dealer named Joseph G. McCoy dreamed of establishing a railroad market which would take Texas cattle and transport them readily to the great packing plants. His scheme met rebuffs and discouragements without number, but it was of the stuff of which empires are created.

He finally built a shipping yard and offices in Abilene, Kansas, then a wretched little hamlet of a dozen ramshackle log huts, with a single street 'so lacking in traffic that a busy and populous prairie dog town existed in the middle thereof'. There also he erected a three-storey frame hotel, the Drover's Cottage, installed a set of Fairbanks scales; and from there he sent emissaries south to meet the northward-wending herds and tell their owners of opportunity awaiting them where, to use his own words, 'Southern drover and Northern buyer would meet upon an equal footing, and both be undisturbed by mobs or swindling thieves.'

He received some cattle, but by no means all he wanted, that first year of 1867. But the experiment worked; word went back to Texas, and in 1868 his shipping yards did a capacity business, so that the Kansas Pacific Railroad, which ran through Abilene, realized at last the immense value to it of this form of livestock freight. Abilene became the first of the booming cow towns.

It was succeeded, as the railroads discovered belatedly an eagerness to win the cattle freight business, by other towns as the railheads progressed west. Ellsworth, Newton, Wichita, Fort Hays, Dodge City and their kindred communities sprouted, mushroomed, and withered as cattle capitals. Each of them encountered the effervescence of the wild riders who came up from Texas with the herds; and each had its lurid chapter of lawless, six-shooter domination; and also its town marshal, grown legendary now, who upheld the peace with smoking revolvers.

Abilene had Bear River Tom Smith and Wild Bill Hickok; Ellsworth had Chauncey Whitney; Newton had Mike Mc-Cluskie and Jim Riley – who fought out Newton's 'General Massacre' in which nine men were killed or wounded in a saloon, the bloodiest fight in all the cattle country's history – and Jack Johnston, who enforced law with a lightning draw; Dodge City had Bat Masterson, Wyatt Earp – who would be heard from elsewhere and later – Mysterious Dave Mathers and others. And so on. The exploits of the gunfighters were spectacular and have been recounted with sufficient detail in countless books, yet they provided little of importance to history, save for local narrative; and though there will always be dispute between Texas and Kansas as to which had the deadlier gunman, the former upholding John Wesley Hardin and the latter Wild Bill Hickok, there is so much legend surrounding them now that the truth probably never will be discovered.

Without exception each railroad town, as it became the goal of the Texas cowboys, had its district of vice. It was Texas Street in Abilene, Nauchville in Ellsworth, Hide Park (from the bare skins of the ladies of the evening) in Newton, and Delano in Wichita. Dodge City provided a generic name, used the world over now, the Red Light district – arising from the old Red Light, a sporting house with blood-red glass in the front door through which the light shone in lurid welcome to the cowboys, and which gave its distinctive title to all the saloons and bawdy houses gathered about it, south of the tracks. Dodge City, incidentally, provided another widely used name – Boot Hill. It buried its dead who passed suddenly to their reward with their boots on – hence by 'lead poisoning' – on a low hill, which soon became rather populous with the dear departed. So appropriate was the designation that Boot Hills afterward were designated all over the West.

But all of this was incidental to the great surge of cattle driving, whereby Texas projected its vast reservoir of livestock into the remotest corners of the Western country from the Canadian to the Mexican line. From driving to immediate market, Texas cowmen began seeking pasturage north and west. When the United States Army finally put the Sioux, Cheyennes and Arapahoes of the Dakotas, Wyoming and Montana on their reservations in 1876-78, this movement was accelerated. What had been buffalo country became cattle country, as the hide hunters wiped out the great bison herds. Ranchers, pushing ever farther and farther, ferreted out each watercourse, valley, mountain pass and stretch of grass; and threw their cattle across the continent, thus bringing civilization (of a sort) all the way up to Calgary, in Canada.

Repeatedly the cattle trail was swung farther and farther westward, until at last it culminated in Miles City, Montana. How many cattle went up that shifting trail nobody will ever know. But a single firm, headed by Captain John F. Lytle,

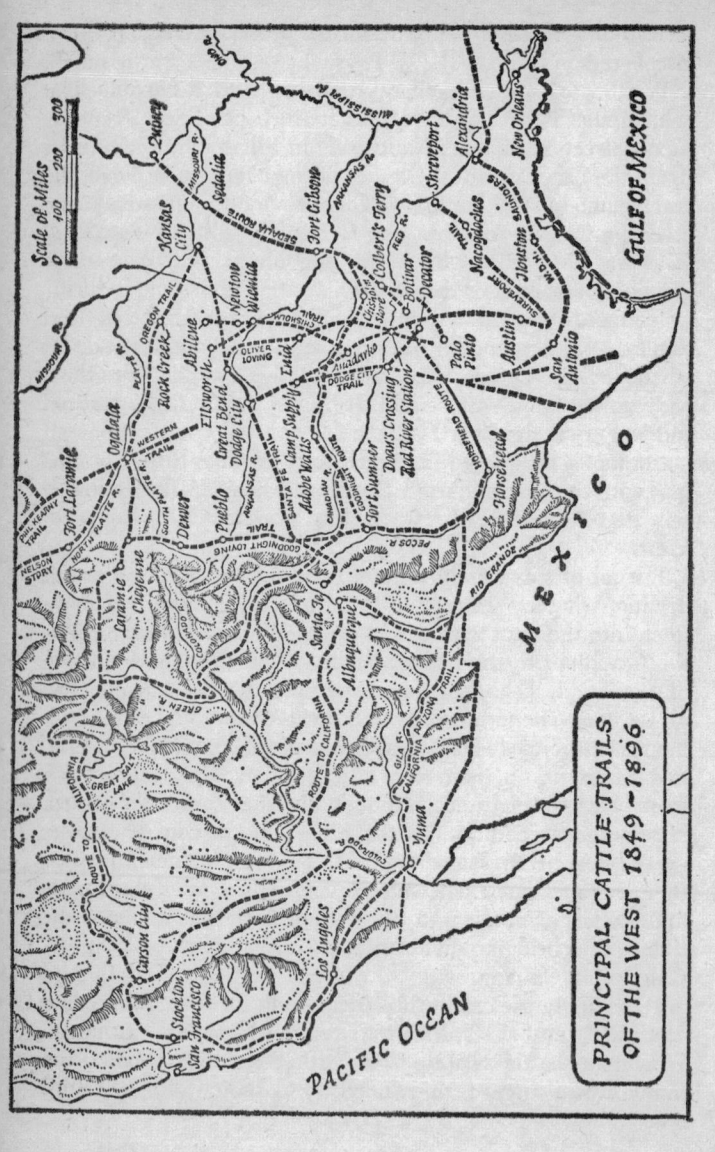

PRINCIPAL CATTLE TRAILS
OF THE WEST 1849~1896

sent 450,000 over it in a period of several years, and in a single season Colonel Ike T. Pryor drove 30,000 cattle north. When one considers other names equally notable – like Shanghai Pierce, Captain Richard King, Mifflin Kenedy, Colonel D. H. Snyder, to name only a few of the giants of trail-driving days – besides scores of less famous drovers, the numbers become fabulous. George W. Saunders, himself one of the great drovers and later president of the Texas Trail Drivers' Association, made the following estimates, which probably are as close as anyone will ever get to the totals.

Saunders said that approximately 12,000,000 cattle and horses were driven north during the trail-driving period. Of these about 6,000,000 crossed the Red River at Doan's Crossing for the Western trail; 5,000,000 at Red River station, farther east, for the Chisholm Trail and the Kansas rail markets; and 1,000,000 at other points for various goals. The sale of these vast herds brought approximately $250,000,000 – a very tidy sum in the dollar of that day, bringing prosperity where there had been ruin in Texas.

Trail driving lasted less than thirty years – until settlement spread westward so far that it was no longer possible to drive great herds of cattle because of towns and fenced farms. The last great Texas trail herd was an XIT bunch which was driven north in 1896, with John McCanles as trail boss. The drive was one long continued, exasperating battle with farmers and city constables, but McCanles finally delivered his herd.

Before this, however, trail driving had practically ceased. The railroads had equalized the cost and Northern ranches were pretty well stocked. Trail driving became history as rapidly as it developed, but the impetus from Texas made Texas talk, dress, actions, modes and habits of thought the familiar fan of all the great plains northward.

Meantime an equally vital trend had been established directly west of Texas. Goodnight and Loving, pioneering the Horsehead route, provided the spur to other cattlemen. While cattle had always been raised in New Mexico, the ranching industry assumed no considerable proportions until after that famous drive of the adventurous partners. Thereafter, however, many drovers competed with Goodnight and Loving; and when more cattle were in New Mexico than its ranges needed, the herds were driven north to Colorado, or still farther west into Arizona, even to Nevada and California.

A certain stimulus was given to this westward movement by those freebooters, the *Comancheros*, who encouraged the Comanche Indians to steal Texas cattle and horses, bought the livestock from the raiders, and trailed the stolen herds across the Staked Plains to New Mexico. In 1872 two Texas ranchers, John Hittson and H. M. Childress, with sixty hard-visaged riders, and armed with powers of attorney from many ranchers in the Lone Star State, suddenly descended on New Mexico, swept through the Pecos Valley, and repossessed cattle wherever good ownership credentials could not be shown. They overawed small ranches which had cattle with Texas brands, so that not a shot was fired; and rode back with 11,000 head they had recovered – all of it, presumably, from the *Comanchero* trade.

CHAPTER THREE

The Buffalo and the Indian

FOR much of the plains country, cattle ranching was at first impractical because of the enormous herds of buffalo which occupied the vast open stretches. Not only did the migrating bison destroy fields and fences, encompass and move off livestock herds, and make settlement almost impossible, but they were the key to the Indian problem.

It is difficult in this day to comprehend the numbers of buffalo existing in the great herds at their height. Alvarado, Coronado's captain, rather helplessly reported, 'There are such multitudes of them that I do not know what to compare them with unless it be the fish of the sea.' E. T. Seton, the naturalist, estimated that 75,000,000 ranged from north New Mexico to central Canada, and from the Alleghenies to the Cascades, in the period just before the Indian acquired the horse. In the 1860's General Sheridan computed 100,000,000 on the southern plains alone.

The wild Indians depended on the buffalo, which furnished them everything they needed for subsistence – meat, robes, tepee covers, bone utensils, sinew for cordage, and countless other articles of savage life. With this ready commissary at hand the Indians could, and did, devote a great deal of their time to warfare against the White man. And it appeared to most persons that the very numbers of the buffalo made it unthinkable that they ever would be eliminated from their feeding grounds.

Yet this seemingly insuperable problem was solved in a single decade, and in a manner so cold-bloodedly methodical that it left the world aghast at the slaughter of those vast herds. The millions of buffalo were wiped out; not by the Indians who lived on them; not by the soldiers who wanted them out of the way to make easier the defeat of the hostile tribes; not by cattlemen who desired room for cattle range, or farmers who wished to preserve their fields from being trampled; but by a new potent army, which appeared and disappeared with equal suddenness – the hide hunters.

Fearless, armed with rifles shooting a very heavy bullet, they were from all walks of life. One of them, killed by Indians near Adobe Walls in 1874, was an heir of a noble British house whose death created serious diplomatic complications. Among them were men of high character, like Billy Dixon, Pat Garrett, J. Wright Mooar and others. But many also were fugitives from justice – murderers, thieves and outlaws.

Sudden discovery in 1870 that buffalo hides were commercially usable sounded the death knell of the bison. In that year J. Wright Mooar sent a shipment of hides experimentally to a New York tanning firm, which found them of value, particularly for machine belting.

Followed as terrible and indiscriminate a destruction as the world ever witnessed. By the thousands hide hunters went out on the plains. A good hunter could kill 150 to 200 animals a day; the number limited only by the ability of his skinners to keep up with him – and the skinners, using horses to strip off the hides, worked fast. So many hunters were at work all the time that old-timers recalled that on a clear morning the firing sounded like a fair-sized battle in progress. The stupidity of the animals made the slaughter possible. If they did not see the hunter, or smell him, as he crouched behind some obstruction or perhaps in a buffalo wallow, they would mill around while, one after another, they sank to the ground before the merciless buffalo gun, only a few fleeing at last.

Their rotting carcasses created an overpowering stench over great stretches of the fairest plains; buzzards, ravens, coyotes and other creatures gorged fat on their carrion; and when their bones whitened they became a source of revenue to men called 'bone pickers' who went about with wagons, gathered the skeletal parts strewn everywhere, and shipped them to Eastern fertilizing companies. By 1889, fifteen years after hide hunting ceased for lack of sufficient animals to hunt, Dr. William T. Hornaday, in a continental survey, found only 1,091 American buffalo still in existence. He awakened the public consciousness, fortunately, in time. Today the bison is secure from extermination, although his fate for all time is to occupy game preserves and parks.

Slowly the Indians began to realize that their natural commissary was disappearing. The army was fighting a desultory and not very successful war with the Sioux and Cheyennes of the northern plains when, in October, 1867, representatives of the southern tribes gathered on Medicine Lodge Creek in southern Kansas, to make a peace treaty.

General W. T. Sherman, commanding general of the army, and General Phil Sheridan, commander of the Division of the Missouri, scoffed at the peace effort as a waste of time. Nevertheless a commission, headed by Generals Harney and Sanborn, met with the Indian tribes which had been doing most of the damage in the Southwest. The record shows that of the Comanches there were 150 lodges; of Kiowas 150; of Arapahoes 175; of mixed Kiowas and Lipan Apaches 85; and of Cheyennes 250 – a total of 810 lodges, or more than 4,000 Indians, figuring the usual average of five persons to a lodge. The Comanches had only about 750 persons present – a significantly small representation from that populous tribe.

From the chiefs at council the commissioners received promises of peace, agreement to relinquish their hunting grounds in the Texas Panhandle, and assurances of willingness to abide on reservations in the Indian Territory assigned to them. In return for this the commissioners divided among the Indians a wagon train of provisions and clothing, and – most delightful of all to the red men – large quantities of ammunition and arms.

It was assumed that the 'Medicine Lodge Peace Treaty' would end Indian troubles in the Southwest. What happened, of course, was the reverse, just as Sherman and Sheridan had predicted. Arms and ammunition furnished by the government figured prominently in the Indian wars that followed. The Cheyennes scourged Kansas and Colorado. The Comanches and Kiowas, far from relinquishing the Texas Panhandle, continued to frequent it. Raids on cattle ranches and settlements went on as before.

'So boldly has this system of murder and robbery been carried out that, since June 1862, not less than 800 persons had been murdered, the Indians escaping from the troops by travelling at night, when their trail could not be followed, thus gaining enough time and distance to render pursuit, in most cases, fruitless,' wrote Sheridan in 1868. 'This wholesale marauding would be maintained during the seasons when the Indian ponies could subsist upon the grass, and then in the winter, the savages would hide away, with their villages, in remote and isolated places, live upon their plunder, glory in the scalps taken, and in the horrible debasement of the unfortunate women they held as prisoners. The experience of many years of this character of depredations with perfect immunity to themselves and families, had made the Indians very bold. To disabuse their minds of the idea that they were secure from punishment, and to strike them at a period when they would be helpless to move their stock and villages, a winter campaign was projected against the large bands hiding away in the Indian Territory.'

Followed the Washita campaign of General George A. Custer, who later was to be the chief figure in the total destruction of his United States cavalry force by the Sioux, on the Little Bighorn River of Montana. In the dead of winter Custer, with his Seventh Cavalry, marched south from Camp Supply, Indian Territory. There was a foot of snow on the ground and the weather was bitter cold when he struck an Indian trail left by a band of warriors who had killed mail carriers between Dodge City and Larned, an old hunter near Dodge City, and two of Sheridan's dispatch carriers.

On the night of November 26, Little Beaver, an Osage scout, smelled smoke. He told Custer an Indian camp was near. With the scout, Custer crept to the top of a low snowy hill, from which his straining eyes made out a dark blotch on the snow – an immense pony herd. Significant noises reached his ears – dogs barking, a bell tinkling in the herd, the faraway wail of an Indian baby. He was right on top of a big Indian village.

Returning to his command, he split it into four detachments – three troops under Major Joel Elliott, two each under Captains Thompson and Myers, and four troops under himself. He was dividing his forces in the face of an enemy, a violation of an old military rule, and the same tactics cost him his life and the lives of his immediate command later at the Little Bighorn when the Sioux defeated his detachments in detail; but on this occasion the plan worked.

Just as the first light of morning broke a bugle sounded and Custer and the Seventh Cavalry rode down on the village from every side. With startled yelps the Indians bolted from their tepees, some running stark naked into the icy waters of the Washita. A few fought and were slain where they stood, but for the most part the troopers simply killed fugitives, including women and children, and mostly unarmed.

The village was Cheyenne, under a chief named Black Kettle. It was pretty thoroughly obliterated. Custer's men killed 101 Indians and captured 53 squaws and children. They destroyed more than a thousand buffalo robes, five hundred pounds of lead, an equal amount of powder, four thousand arrows, all the lodges, and slaughtered seven hundred captured ponies.

But in the middle of the morning, when the fight should have been over, more warriors were seen riding up the valley. Custer did not know it then, but the village he had attacked was only one of several strung up and down the Washita, including Kiowas, Arapahoes, Comanches, Lipans and Cheyennes. There were perhaps two thousand warriors within riding distance.

The Indians cut off and killed Major Elliott and fourteen troopers, but Custer extricated the rest of his force and retreated. Including the Elliott group, he lost 21 officers and men dead, and 14 officers and men wounded.

Two other columns under Colonel A. W. Evans and General Eugene A. Carr, at about the same time, scouted up and down the Canadian River in Texas, where they made the country so unhealthy for Indians that a large number of hostiles came in and went on the reservations assigned to them.

But the next year, 1869, the hostile tribes again ranged all over the plains from north of the Platte to the Mexican border, and 1870 saw more of the same. In New Mexico the stage routes were closed. Thirty separate raids and engagements with Indian war parties were recorded in Texas and New Mexico in those two years, an unrecorded number of American and Mexican settlers were murdered, and hundreds of head of livestock driven away, to say nothing of ranches looted and burned.

But the tide was about to turn. In 1871 General Sherman made a personal tour of inspection of the frontier posts. He was critical of the carelessness of the border ranchers. 'They expose women and children singly on the road and in cabins far off from others, as though they were safe in Illinois,' he wrote. 'If the Comanches don't steal horses, it is because they cannot be tempted.'

He saw no Indians who could be described as hostile until he reached Fort Sill, Indian Territory, but while on his tour, at Fort Richardson, Texas, a man named Thomas Brazeal staggered in with a gunshot wound in one foot. He told of an attack by Indians on a wagon train a few miles from where Sherman had slept that night. Four men escaped the Indians, three of them, including Brazeal, being wounded. Seven were killed. The bodies of the slain men, all mutilated, and one charred and suspended face down over a fire by a chain on a wagon pole, indicating that he was tortured to death, destroyed any scepticism Sherman might have had concerning the ferocity of savage warfare.

When he reached Fort Sill, he at once asked Lawrie Tatum, the Indian agent, if any Indians recently had been off the reservation. Tatum thought a few Kiowas had gone. When these Indians arrived a couple of days later to draw their rations, Sherman had the agent bring some of them to the headquarters of the fort.

The general began by asking which of them were involved in the destruction of the wagon train near Fort Richardson. To his amazement, Satanta, one of the chiefs, said he was the leader of the attack. 'He openly admitted the affair,' Sherman wrote, 'and described the attack exactly as the man did to me at Fort Richardson, only denying that anybody was tied to the wagon pole and burned; but as Gen'l MacKenzie found the body, it does not admit of dispute.'

With that, Sherman ordered that Satanta and two other chiefs Satank and Big Tree, be arrested and sent to Texas to be tried for murder.

William Tecumseh Sherman was internationally famous as a soldier, the commanding general of the United States Army, and being mentioned at the time as presidential timbre. But in those next five minutes he stood as tensely close to death as ever in his career.

At the mention of arrest, Satanta threw back his blanket and grasped the handle of a revolver at his belt. He could have killed Sherman and nobody could have stopped him.

But for some reason the Indian hesitated. As cool as if he had all day, Sherman gave an order, and the windows of the headquarters building opened, revealing a squad of soldiers with levelled carbines.

Satanta said, 'No shoot!' and took his hand off his gun.

But Kicking Bird, another chief, began to harangue, saying that he had been a good friend to the white man – which was true – and asking that his three chiefs be released.

Sherman stood grimly firm. 'I am going to take them with me to the place where they killed those boys,' he said. 'There they will be hung, and the crime will be paid for.'

Kicking Bird grew excited. 'You have asked for those men to kill them!' he exclaimed. 'I will not let you have them. You and I are going to die right here!'

At this juncture, Big Tree attempted to escape. He knocked down a trader and dove through a glass window headfirst. Soldiers pursued him, firing, and a bullet creased his scalp. He stopped running and surrendered.

Meantime Lone Wolf, one of the most dangerous fighters in the Kiowa tribe, came to the porch carrying two Spencer repeating carbines, a bow and quiver, and a revolver. He distributed these weapons among the Indians crowding about the porch, saying as he handed the revolver to one of them, 'If anything happens, make it smoke.'

Stumbling Bear, who received the bow, promptly strung it and put an arrow to the string. 'I want to kill the big soldier chief,' he said, and drew the arrow to the head, pointing it at Sherman. But as he released the shaft someone knocked the bow up and the arrow sailed harmlessly overhead.

Lone Wolf aimed his carbine at Sherman, but Colonel B. H. Grierson, commandant at Fort Sill, seized him and fell with him, kicking on the floor.

A flurry of shots sounded. Near the guardhouse some

Kiowas had fired on a group of soldiers, wounding one. The soldiers shot back, killing one of the Indians.

Through all this furious excitement, amidst the yelling of the Indians, the shots and the scuffle, the one person who remained completely calm was General Sherman. He had looked death in the eyes three times in five minutes, and he did not turn a hair.

His monolithic coolness subdued the Indians. Leaving their chiefs, Satanta, Satank and Big Tree, manacled, they departed for their camp.

While being taken to Texas, Satank 'committed suicide' in a novel manner. He sang his death song, told another Indian that by the time they reached a certain tree he would be dead, then somehow managed to free himself from one of his manacles, wrenched a carbine from a soldier, and stabbed a corporal in the leg with a knife he had secreted. A moment later he was dead as he predicted, with seven bullets in his body.

Satanta and Big Tree were not executed, but were confined in the Texas penitentiary at Huntsville.

Even the presence of Sherman and his awesome display of intrepidity in the face of deadly peril, followed by the arrest of the Kiowa chiefs, did not, however, bring any betterment of conditions on the plains. Many of the Comanches had never gone on the reservations, and this contingent, the Quahadas, was led by Quanah Parker – son of Cynthia Ann Parker by Peta Nokoni – who had developed into the chief daredevil of the Comanche people. Late in September, 1872, Colonel Ranald S. Mackenzie surprised a Quahada Comanche village on McClellan Creek and routed the Indians, killing 23 and capturing more than 100, with a loss of only 3 killed and 7 wounded. He rounded up the herd of Indian ponies and let his Tonkawa scouts take the pick of them for racing and hunting steeds.

That night, however, Quanah Parker led his braves in a wild dash through Mackenzie's camp, ringing horse bells, blowing whistles, yelling, and dragging bouncing buffalo robes at the ends of lariats. The whole horse herd 'spooked' and stampeded, and the Comanches got not only their own animals but all the horses of the Tonkawa scouts as well. Next morning Mackenzie faced his chagrined Indian allies, who had only a solitary and forlorn burro left, of all their animals.

Mackenzie's punishment, while severe, did not drive the Comanches on their reservation. They still hid their villages on the breaks of streams coming from the great canyons in the escarpment of the Staked Plains, and caused continual trouble. Then, after two years of prison, Satanta and Big Tree, the Kiowa chiefs, were released in October, 1873, over the protests of Agent Tatum, who resigned because of it. The Kiowas had behaved themselves, believing their chiefs were being held as hostages. But with the return of the two, they shortly drifted away from the agency and out on the plains. And in the spring of 1874 all hell broke loose.

Destruction of the buffalo herds caused the final desperate flurry of fighting. By 1874 the hide hunters had done their job of extermination so well that only a few stragglers of the once teeming millions remained on the southern plains. It upset the whole way of life for the Indians, and together they rose – Comanches, Kiowas, Cheyennes, Arapahoes and Lipans – with a fury and unanimity as shocking as it was surprising.

Through New Mexico, northern Texas, Colorado, Kansas and the Indian Territory their war parties swept; and a partial list of their victims among the settlers, including no casualties of soldiers or scouts, shows 190 killed.

Chief resentment of the Indians was against the hide hunters. And the hide hunters had a stronghold – a primitive outpost of a few sod and log structures whose outer walls formed a palisade – situated near the juncture of Bent's Creek and the Canadian River, near which stood an old trading post built and long ago abandoned by the fur company of Bent & St. Vrain. The ruins were called the Adobe Walls, and from them the fort took its name. ·

About the middle of June, when the hunters were scattered at their killing, the war parties began their work. Here and *here they surprised and killed hunters. The survivors found the bodies of their friends and partners butchered and scalped, and took the hint. From every direction they hurried to the fort.

The night of June 26 was sultry, with heat lightning playing on the horizon. At Adobe Walls that night slept twenty-eight men and one woman – Mrs. William Olds, wife of a man who ran a sort of restaurant for the hunters. In the darkness Comanches, led by Quanah Parker and Isa-tai, a medicine man who promised them invulnerability against the white man's bullets, Cheyennes under Iron Shirt, and Kiowas and Lipans under Satanta and Lone Wolf, stole up around the post.

A remarkably timely accident saved the white people. One of the structures at the post was a sod house, in which James Hanrahan ran a saloon. The roof was of slabs of sod, so heavy that the cottonwood ridge pole was too weak to uphold it. That ridge pole selected as its time to break, with a loud crack, two o'clock on the morning of June 27.

The people in the post were aroused, and since the whole roof threatened to collapse – on all that precious whiskey! – everyone took a hand in repairing it. So all were awake when the first pink light of pre-dawn tinged the eastern sky, and Billy Dixon, a great hunter and scout, stepped out of the fort to get his pony from the corral. It was he who discovered the Indians and, firing his rifle, gave warning.

As soon as they knew they were seen, the Indians, believing in their 'medicine' of invulnerability promised by Isa-tai, charged with remarkable boldness directly at the fort. Two hunters, the Shadler brothers, who had slept outside because of the heat, were shot down or lanced before they could reach safety. Then the Adobe Walls blazed with the roar of the hunters' heavy guns.

In the little fort were some of the finest shots in the world. Indians fell fast. They rode into the stockade and hammered on doors and windows of buildings with their rifle butts, but the hunters inside never ceased spreading death.

Very quickly the warriors retired from that hot enclosure, amazed and angered at seeing so many of their best fighters dropping, and more than dismayed by the failure of Isa-tai's promise. For a time they tried a long-range duel with the hide hunters, but there the hunters held all the top cards. Their rifles outranged those of the Indians and about four o'clock in the afternoon, carrying off all their dead and wounded whom they could reach, the hostiles withdrew.

The hunters had four dead, including William Olds, husband of the only woman in the post. Nobody learned the extent of the Indian losses, but thirteen dead warriors were found close about the fort in spite of daring efforts made by the Indians to carry them away. The heads of these thirteen decorated posts of the palisade when, a few days later, a relief expedition reached Adobe Walls from Dodge City.

After the bloody repulse, the allied tribes went out for revenge. Not a road in western Kansas, eastern Colorado, the Texas Panhandle or the Indian Territory was safe. Agencies, ranches, even military posts were attacked and wagon trains ambushed and the drivers butchered. The frontier yelled for the army, and the army took the field.

General Nelson A. Miles campaigned in the Sweetwater Valley, and a detachment of his men under Lieutenant Frank D. Baldwin smashed the village of Gray Beard, sending these Indians back to their reservation and securing also the release of four white girls, sisters by the name of German (or Germaine). They were Catherine, seventeen years old; Sophia, fifteen; Julia, ten; and Adelaide, five. All had been captured in a Cheyenne raid near the Smoky Hill River, in Kansas.

The experiences of the girls, particularly the older ones, were terrible, of course; and when the Cheyennes surrendered, the men were lined up and the girls pointed out a number of them, who had been chiefly guilty in the murders of their parents, and in offences later while the girls were prisoners in the Indian camp. These men were sent to Fort Marion, Florida, to be imprisoned. Great pity was aroused over the girls, but General Miles became their guardian, sufficient funds were taken from the Cheyenne annuities to support them, and all of them lived normal and happy lives, married, reared families, and survived to a ripe old age.

But the heaviest blow was struck by Colonel Mackenzie. Hunting Indians in the Staked Plains, he encountered José Tafoya, a *Comanchero* who had grown rich buying blood-spattered Indian loot and was heading out with his caravan to make some more profitable transactions. Mackenzie questioned him. When the old *Comanchero* refused to talk, Mackenzie had a wagon tongue propped up and from it suspended Tafoya by the neck. As his breath grew short the *Comanchero* recovered the use of his tongue. Through him Mackenzie learned that the hostiles were in Palo Duro Canyon.

Led by his scouts to the rim of the great chasm in the night of September 26, he sent his men clambering down a precarious trail to hit the big Indian village which was in the canyon. Before they reached the bottom they were discovered and shooting began; but the main body of Indians was farther along the gorge, and though bullets smacked the rocks about them or ricocheted off through the darkness, howling like lost souls, the soldiers reached firm ground on the bottom before they were seriously attacked.

Now powder smoke made a grey cloud in the gloom-filled gorge and the multiple clatter of rifles was doubled and trebled by the sounding echoes. Mackenzie drove the Indians, but encountered fierce resistance. The camp was Lone Wolf's Kiowa village and the chief managed to get the squaws, children and most of their lodges and equipment out, although it cost him some warriors. The troops captured and burned about a hundred tepees and killed some fourteen hundred captured ponies.

After the Palo Duro fight the Kiowas and Cheyennes surrendered by hundreds and when winter came in 1874 the war was practically over. A few Comanches still remained out, but in February, 1877, one of the last of these bands encountered and was severely defeated by forty-five hide hunters led by Hank Campbell. They lost thirty-five dead in the little fight on the Staked Plains, and when Captain P. L. Lee, with a troop of the Tenth Cavalry, rounded them up weeks later near Lake Quemado, they were ready to surrender.

The Comanches never went on the warpath again. They and their allies were convinced there was no place for them to hide any longer, and peace was their only course. The buffalo were gone, the Indian menace abated, and the cattle moved in.

CHAPTER FOUR

"The Incorrigibly Hostile"

In the farther Southwest the problem of hostile Indians was even more difficult. There were, to be sure, fewer of the Apaches than of the Comanches and their allies of the plains, but what they lacked in numbers they made up for in sheer endless murderousness and in the skill with which they used the desert reached for their warlike purposes.

As nearly perfect at self-subsistence as any fighting man in the world's history was the Apache warrior, even though his chosen campaigning ground was ferociously sterile desert. No clumsy commissary accompanied him, nor any pots, frying pans or other utensils, save for the knife sheathed at his belt. In addition to the white man's sheep and cattle, which he took without hesitation or qualm of conscience, his range was the habitat of many kinds of game – deer, *javalinas* (desert peccaries), rabbits, wild turkey and desert mountain sheep. Nor was he dainty in his tastes. When other meat lacked he did not disdain mice or pack rats, dug from their small lairs, or lizards killed with a switch, or even the grey flesh of the coiling rattlesnake. When all else failed, his pony always was a last resource. Killed when perhaps too exhausted to move farther, it furnished a stock of jerked meat and a unique water carrier – the long intestine, which, cleaned (after somewhat rudimentary Apache notions of cleaning), could be filled with water and wound several times about the body of another horse, to furnish life-giving if somewhat offensively smelling and tasting water for days. It is no wonder that the frontier troops, handicapped by pack trains and equipment, had difficulty in coping with their wily and resourceful foe.

But the Apache was more than a mere Spartan in his living. He took and utilized every modern implement of war on which he could lay his hands. The best rifles and revolvers were his – by capture, or by purchase from sneaking traders who got the highest price for their illegal merchandise – and the Apache knew how to use them to deadliest effect. He cached spare ammunition and arms at strategic hidden places, so that he usually could get new supplies when needed. He even had field glasses – the finest – to supplement his already marvellous eyesight. And he was a master at camouflage and concealment.

His natural ferocity was brought to peak by treacheries such as the murder of Mangus Colorado, the 'Pinal Treaty,' the scalp hunters' slaughters, and the Camp Grant massacre, in which, on April 30, 1870, a camp of Aravaipa Apaches, who had surrendered, was attacked by a mob from Tucson, and eighty-five of them slaughtered, all but eight being women and children.

Most active and murderous of the Apaches for a time were Cochise and his Chiricahuas. A spare, grey-eyed, slightly stooped, sandy-haired man, with a five-foot-seven-inch frame of whale-bone endurance, was their ablest and most untiring foe. He was Lieutenant Howard B. Cushing, of a famous military family.

For a time the honours were with Cushing in his duel with Cochise. But Cochise had the last say. On May 5, 1871, the Chiricahua chief lured his arch-enemy and twenty-two men into an ambuscade near Bear Springs in the Whetstone Mountains. So perfect was the trap that Cushing and his men did not even suspect it until they were well within it. At the tearing volley from the Indians, Cushing dropped dead. Down the sides of the canyon bounded the yelling Apaches, fighting the soldiers hand to hand. Half the soldiers were dead and most of their horses lost when the survivors escaped, leaving their fallen leader.

The following July, General George Crook took command of the Department of Arizona. Before he could move, however, President Grant appointed Vincent Collyer to go to the Southwest with plenary powers to bring about peace with the Apaches. Collyer knew the President's kindly attitude toward the Indians and worked hard, though without complete success.

One paragraph of his report indicates that the Apaches had good reason to hate the white race : 'The Apaches were friends of the Americans when they first knew them . . . the peaceable relations continued until the Americans adopted the Mexican theory of "extermination," and by acts of inhuman treachery and cruelty made them [the Apaches] our implacable foes . . . this policy has resulted in a war which, in the last ten years, has cost us a thousand lives and over forty millions of dollars, and the country is no quieter nor the Indians any nearer extermination than they were at the time of the Gadsden purchase.'

Collyer did induce Cochise to quit the warpath. Early in September, after some negotiations, the Chiricahua chief met General Gordon Granger and a peace commission in the Cañada Alamosa. One of those present, Dr. A. N. Ellis, described this remarkable Indian as he sat in council : 'Evidently he was about fifty-eight years of age, although he looked very much younger; his height, five feet, ten inches; in person lithe and wiry, every muscle rounded and firm. A silver thread was now and then visible in his otherwise black hair, which he wore cut straight around his head about level with his chin. His countenance displayed great force.'

Cochise's speech revealed the essential sadness of the red man and his perplexity at facing the insoluble problem of white encroachment. Toward the close he said : 'When I was young I walked all over this country, east and west, and saw no other people than Apaches. After many summers I walked again and found another race of people who had come to

take it. How is it? Why is it that the Apaches want to die –
that they carry their lives on their finger nails? They roam
over the hills and plains and want the heavens to fall on
them. . . . Tell me, if the Virgin Mary has walked through all
the land, why has she never entered the lodge of an Apache?
Why have we never seen or heard her?'

He finished by promising to remain peaceful, stipulating
that his reservation should be the territory about the Cañada
Alamosa. This was promised – and the promise promptly
broken. Told he must go on the Tularosa reservation,
Cochise simply took to the mountains with his people and
war flared all over the Southwest again. In the next year
fifty-four Indian attacks were made in Arizona alone, forty-
four soldiers and civilians killed, sixteen wounded, several
children taken captive, and hundreds of head of livestock
stolen, besides other damage.

Cochise, however, was getting old and found less zest in
the labours and self-denials of the warpath. A few months
later General O. H. Howard arrived in Arizona, with orders
to find Cochise, rectify the errors made concerning him, and
bring him back once more to peace.

The only white man who could claim friendship with
Cochise was Tom Jeffords, a lean, tall frontiersman, with
red hair which he generally wore about as long as any
Apache, and a dangling red beard which no Apache could
match. He was given to sartorial eccentricity – no matter if
he was on the roughest kind of border scouting duty, he wore
a black derby hat and a long-tailed black frock coat, both
somewhat rusty as to hue and frayed by use, which gave him
a most incongruous appearance among the scouts, Indians
and soldiers. He had won the regard of Cochise, even –
according to one account – becoming blood brother with
him 'through the mystic ceremony of commingling and
quaffing each other's blood.'

Enlisting the help of this whimsical and droll personage,
Howard sought out the camp of Cochise in the Dragoon
Mountains and talked peace with him. The chief was con-
ciliatory. He had two demands – that his people have their

reservation in the mountains and valleys of their present hunting grounds, and that Jeffords be their agent. When this was agreed, Cochise said, 'Hereafter, the white man and the Indian are to drink the same water, eat the same bread, and be at peace.'

He was true to his word. As long as he lived – his death came June 8, 1874 – his Chiricahuas stayed on the reservation, as a people; although some of the young braves perhaps 'wandered off' occasionally to join some of the 'bronco' Indians.

With the most formidable Apache chief pacified, Crook reorganized his forces, enrolling numbers of Apaches as scouts, and announced a policy of dealing justly with peaceful Indians while proceeding to 'punish the incorrigibly hostile.'

The 'incorrigibly hostile' were many and agile as fleas, but Crook was one of the greatest of all Indian fighters. He was a lean, quiet, muscular man, with chin whiskers and moustache, and averse to outward insignia. When not absolutely obligatory he never wore a uniform, and in his campaigns usually was attired in a duck suit and white canvas helmet.

Crook's first move was against the Apaches of the Tonto Basin. There were several depredating bands there, led by daring chiefs such as Del-she, Chuntz, Nata-totel and Naqui-naquis. November 15, 1871, was chosen as the start of the campaign because it was the beginning of winter and snows in the higher mountains made it difficult for the hostiles to climb into them, while camp fires were necessary, with resultant smoke which could be spotted by Crook's keen-eyed scouts. To sweep the Tonto Basin clear the general sent out several columns, each self-sufficient but operating on a central plan.

Results were immediate and decisive. On December 27, Major William H. Brown, with a battalion of the Fifth Cavalry and 140 Indian scouts, surprised Chuntz's band of Tonto Apaches in the Salt River Canyon. The Indians took refuge in a large rock cave, but the soldiers killed 74 of them and captured 18. Chuntz, the chief, escaped and next day joined Del-she's band.

Chuntz and Del-she raided south toward Wickenburg, where they overwhelmed a party of young Englishmen who had just come into the country. Most of the party were killed at once, but two were tortured to death. Wrote Captain John G. Bourke : 'The assailants . . . tied two of them to cactus, and proceeded deliberately to fill them with arrows. One of the poor wretches rolled and writhed in agony, breaking off the feathered ends of the arrows, but each time he turned his body, exposing a space not yet wounded, the Apaches shot in another barb.'

It fell to Major George M. Randall to pursue these raiders, who took refuge on top of Turret Butte, a mountain named from the fact that it resembled a turret on an old-style battle-ship, with very steep walls and a comparatively flat top. Up the sides of this primitive Gibraltar Randall sent his men clambering the night of April 22, 1872. Their arrival at the top in the darkness took the Apaches by surprise. In a few blasting volleys the fight was over. Some warriors, in despair, leaped over the precipice and were dashed to death hundreds of feet below, but most of the band, including Chuntz and Del-she, surrendered.

The Turret Butte fight cleaned out the Tonto Basin. Crook dealt fairly but firmly with his captives, setting them to work on irrigation projects for their own benefit, and paying them for their labour. Abuses by white men continued, but so long as Crook remained in Arizona comparative peace existed. The Indians themselves dealt with outlaws among them. On one occasion, a group of scouts came to the general and dumped out from a sack they carried seven bloody, grinning, human heads. They had been told to bring in the renegade Apaches dead or alive and, lacking other proof that they had disposed of them, brought in their heads.

But Crook was transferred, in March, 1875, to the Department of the Platte, far to the north, where already ominous signs foretold the outbreak of the Sioux, which would climax in 1876 at the Little Bighorn.

After his departure things grew worse in Arizona. On June 7, 1876, a band of Chiracahuas – deprived now of Cochise's steady influence – killed a corrupt stage station agent named Rogers and another man named Spence, who had been selling them bad whiskey, and, fearing punishment, left their reservation. There were seventy-five or eighty warriors, with their women and children, led by two new chiefs named Geronimo and Juh. The first of these was to win especial lurid fame in history. Not for many months were the Chiricahuas brought back on the reservation. Geronimo, an ugly and morose Indian, was for a time lodged in jail, which did nothing to improve his temper.

At this time, however, he was overshadowed by a Mimbreño chief named Victorio, who jumped his reservation at Ojo Caliente, when told he must move to the hated San Carlos. Victorio had been trained under the great Mangus Colorado and knew every trick and stratagem of Apache fighting tactics.

From the time he first crossed over into Mexico, in April, 1879, until his finish, he provided the most baffling series of manœuvres the army ever had to combat in Indian campaigns. Toward the Mexican sheep-herders and small ranchers he pursued a settled policy; so long as they furnished him with arms, food and ammunition Victorio allowed them to live. When they ceased doing so they died. All of them knew this, and when the savages, with their steel-trap mouths, rode up, the Mexicans gave them anything they demanded, being only too glad to get off with their lives. Replenishing his supplies thus, and knowing every foot of the country, Victorio for many months outwitted and outfought the best the United States and Mexico could send against him.

In September he crossed from Mexico into the Big Bend country of Texas, made a sweep westward into New Mexico, fought three detachments of white men and defeated them each time, killed twenty-six persons and wounded many more, captured scores of horses and other booty, and picked up reinforcements of warriors who joined him from the reservations – all without losing, so far as is known, a single brave.

Returning safely to Mexico, he trapped a body of men from Carrizal who were out looking for him, killed all fifteen of them; then, with cunning such as would hardly have suggested itself to any other Indian, used the dead bodies of the first party to catch a second party fram Carrizal. These went out to discover what had happened to the first group. They found the dead bodies and began burying them, not dreaming that Apaches lay all around them. At Victorio's signal the deadly fire broke out and every man of the second party died.

Now began the biggest manhunt in the Southwest's history. Back and forth, crisscrossing the international boundary, went Victorio, always throwing off his pursuers, sometimes fighting them, seeming to grow more savage as the pursuit continued. Upwards of a hundred Mexicans and Americans were officially listed as killed in this campaign by the Apaches, and the fate of many others was never known.

At last, however, Victorio was forced back into Mexico and to his fate. By accident, rather than design, a large force of Mexicans caught him in a canyon in the Tres Castillo Mountains and killed him with many of his warriors.

Ralph Emerson Twitchell, in *Leading Facts of New Mexican History,* made this comment : 'He [Victorio] outwitted two generals of the American army and one in command of the Mexican forces. . . . He and his warriors killed over two hundred New Mexicans, more than one hundred soldiers, and two hundred citizens of the Mexican republic. . . . This war was the result of the greed of the settler and the corrupt policy of the government in the management of Indian affairs in the Southwest.'

Yet though their ablest chief was dead, the Apaches still remained 'incorrigibly hostile.' In June, 1881, occurred a raid into the United States led by Nana, a superannuated old chief about seventy years old, short, fat, wrinkled and much troubled by rheumatism, so that he usually moved slowly, often feebly. On occasion, however, he was capable of tremendous energy, as he now proved. With forty warriors he swept through New Mexico, killing sheepherders and ranchers. After a skirmish July 17, with a detachment of cavalry, and pursued by converging columns of soldiers, the Apaches reached the San Andreas Mountains, evaded the troops sent to catch them there, surprised a civilian posse in the San Mateo Mountains, killing eight of them, and left the soldiers plodding in frustration in their rear. After two skirmishes with Ninth Cavalry detachments, Nana and his warriors disappeared into Mexico, leaving only a mocking trail fading in the dust. In two months they had raided over a thousand miles of territory, fought eight battles and won them all, killed anywhere from thirty to fifty enemies, captured not less than two hundred horses and mules, and eluded pursuit by more than a thousand soldiers and perhaps four hundred civilians – with a force never exceeding forty warriors and sometimes as few as fifteen. Their only loss was four men wounded, and they all got back to Mexico.

In the spring of 1882, after Nana's wild ride of 1881, Loco, another Mimbreño chief, fled the San Carlos reservation and made for Mexico. He beat off an attack by General George A. Forsyth in the Steins Peak range, and, crossing into Mexico thought himself safe. There, however, he was cut off by Colonel Lorenzo García with 250 Mexican soldiers. In a furious battle in which García lost 19 killed and 16 wounded, the Mexicans killed 78 Apaches, chiefly women and children. Most of the warriors escaped, including Loco, but it was the most severe defeat the Apaches had suffered in years.

It was followed by another setback, when White Mountain Apaches, under Nan-tia-tish, broke off their reservation July 6, 1882, ambushed J. L. (Cibicu Charley) Colvig, agency police chief, and killed him and seven of his Indian scouts, then rode wildly north. They destroyed property worth many thousands of dollars and murdered eight ranchers before ten troops of cavalry brought them to bay in Chevelon's Fork of the Canyon Diablo, a gigantic slash through

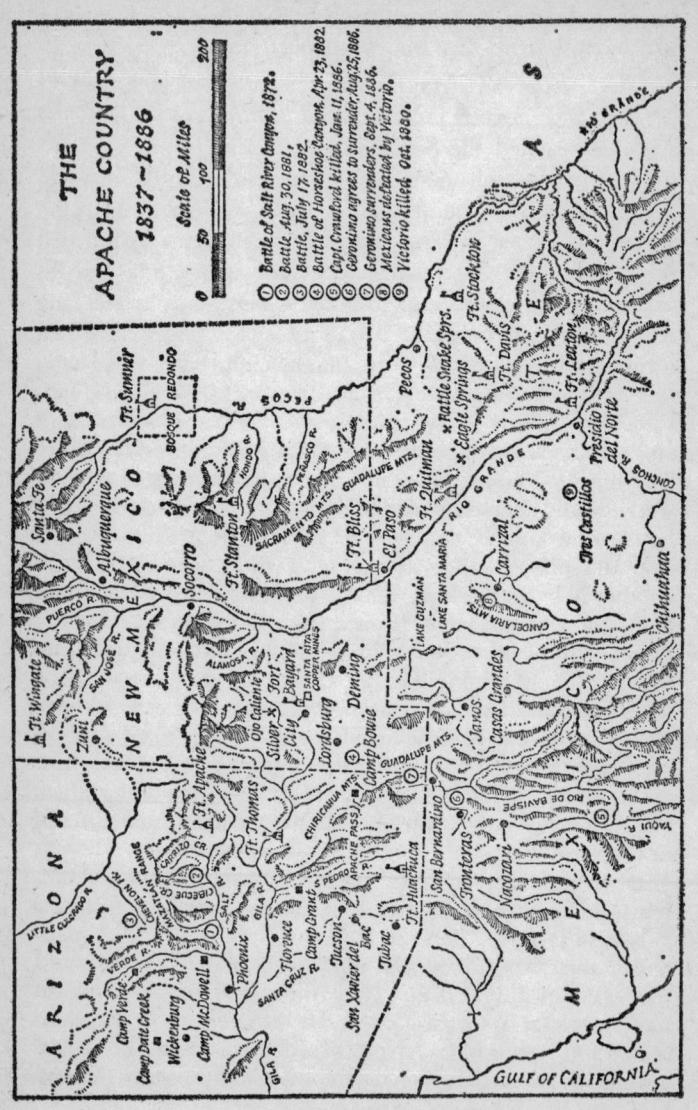

THE
APACHE COUNTRY
1837~1886

Scale of Miles
0   50   100   200

① Battle of Salt River Canyon, 1872.
② Battle, Aug. 30, 1881,
③ Battle, July 17, 1882,
④ Battle of Horseshoe Canyon, Apr. 23, 1882.
⑤ Capt. Crawford killed, Jan. 11, 1886.
⑥ Geronimo agrees to surrender, Aug. 25, 1886.
⑦ Geronimo surrenders, Sept. 4, 1886.
⑧ Mexicans defeated by Victorio.
⑨ Victorio killed, Oct. 1880.

GULF OF CALIFORNIA

the Mogollons, which in places is fully a thousand feet deep with sides so steep they frequently overhang.

Nan-tia-tish, who had only fifty-four warriors, tried to set an ambush for the troops, but under Captain Adna R. Chaffee's directions, the soldiers, outnumbering the Indians ten to one, outflanked them, and in the spitting, snarling rifle duel that followed, twenty-six Apaches were killed, including Nan-tia-tish. The rest, many of them wounded, hastened back to their reservation and the White Mountain uprising was over. The troops, with overwhelming superiority in fire power, lost only two dead and seven wounded.

In the midst of these difficulties General Crook returned from the Sioux campaigns to resume command in Arizona, September 4, 1882. At once he set out to rectify wrongs. White squatters and unauthorized miners were expelled from Indian lands, trusted officers were placed in charge, the growing crops and livestock was encouraged again. The Indian Ring – of government contractors and traders – took the usual dim view of this, since if the Apaches became self-supporting the profits to the Ring would cease. Began again the long-drawn political fight which ended only when Crook left the territory.

Yet Crook almost succeeded in pacifying the Apaches; he would have done so had it not been for Geronimo. That Indian, whose real name was Go-ya-thle (He Who Yawns), hated all peoples who were not Apaches and he had a long record of blood, particularly in Mexico. Crook called him 'the human tiger.' General Miles referred to him as 'the worst Indian who ever lived.' He was cunning, bloodthirsty, incredibly cruel, and combined many savage talents. Though he gave an impression of cowardice with his skulking tactics, on occasion he was courageous. Of his appearance, Charles F. Lummis wrote :

'He was a compactly built, dark-faced man of one hundred and seventy pounds, and about five feet, eight inches in height. The man who once saw his face will never forget it. Crueller features were never cut. The nose was broad and heavy, the forehead low and wrinkled, the chin full and strong, the eyes like two bits of obsidian with a light behind them. The mouth was a most noticeable feature – a sharp, straight, thin-lipped gash of generous length and without one softening curve.'

Geronimo was in the fastnesses of the Sierra Madre of Mexico when Crook returned to Arizona. In March, 1883, one of his chiefs, Chato (Flat Nose), raided north of the border. In this raid the Indians killed seven persons. Most notable of their victims were Judge H. C. McComas and his wife. Judge McComas was a federal judge and Mrs. McComas, cultured and accomplished, was a sister of Eugene Ware, the then popular poet 'Ironquill'. Their little son Charley was carried away. The McComases were driving by buckboard for a session of court at Leitendorf, near Silver City, New Mexico, when the Apaches attacked them.

Owing to the prominence of these victims, a national sensation was created and Crook was ordered to pursue the raiders, punish them, and try to recover the little boy. Taking advantage of a treaty recently signed with Mexico, whereby troops were permitted to cross the border in pursuit of hostile Indians, Crook was in the Sierra Madre by May 8. Captain Emmett Crawford, with a company of Indian scouts, surprised a camp high in the mountains May 15 and defeated the hostiles. Shortly after, most of the Apaches, including Geronimo, Nana, Chato and Loco, surrendered and returned to their reservation.

Charley McComas was not recovered. Crook was told by the Indians that the child was dead, but there is a strange story, at least partly substantiated, that the boy lived and grew up among the Apaches in Mexico, eventually became a chief in the wild bands of the Sierra Madre, and died only comparatively recently.

With the exception of a few bronco (outlaw) bands, all the hostiles now were back on the reservation. Many even of those came in later, for Juh, the last chief of consequence who remained out, got drunk and unromantically drowned when he fell from his horse while fording a river near Casas Grandes, Mexico.

The breathing space did not last long. On May 17, because their agent told them to stop drinking *tiswin* – a native beer that made them ugly and quarrelsome – thirty-two warriors, eight well-grown boys and ninety-two women and children left the Fort Apache reservation and headed for Mexico. At their head was Geronimo. With him went Nana, Nachite (son of Cochise), Mangus (son of Mangus Colorado), Chihua-hua and Ulzana, all notable leaders, besides the pick of the warlike Apaches.

Army pursuit was prompt and vigorous but pretty futile. In the next six months of campaigning the troops and their Indian allies killed six warriors, two women and a child of the Apache outlaws. In the same period, according to the official records, seventy-three soldiers and settlers and twelve reservation Indians were slain by the hostiles in American territory besides an unknown number of *vaqueros,* sheep-herders and peons below the Mexican border.

Most spectacular episode of this period, and worth special examination because it so well illustrated the peculiar aptness for murder and stratagems of the Apaches, was Ulzana's raid.

A dour fighter and cunning as a wolf, Ulzana with ten warriors slipped across the international line into Arizona early in November, 1884. In the full knowledge that they were braving the efforts of two thousand soldiers and many Indian scouts, as well as all the settlers and ranchers in the country who were unanimously anxious to cut them off and exterminate them, the eleven Apaches travelled over the roughest mountains to the Gila River. There, the hue and cry having been raised, they scattered and disappeared. The pursuit was called off, simply because there was nobody to look for.

Nothing was heard from the Apaches for nearly three weeks, while Ulzana hid in the mountains of New Mexico, planning his foray. Then he gathered his braves, and on the night of November 26 he struck.

The renegades were bitter against their kinsmen who refused to join them and that night Ulzana descended on a village of White Mountain Apaches near Fort Apache, Arizona. Guns thudded, white-hot flashes lit the gloom, there were wild yells and scurrying figures in the darkness. Before the cavalry could come from the fort Ulzana was gone, leaving the bodies of twelve Indians friendly to the whites, and one of his own warriors, who had been killed by a reservation Apache with an axe.

From then on Ulzana's band, now numbering exactly ten warriors, led a career both bloody and thrilling. Flashed by telegraph, news that the terrible Apaches were on the prowl again went to every fort and town in the Southwest. Troops swarmed to the pursuit from Fort Apache, San Carlos, Fort Thomas, Camp Grant and Fort Bowie.

At first Ulzana made for Mexico via the old route between the Dragoon and Whetstone Mountains which had been used ever since Coronado first came that way centuries before. On December 2 he was in the vicinity of Solomonville, on the Gila River, signalizing his arrival when his warriors killed two brothers named Wright near that town and Dick Mays next day on the Coronado ranch.

Knowing Apache ways, Crook concealed five companies of soldiers in the valley between the Whetstones and Dragoons; but Ulzana perceived and was contemptuous of this obvious device. Instead of continuing south he turned east up the Gila and crossed into New Mexico with cavalry and scouts pressing on his trail.

Pursuit he really did not fear, since he changed horses of his band every time a new ranch herd came into view, while the troops were forced to husband the strength of the animals they rode, no remounts being handy for them. So on December 9 and 10 the Apaches stopped on the upper Gila long enough to kill four ranchers. Then, abandoning their horses and much of the plunder they had picked up, they scattered like so many coyotes. Once more Ulzana's band had disappeared as if into thin air, and nobody could tell where or when it would next assemble.

Wildest panic, by this time, prevailed in Arizona and New Mexico. Every effort was made by the government and by private citizens to notify all ranchers, farmers, prospectors and travellers of the presence of Apache death in the country, but to reach all was impossible.

Ulzana manifested himself again December 19, when he and his braves fought a brief little battle with a detachment of the Eighth Cavalry in Dry Creek Canyon. Dr. Maddox, an army surgeon, and four enlisted men were killed. The Apaches suffered no losses. Evidently the hostiles once more were heading south, and Crook, who had not for one moment relaxed his grim alertness, posted five companies of cavalry between the Chiricahua and Peloncillo ranges, while he kept a company of Navajo scouts, under Lieutenant Scott, pushing behind the raiders to keep them from turning back.

Two men, named Snow and Windham, were killed by the hostiles near Carlisle, New Mexico, November 26, and the same day they crossed over into Arizona and butchered two more men near Galeyville. One was Caspar Albert. The other has not been identified to this day.

At this point it appeared that Ulzana and his warriors were caught between Scott's scouts and Crook's cavalry. But at the last minute, just before the nutcracker closed, a heavy snowstorm began. It lasted for three days. To trail the Indians now was manifestly impossible. Sometimes in that period Ulzana, using an unknown game trail over the mountains, passed through the military screen and was once more out of reach of the troops in the Sierra Madre of Mexico.

In four weeks Ulzana had led his men not less than twelve hundred miles through enemy country, maintaining himself and his warriors as he went. His band killed thirty-eight persons, captured and wore out two hundred and fifty horses and mules, changed mounts at least twenty times, twice left all their animals and scattered on foot to evade pursuit; and yet, in spite of the efforts of two thousand soldiers, many Indian scouts and hundreds of civilians, eventually got back to Mexico with the loss of only one brave – killed by a White Mountain Indian near Fort Apache.

Crook was convinced by the Ulzana raid that he could not catch the will-o'-the-wisp Apaches when they made their lightning forays into the United States. He reorganized his plan and prepared to send detachments down into Mexico after them.

Best of his Indian fighters was Captain Emmett Crawford, who with a contingent of lean, fierce Apache scouts was the chief spearhead of the pursuit. Crawford almost caught Geronimo. He did capture the renegade's camp, with all his supplies, and a squaw came as a messenger from Geronimo, suggesting a peace talk. Delighted, Crawford agreed. But he never held the conference. Next day, January 11, 1886, a Mexican contingent was encountered in the mountains. The Mexicans thought Crawford's scouts were hostile Apaches. In the confusion shots were fired and Crawford was mortally wounded. Furious at the fall of their leader, the scouts returned the fire, and killed two officers and two enlisted men of the Mexican force.

Carrying their captain, who died a few hours later, the scouts fell back toward the American line. That night Geronimo met Lieutenant Marion P. Maus, who succeeded Crawford in command, and promised to confer with General Crook, 'in two moons'. At the same time old Nana, weary of war, surrendered with eight other Indians and returned with Maus.

True to his promise, Geronimo and his warriors met Crook and an escort of officers, men and scouts at the Canyon des Embudos, south of the Mexican border. Followed a long, three-day council, at the end of which Geronimo shook hands with Crook. 'Two or three words are enough,' he said. 'I surrender myself to you. Once I moved about like the wind. Now I surrender to you and that is all.' Again he shook hands with the general.

But a conscienceless, money-grabbing white man spoiled everything. An American bootlegger named Tribolet sneaked into the Apache camp that night and began selling liquor to them. Before morning Geronimo, in the light of his new alcoholic courage, repented of his peace agreement and skipped out with Nachite and twenty warriors, thirteen women and six children. All the others of his band, including the ferocious Ulzana, kept their promise and returned to their reservation.

The escape of Geronimo, the dreaded, aroused a typhoon of angry criticism of the commanding general in Arizona. Crook, who had been hectored by the Indian Ring throughout his tour of duty, had enough. He wired General Sheridan a long message, outlining his policy of fairness both to red men and white, and ended by requesting to be relieved of command.

Next day, April 2, General Nelson A. Miles was assigned to command the Department of Arizona. A famous and successful Indian fighter, who had campaigned against the Comanches, Sioux, Nez Percés and other tribes in wars extending over more than a decade, Miles set out to capture Geronimo.

It was a big problem, yet actually the Apache was doomed. In twenty-five detachments, Miles set his troops to combing the country. Every water hole, no matter how small, and every ranch had its garrison. Flying columns penetrated into Mexico. Mountain peaks were equipped with heliograph stations, from which the campaigning units were kept informed of every report concerning their enemy.

Yet once more Geronimo swept into southern Arizona. On April 27 he butchered several cowboys on the Peck ranch in the Santa Cruz Valley and compelled the rancher, Peck, to witness the torture of his wife until he went temporarily insane. The superstitious Indians released the crazed rancher but carried away his thirteen-year-old daughter.

Pursuing with a company of scouts, Captain H. W. Lawton recovered the girl, but the Apaches were back in Mexico, leaving a trail of blood. They killed seven Mexican irregular soldiers south of the border, five or six Mexican placer miners a little farther on, seven woodchoppers next, and thus continued into Sonora with murders marking their passing.

In the Pinito Mountains Geronimo repulsed a cavalry attack, and again did so between the San Pedro and Santa Cruz rivers. But Lawton had begun what was to be an endless pursuit. For three months it continued, a never ceasing, bloodhound following of the hostile's trail, with the heliograph signals always directing him. Pressed as he was, Geronimo vented his hate in slaughter. During his pursuit Lawton picked up as many as ten butchered Mexicans a day, and Governor Luis E. Torres of Sonora reported between five and six hundred of his people killed during the campaign.

On June 6, Lawton captured Geronimo's camp with most of the Apaches' ammunition. Late in July two squaws stole into Fronteras, Mexico, with word that the hostiles wanted to give up. Lieutenant Charles B. Gatewood, best liked by the Indians of the army officers since Crawford's death, with two Indian scouts, went on an assignment of immense peril – to find Geronimo and verify the message of the squaws.

Gatewood met the chief at last, and boldly laid down Miles's terms. 'Surrender and you will be sent with your families to Florida, there to await the decision of the President as to your final disposal. Accept these terms or fight it out.'

Geronimo passed his hand over his eyes, and as he did so, Gatewood saw it tremble. The iron chief was shaken at last.

On September 3, 1886, Geronimo and his band met Miles and his escort at a place named as if by inspiration for such a scene – Skeleton Canyon. There the final fragment of a warlike race and the sole remaining fighting chief of the Apaches surrendered.

The captives were sent to Fort Marion, Florida, from which after many years the survivors were removed to Fort Sill, Oklahoma. A lasting infamy is the fact that many Chiricahua and Mimbreño Indians, who had remained peacefully on the reservation, including some of the very scouts who bravely helped capture Geronimo's band, were lumped in with the renegade prisoners and all shipped away together, to exile and misery.

Old Nana died at Fort Sill, at a great age, saying, 'I feel that I have no country.' Geronimo died there also, in 1909. Peace, as far as the Indians are concerned, has reigned in the Southwest for three quarters of a century. But because of that final episode it can hardly be called peace with honour.

CHAPTER FIVE

Six-shooter Vendettas

THE invention by Samuel Colt of the repeating pistol with a revolving cylinder revolutionized the firearms industry and had a mighty effect on the history of the West. Colt revolvers first became popular in Texas as early as 1839, because they were ideal horseback weapons, could be put in action quickly, and hence were, as one Texas Ranger said, 'the best answer to a Comanche.' The handiness of the new firearm soon caused it to supplant the bowie knife as the universal weapon of the frontier. So much a part of the equipment of every range rider did it become that until comparatively recently a cowboy felt hardly decently garbed without his cartridge belt and six-shooter.

After the destruction of the buffalo herds and the sub-duing of the hostile Indian tribes, a tidal wave of cattle swept out from Texas. Within a little more than two decades the thrust of ranching expansion occupied the whole of the unsettled portions of the United States, bringing the half-outlaw precursor of civilization to a territory comparable in size to that which required three centuries to win east of the Mississippi.

To cattle and sheep ranching was added gold prospecting, and mines of many materials were developed in the Southwest, among which silver and copper were the most important. In such a period of vast enterprise and exploitation, when rights to properties of great value were in frequent dispute, and where almost every man carried a lethal weapon on his hip, violence was inevitable. Outlawry was common, robbery and murder frequent, and the six-shooter was very often the arbiter of disputes in the mountains and on the plains. Feuds broke out – between ranch and ranch, between big operators and little ones, between claim owners and claim jumpers, between cattlemen and sheepmen, between stockmen and rustlers, between man and man.

Though the army finally cornered the last of the hostile Indians, it by no means followed that there was peace in the Southwest. Revolvers barked out their staccato messages of death in saloons and dives, along the trails and in the open. Road agents and rustlers fought posses, town marshals sought to enforce peace with bullets, men sometimes shot it out in simple rivalry over which had the greatest lethal virtuosity with the nimble weapon he swung at his belt. In this era it was notable that bullies were scarce in the West; and that a high degree of almost stately politeness existed between men. This was for the reason that all were measured by the standard of the six-shooter, and a big man could be cut down as quickly as a little man by a leaden slug.

Billy the Kid was an undersized youth, physically no match for any able-bodied man of normal size and strength, yet he was a terror in half of New Mexico and part of Texas. Doc Holliday was a skeletonic consumptive, but his name brought respect from men far bigger, healthier, and fully as brave as he. The holstered death at their sides made these two – and others – greater than themselves. In the West they spoke of the six-shooter as 'Colonel Colt's Equalizer'.

A long struggle took place before law and order were brought to the land and men were induced to lay down their weapons. In Texas the Rangers proved themselves a holy terror to evildoers, and although they could not quite boast that they always got their man, chiefly because of state and international boundary lines across which they could not operate, they imprisoned or killed men like John Wesley Hardin, Sam Bass, Juan Flores – and in later years Bonnie Parker and Clyde Barrow – to name only a few. They broke up county feuds and suppressed banditry by both American and Mexican outlaws, until Texas became relatively law-abiding.

Elsewhere no such efficient peace-enforcement weapon as the Rangers existed, and feuds and factional 'wars' were correspondingly explosive. In the Pleasant Valley War of Arizona, from 1887 to 1892, for example, between twenty-eight and fifty men were killed before the last man of the Tewksbury faction slew the last man of the Graham faction and thus brought to an end by sheer attrition, the feud.

Among the hundreds of episodes in which the six-shooter played its deadly role, the two most celebrated serve to give a general example: the Lincoln County War of New Mexico, 1876-78, and the Earp-Clanton feud of Tombstone, Arizona, 1880-81.

The Lincoln County War begins with John Chisum and Major L. G. Murphy. Chisum, a considerable cattleman from Texas, established his ranch on the Pecos River and gained possession of riparian rights – by squatter claim – on both sides of that stream, from Fort Sumner to the Texas line, two hundred miles southward. His cattle holdings were said at one time to be the largest in the world. Murphy operated a store, saloon, hotel and flour mill at the little town of Lincoln, about sixty miles west of Chisum's headquarters. In addition to these enterprises the major had some cattle in the hills, and since his herd multiplied far faster than natural increase might account for, Chisum, a forthright personage, accused him of rustling from the Chisum herd.

Bitterness between the two men was increased when Alexander A. McSween, a young lawyer from Kansas who once had hoped to enter the ministry and still had pronounced views on ethics and violence, refused to defend some of Murphy's men who were charged with cattle theft, and shortly after began to represent Chisum instead. When McSween set up a store in rivalry to Murphy's emporium in Lincoln, the major felt even more aggrieved, for he charged that Chisum was behind the enterprise. This McSween denied, saying that his only backer was a young Englishman, J. H. Tunstall, who was enamoured of the American West and had bought a ranch on the Rio Feliz, thirty miles from Lincoln. Some of Murphy's ire turned on Tunstall.

The major was a political as well as a financial power. He controlled the town of Lincoln, which was the county seat of Lincoln County, then including the present New Mexico counties of Lincoln, Chavez, Eddy, Otero and part of Doña Ana – one fifth of the state, an isolated mountain country, cut off from outside civilization by barriers of desert. Its people traded naturally at Lincoln and prior to McSween's mercantile venture Murphy controlled that trade, as he controlled the votes of the area. The sheriff, James A. Brady, was his man.

One of Tunstall's cowboys was a youth named William Bonney, much better known as Billy the Kid, a name given him with indulgent humour by his fellow cowboys before he became terrible. About Billy the Kid there was nothing to impress one who saw him. A damaged photograph of him exists and it coincides with a description of him given by a man who knew him well, Frank Collinson, of El Paso, Texas :

'A slight, boyish-looking chap, badly weather-beaten . . . not much to look at. About five feet seven or eight inches, not over one hundred and forty pounds at the outside. Rather sloping shoulders, no chin, good nose, very good blue-grey eyes . . . everything he wore, from his old black hat to his boots wouldn't have cost ten dollars all together when new.'

Yet this unlikely-looking individual was, in many respects, the most notable six-shooter killer of history.

The Kid was born in New York's Bowery and was taken, as a baby, by his parents to Coffeyville, Kansas, a tough border town where later the Dalton bandit gang was wiped out in a street battle. His father died and his mother took him to Colorado, where she married a man named Antrim. Later they moved to New Mexico and the Kid is said to have killed his first man at the age of twelve – a Silver City blacksmith who spoke slightingly of his mother.

Thereafter the boy took to the hills. He never saw his mother again. In the next years he roamed the Southwest, becoming an unparalleled expert with the six-shooter, almost equally dexterous with cards, doing some cattle rustling, and killing a man now and then in saloon fights – a deadly youth, whose moods and technique men learned to dread and respect. Yet he had some good points, too. Women often idolized him, and some men remained faithful to him to the death. He had a certain oblique code of honour and made good his word, whether it was a threat or a promise. Above all he possessed superlatively the virtues that counted most in the wild cattle land – nerve and courage.

Tunstall had befriended Billy the Kid; and the Kid, in turn, idolized the bluff Englishman. What took place February 13, 1878, therefore, drove the youth berserk.

On that day Murphy sent a posse to the Rio Feliz ranch to take over Tunstall's property, in lieu of a debt the major alleged was owed him by McSween, the Englishman's partner in the Lincoln store. Tunstall indignantly objected. The possemen were drunk and irresponsible. They shot the Englishman and left him lying dead. Over Tunstall's grave, later, Billy the Kid said with chill solemnity, 'I will kill every one of the men that had a hand in this murder, or die trying. You were the only man who ever treated me like I was free-born and white.'

Those two sentences, uttered by a lonely youth to a man in his grave, constituted the declaration of war in Lincoln County.

Through his lawyer, McSween, Chisum managed to get Dick Brewer, Tunstall's foreman, appointed constable. That made two rival law-enforcement heads in Lincoln County – Murphy's Sheriff Brady and Chisum's Constable Brewer. Wild to avenge Tunstall, Brewer appointed as his deputies some of the choicest desperadoes in the West. Among them were Billy the Kid, Charlie Bowdre, Tom O'Folliard, Doc Skurlock, Hendry Brown, Frank McNab, Jim French, John Middleton and George and Frank Coe.

A few days after Tunstall's murder, Brewer's men captured two members of the posse that had killed him – Billy Morton and Frank Baker. The prisoners were fearful that they would be lynched. As they rode toward Lincoln a member of the posse named McClosky tried to reassure them by saying that before they were harmed he would have to be killed first. He uttered his own death sentence. Another posseman, Frank McNab, shot McClosky dead off his horse. Knowing that their own death was certain, the two prisoners spurred to get away, but Billy the Kid, sitting in his saddle, fired twice. Morton and Baker spun lifeless out of their saddles. Leaving the three bodies to the buzzards, the Brewer deputies rode back to Lincoln.

March passed. On April 1, as Sheriff Brady, with Deputy George Hindman, Billy Matthews, the court clerk, and George Peppin – all Murphy men – walked past the Mc-Sween place in Lincoln on their way to open court, a clatter of shots echoed from the canyon wherein stood the town. Down went Brady, dead in the dust. Hindman, mortally wounded, with a bullet between his shoulders, crawled in a trail of blood to the steps of San Juan church, where he died. The other two, dodging and bounding, reached safety around a corner.

Over the patio wall vaulted the Kid and Fred Wayte. The Kid wanted Brady's guns. As he stooped over the fallen man, Matthews, from the door of a Mexican house, fired and wounded Wayte in the thigh, the same bullet cutting a slight flesh wound in the Kid's hip. The two jumped back to the protection of the wall, but the Kid stopped long enough to gather up the guns and fire a *coup de grâce* shot into Brady's head. Charlie Bowdre, Tom O'Folliard, Jim French and Frank McNab took part in the ambush, with the Kid and Wayte. But the Kid personally accounted for Brady, the man who had sent out the posse that murdered Tunstall.

Thereafter things happened rapidly. With a posse of thirteen men, Brewer tried to arrest Andrew J. Roberts April 14. The 'wanted' man was known as Buckshot Roberts because of the amount of lead he carried in his frame owing to a career as a soldier and Texas Ranger, and he was marked as a Murphy partisan. They found him at Blazer's mill on the Mescalero reservation, but he refused to surrender. Though mortally wounded by a bullet fired by Bowdre, and haemorrhaging to death, Roberts propped himself up at a window and fought like a dying wolf. One of his bullets passed through Jack Middleton's body. A second took off George Coe's trigger finger, knocking the revolver out of his hand. A third, fired from a huge-bored buffalo gun, neatly removed the top of Brewer's head and with it his life.

The posse withdrew with its wounded. Roberts quietly bled to death in the mill. Next day he and Brewer were buried side by side – some say in the same grave – near the scene of their battle.

Brewer, leader of the McSween faction, and Brady, head of the Murphy people, were both dead. But instead of ending, the war spread. Out on the range shooting occurred. McNab, who had killed McClosky, was himself killed and two or three other men wounded in a clash between rival posses in Bonito Canyon. The Kid, with five or six followers, fought a long-distance gun battle with a posse that tried to arrest him on the Chisum ranch; and then escaped with his men to the refuge of the McSween house in Lincoln.

There, the night of July 17, George Peppin, who had been appointed sheriff after Brady's death, surrounded them with sixty men. Shortly afterward McSween rode into town with reinforcements – perhaps twenty men. Though still far outnumbered, the Kid laughed scornfully at Peppin's call to surrender.

McSween, with both legal and moral scruples against violence, begged for a peaceful adjustment, but he was caught in a storm of conflicting forces over which he had no control. Even as he pleaded, the first shots crackled out, and the 'Three Days' Battle', as famous as any in Western history, was on. Billy the Kid was only eighteen years old. Yet he was the dominating figure, the leader, the maker of decisions, to whom men greatly his senior in age and experience turned for orders, in the fighting that followed.

Although the shooting was rather continuous nobody at first was hit on either side, because these men were too adept at finding and using cover. The Kid did no firing for a time. He was a little bored and said with a yawn, 'I'm waiting till

I get a good square crack at someone.' To poor McSween, imploring him to trust the Lord and keep the peace, he said, 'Go ahead and trust the Lord. The rest of us will trust our six-shooters.'

A small peak lifts its head just above the town and when night fell, silencing the guns, two of Sheriff Peppin's best shots, Lucio Montoya and Charlie Crawford, posted themselves there. From it they could look down into the patio of the McSween house.

As dawn came a man crossed the yard. Both Montoya and Crawford fired at him, but missed. He dodged back into safety.

Down in the patio, Fernando Herrera, an old Mexican buffalo hunter who had espoused the cause of 'the Keed', crouched with his heavy Sharp's rifle. When Crawford raised his head to look down from the pinnacle, which loomed about a quarter of a mile distant, Herrera's gun boomed, and Crawford, a bullet through his skull, toppled over lifeless and rolled all the way down the cliff. Montoya, in his excitement, leaned over to see where his companion had fallen and a second slug from the buffalo gun smashed his leg.

From then on both sides took added care to keep in concealment, and though windows were smashed and doors punctured, nobody was wounded in the long hours of the day. The second night came and again the guns ceased speaking, although everyone was tensely watchful. On the third day, July 19, the shooting began again, an indeterminate stalemate now, until a new force appeared in the afternoon.

Notified of the battle in Lincoln, Colonel N. A. M. Dudley rode into the town with two troops of Negro cavalrymen and a couple of Gatling guns. After he conferred with the leaders on both sides, he withdrew and camped outside the hamlet. He had concluded, as he later reported, that the legal sheriff of the county, with a legitimate posse, was in combat with men who were at least technically outside the law. It was a civil affair and Dudley could interfere only if asked to do so by the proper authorities. Peppin, who seemed to be the 'proper authority', wanted no help, and certainly no interference from the military.

The parley occurred toward evening. While all attention was focused on it, some of the Peppin men crept to the rear of McSween's house and set it on fire. After the soldiers departed and the shooting again began, the flames were suddenly discovered. Efforts to control them were vain, because water was lacking. The beleaguered forces of the Kid had to burn to death, surrender, or fight their way through the cordon surrounding them.

Mrs. McSween and two other women came out of the blazing building. Not a shot was fired as they hurried to safety.

But with the men it was different. Harvey Morris and Francisco Semova made the first dash for life. Outlined in the glare of the flames, they fell dead, riddled by bullets. Vicente Romero was next to try – and die. Then McSween stepped forth. He carried his Bible in his hand and called, 'Gentlemen, I am McSween.' It was no use. A dozen rifles from the darkness crumpled him lifeless on the ground.

Suddenly the men in the burning and untenable house came hurtling out in every direction, running for life. So unexpected was the rush, and the fugitives burst forth in such numbers, that it seemed to confuse the Peppin men. A ragged volley roared out, but only two of the fugitives were hit, both wounded. The others, leaping and dodging, threw themselves over the adobe wall at the rear and plunged into the safety of the brush along the Rio Bonito which cut through the town.

Last to emerge was Billy the Kid. With a revolver blazing in each hand, he sprinted across the McSween patio, bullets singing and thudding about him. Bob Beckworth pitched forward, dead from one of the Kid's leaden slugs. Two other Peppin men were wounded. Then the Kid was gone – diving headlong down into the ravine and lost in the brush. Guts and murderous skill with his six-shooters had saved him.

The three-day fight produced six corpses and several

wounded. It firmly established Sheriff Peppin in power, but it did not end the feud. Hatreds grew worse, if anything. Out in lonely canyons and on wild sagebrush flats cowboys were 'dry-gulched'. Rustlers continued to steal cattle and herders died defending them. Billy the Kid, small, slope-shouldered and deadly, led and directed the outlawry.

General Lew Wallace, governor of the territory – and then working on his famous novel, *Ben Hur* – sent for the Kid, under a promise of safe-conduct, and, when the latter showed up, offered him amnesty if he would leave New Mexico. The Kid shook his head. 'This is my country,' he said, 'and I'm staying in it.'

He still had some accounts to square for the killing of Tunstall. Revenge was the great driving motive of his life. He left the governor and rode back to his wilds.

But a new adversary entered the arena when a six-foot-four-inch former buffalo hunter, Pat Garrett, became sheriff in place of Peppin. Garrett knew Billy the Kid and had once been his friend, but when he accepted his office he solemnly accepted with it the duty of bringing in the outlaw. Months passed in a widespread man hunt and the Kid killed and killed, until his total of dead was nineteen. At last Garrett's relentless pursuit cornered him. Surrounded in an abandoned stone house by a posse, the Kid at first fought back, but when his two companions, Bowdre and O'Folliard were killed, he surrendered.

Tried at Mesilla and sentenced to hang, he was returned to Lincoln for execution. But the Kid wasn't ready to die yet. While Garrett was out of town – making arrangements for the gallows – the young outlaw took advantage of the carelessness of one of the two deputies set to guard him, and managed to get the man's own revolver and kill him. Then he shot the other guard from the window as he came running from where he had been eating lunch. With a Winchester in his hands, taken from the jailer's gun rack, the Kid cowed the crowd of people that gathered at the shots, made someone free him of his manacles and leg irons, and, commandeering a horse, rode away.

Garrett's work was all to do over again. Doggedly he began it and for months he maintained his hunt, knowing now that it was Billy the Kid or himself – one or the other must die before it was over.

Billy the Kid's one weakness – for a woman – finally undid him. A girl who lived at Fort Sumner fascinated him. He went to see her. Learning of it, Garrett followed and on the night of July 14, 1881, stole into the house of Pete Maxwell where the Kid was staying.

In the darkness his presence was felt rather than seen by the outlaw.

'*Quién es?*' called the Kid.

Two instantaneous flashes lit the interior for the wink of an eye as Garrett pulled his trigger twice.

Billy the Kid plunged lifeless to the floor. He was just twenty-one years old.

How many men died in the Lincoln County War nobody will ever know. The Kid's own total killings was twenty-one – a man for every year of his life – but of these only eight died by his hand in the Lincoln County feud. The authenticated list, starting with Tunstall, is in the neighbourhood of twenty. But this does not take into account killings which took place out in the hills and canyons, of which no record was kept, and which perhaps were never known except to the slayer, until someone stumbled across a whitened and unidentifiable skeleton in later years.

Meantime, while the later stages of this stark vendetta of the hills were being enacted, a feud equally as spectacular began in another frontier town, hundreds of miles to the west.

A prospector named Ed Schieffelin had discovered a fabulous silver lode in southern Arizona in 1877. In that year the Apaches still were very active in the area. When Schieffelin told his friend, Al Sieber, chief of the army scouts, that he was going to prospect for 'stones' (quartz specimens), the latter said, 'The only stone you'll ever find out there is your tombstone.' Because of that remark Schieffelin sardonically named his diggings Tombstone.

In the rush that followed his discovery the town of Tombstone grew up nearby, with other mining towns, such as Bisbee, near. The mushrooming growth of population created a market for beef, and certain gentry made shift to provide that beef – by stealing cattle in Mexico and driving them north over the border. The stolen cattle were held in southern Cochise County, then a wild stretch of mountains, gulches and desert on the international boundary, where men who did not particularly wish to have their past known found a convenient hiding place.

Headquarters of these stock thieves were at two ranches: the Clanton ranch in the San Pedro Valley, where N. H. (Old Man) Clanton and his three hard-eyed, hard-shooting sons, Ike, Phin and Billy, held sway; and the McLowery ranch, run by the brothers Frank and Tom, both quick and deadly on the draw. About these gathered as malign a group of desperadoes as ever lived, including men like Curly Bill Brocius, John Ringo, Joe Hill, Jim Hughes, Pony Deal, Frank Stilwell, Billy Claiborne, Zwing Hunt, Billy Leonard and others, all killers, all outlaws, living in that rustlers' paradise.

After Old Man Clanton and four of his men were waylaid and killed by Mexicans while running stolen cattle across the border, Curly Bill Brocius assumed the leadership of the rustlers and Clanton's sons carried on with him, the McLowerys and the others. Not only cattle theft but other crimes, including stage robbery, murder and a reign of terror in all southeastern Arizona, emanated from the outlaw domain of Cochise County.

A deputy United States marshal named Wyatt Earp arrived in Tombstone December 1, 1879. Remarkable even on the border, which had many remarkable men, was Earp. When he arrived in Tombstone he was thirty years old, but already he was famous as a gun fighter, having served as a peace officer in Ellsworth, Wichita, Dodge City and other Kansas cow towns in the era of trail driving and six-shooter law. A tall, loose-limbed, powerful man with lightning reactions, his face was unforgettable, with its grim jaw, sweeping blond moustaches and blue-grey eyes, piercing, cold, continually watchful.

He was shortly joined by three others – his brothers Morgan and Virgil, and a close friend of all of them, John H. Holliday, always known as Doc, lean, consumptive, sardonic and deadly. The brothers, Morgan and Virgil – and Warren, who came into the picture later – were similar in mould to Wyatt : tall, moustached men, but a little less striking than he. All four Earps were fond of and intensely loyal to each other, a loyalty joined in by and extended to Doc Holliday.

Concerning the feud that followed there is to this day an extremely wide divergence of opinions. Billy Breakenridge, who later became sheriff of Cochise County, wrote a book called *Helldorado*, in which he referred to the Brocius-Clanton-McLowery crowd merely as 'cowboys' and stigmatized the Earps as aggressors, mistreating the inoffensive sons of the saddle until they were goaded into action. On the other hand, such writers as William MacLeod Raine, Walter Noble Burns and Stuart Lake take the position that the Earps were peace officers legitimately fighting crime and the Cochise County crowd were rustlers, desperadoes and outlaws – in which the record rather seems to back them up. In the Southwest these differences in belief still hold true, but the fact remains that the Earps broke the power of outlawry and when they moved on the clean-up that followed was possible.

In the summer of 1880 the Bisbee stage was held up and Sheriff Johnny Behan arrested Frank Stilwell and Pete Spence, of the Brocius-Clanton crowd, for it. After they were arraigned and about to be released upon bond, Wyatt Earp, as deputy U.S. marshal, rearrested them for robbing the United States mails, for which they were again arraigned and bonds much heavier placed upon them. The friends of the two considered the second arrest gratuitous and Earp began to receive threats.

Into Tombstone, the evening of October 27, rode a crowd of men. Curly Bill Brocius was at their head. He was accompanied by Ike and Billy Clanton, Frank and Tom McLowery,

271

Frank Patterson, Pony Deal, and a few others. By the time they had made a round of the saloons they were drunk and ugly, Fred White, the city marshal, set out to arrest them, and asked Wyatt Earp to help him.

Tragedy followed. In a struggle for Brocius' gun, White was shot through the bowels and carried away dying. Earp 'pistol-whipped' Brocius, dragged him unconscious to the jail, and locked him up. Then he set out grimly to arrest the other ringleaders. One after another he hunted down Frank Patterson, both McLowerys, Pony Deal and Billy Clanton. Each he handled in the same way – a tremendous blow on the skull with the barrel of his pistol, then a cell for the senseless man.

Before he died, however, Fred White exonerated Brocius, saying the shot that killed him was accidental. The prisoners were freed and rode back to their ranches, furious at Earp and with aching heads.

Feeling now was tense but almost a year elapsed before the climax came. On October 25, 1881, the Clantons and Mc-Lowerys once more rode into Tombstone and began to 'licker up'. Ike Clanton and Doc Holliday met in a saloon and exchanged fiery words, but were parted.

Early next morning the Earp brothers were notified that the Clanton gang was gathering. There had been some loud talk and threats with guns on the street. Finally direct word came, to the following effect:

'Tell the Earps that we're waiting at the OK Corral, and if they don't come down and fight it out, we'll pick them off the street when they try to go home. If Wyatt Earp will leave town, we won't harm his brothers but if he stays the whole outfit will have to come down and make its fight.'

It was a formal cartel of the West. In the OK Corral waited Ike and Billy Clanton, the two McLowerys and Billy Claiborne, five very dangerous gunfighters. To meet them went the three Earp brothers and Doc Holliday, refusing an offer by some of the citizens, who had formed a vigilance committee, to go down and disarm the troublemakers.

There, in the OK Corral, the five Clanton gunmen were

confronted by the four Earp fighters. A sudden shattering clatter of many guns fired at once – and save for a haze of smoke drifting slowly across the corral, it was over in sixty seconds.

Morgan Earp had a bullet in his shoulder and Virgil Earp one in his leg. But Frank and Tom McLowery were dead, Billy Clanton was dying of haemorrhage, and Ike Clanton and Claiborne were running for their lives.

By no means, however, was the feud over. Weeks later Virgil Earp was wounded again, by an unknown sniper. Morgan Earp, five months after the corral battle, was killed by a shot through a window as he was playing billiards.

The surviving Earps grimly began to collect blood-payment. Within forty-eight hours, in Tucson, Wyatt Earp killed Frank Stilwell, who, he believed, had murdered Morgan Earp. Sheriff Behan made a half-hearted effort to arrest Wyatt, but public opinion favoured Earp and other officials refused to co-operate. Warren Earp, the fourth brother, arrived in Tombstone to take Morgan's place and the hunt went on, as the Earps, with a posse of fighting men, strode relentlessly through the wilds of Cochise County.

Indian Charlie, a half-breed member of the rustler crowd, was killed at the camp of Pete Spence. Before he died he said it was Spence who had killed Morgan Earp – for which Spence later served a penitentiary sentence.

Curly Bill Brocius elected to fight it out with Wyatt Earp at Iron Springs. He got in the first shot but was cut down by a blast of buckshot from Earp's shotgun. Other leading rustlers, including Ike and Phin Clanton, John Ringo, Hank Swilling and Pony Deal, scampered into Mexico.

Their work was done and the Earps left Tombstone. They encountered legal difficulties over their killings, but the governor of Colorado refused to honour a request for their extradition and later all charges against them were dropped. A few years afterward Wyatt Earp was offered the position of U.S. marshal for Arizona by President McKinley, but refused it on the ground that he did not want to stir up old hard feelings. Wyatt Earp lived to be more than eighty years old. He became fairly wealthy in oil and died peacefully at his home in Los Angeles, California, January 13, 1929 – one of the few frontier gunfighters to attain a considerable age.

The record of what happened to the once powerful rustler crowd shows the thoroughness of the Earps' campaign. Old man Clanton and Billy Clanton were dead. So were both McLowerys. Ike and Phin Clanton were in Mexico; but Ike was killed soon after, along with Pony Deal, by Sheriff Commodore Owens, and Phin went to the penitentiary for stealing cattle. Curly Bill Brocius was dead and also Frank Stilwell, John Ringo. Harry Head and Billy Leonard were killed later. Joe Hill surrendered and confessed to some of the activities of the gang – incidentally exonerating Doc Holliday of all connection with an attempted holdup which enemies of the Earps had attempted to pin on him. Others simply disappeared and made themselves 'mighty scarce' in Arizona thereafter. Law and order had come to Cochise County ... after a fashion.

CHAPTER SIX

"The Night Sky Blazed Noon-day Bright"

SIXTY and more years have passed since the end of the last great outlaw-vendetta – the Pleasant Valley War – and settlement, civilization and law have come to the Southwest. Rangers, sheriffs, marshals and vigilance committees, backed by public opinion, played their part here and there; and courageous and often highly informal courts – people's tribunals, convening in the back room of a saloon or store, with the presiding officer's revolver butt as a gavel and the nearest cottonwood tree or windmill as a gallows – dealt sternly with outlaws and criminals.

Picturesquely whimsical characters sometimes dispensed justice (of a sort), like the one in Langtry, Texas, whose sign read, *Judge Roy Bean, Notary Public – Justice of the Peace – Law West of the Pecos – Ice Beer*. There were ferocious ones, too, like Judge Isaac Parker, 'the hanging judge,' of Fort Smith, Arkansas, the scourge of the outlaws of the Southwest who made the almost unorganized Indian Territory their haven; in twenty-one years on the federal bench Parker sent eighty-one men to the gibbet; and he twice had six, and three times five, culprits executed at the same time and on the same gallows – which were built, at his order, to accommodate as many as twelve at once, if necessary. And there were grave judges whose sense of duty impelled them to defy threats and even murder in dispensing justice, whose monument is a land of peace and safety.

The nation fought wars in those sixty years. In the war of 1898 against Spain, the Southwest's old suzerain, the most widely publicized single regiment in American history – the Rough Riders – was recruited chiefly from the cattle ranches, mining camps and law-enforcement bodies of the Southwest. Headed by fiery and colourful Colonel Theodore Roosevelt, its personnel offered brilliant copy to the uncensored and uninhibited war correspondents of the era. In the Cuban campaign, from Las Guásimas to San Juan Hill, the Rough Riders lived up to their advance publicity, and though the fighting methods of the Southwest troopers were sometimes unconventional, they were usually highly successful. And they provided a springboard from which Roosevelt went on to the presidency.

Later, in 1912, trouble flared south of the border when the twenty-six year despotic rule of Portfiro Díaz was broken in Mexico and warring factions struggled for power. Most theatrical of the bandit-generals who campaigned gleefully for loot and ascendancy was Pancho Villa, whose operations close to the American border made continuous trouble. Villa's bullets frequently flew across the international line, as at El Paso when he captured Juárez just across the Rio Grande; Villa's *charros* made incursions into Arizona and New Mexico, looted ranches, and killed American citizens; and at last Villa, infuriated at the recognition by the United

States Government of General Venustiano Carranza, his enemy, as *de facto* president of Mexico, attacked Columbus, New Mexico, in the dark hours of early morning March 9, 1916.

The attack was a surprise, accompanied by no declaration of war, and Villa stealing up with between four and six hundred men on the unsuspecting town, burned the hotel and several other buildings, and killed seven soldiers of the garrison and eight civilians, besides wounding five soldiers and two civilians (one a woman). But the Thirteenth Cavalry, which was in barracks at Columbus, fought back savagely and Villa discovered he had stirred up a wildcat. He retreated precipitately back across the border, pursued by the raging Thirteenth, and leaving forty-three dead to be picked up after the battle, besides suffering other losses never ascertained in dead and wounded who were carried away.

The American people yelled for revenge after the Columbus raid. The patience of President Woodrow Wilson was exhausted. A punitive expedition under General John J. Pershing, later commander of the American Expeditionary Force in World War I, chased Villa five hundred miles down into Mexico, fought six skirmishes, lost about twenty men killed and fifty wounded, and killed and wounded an indeterminate number of Mexican *bandidos*. But nobody in the expedition even caught sight of Villa himself.

The expedition cost about $150,000,000. It was almost a complete failure, and Pershing found his job more difficult than when he later commanded the A.E.F. The Mexican people were understandably exercised over the invasion by the American troops. Even if Villa was a bandit he was *their* bandit and they wanted to deal with him themselves. Pershing and his men were ordered back to the United States as a result of diplomatic representations by the Carranza government, and returned with a profound feeling of frustration.

Nevertheless, two important results were gained : Villa's prestige received a blow from which it never recovered; his career went downgrade from then until he was killed in

1923. And as a result of the raid the National Guard was mobilized and set to guard the entire border of the Southwest. The latter event was of profound importance in our national history. It was the beginning of a new era in national defence, led to congressional action whereby National Guard units became federal instead of state troops, and vastly increased the combat value of those units for the coming test on the battlefields of France in 1918.

In the two World Wars and the Korean War, young men from the Southwest did magnificent service in the armed forces – at places sometimes so far from their homes that they had never heard of them before they battled for them. But these wars, in so far as the Southwest itself was concerned, were remote and part of the national rather than the regional history.

Meantime population grew, cities sprang up and developed in some cases to immensity, universities, schools, hospitals, scientific centres, art colonies and industries – the evidences of settled civilization – flourished. And New Mexico and Arizona – separate territories since 1863 – became states in 1912, New Mexico on January 6 and Arizona on February 14.

Some of this spectacular development was due to a new factor which entered the life of the Southwest. 'Rock oil' – later called petroleum, which means the same thing, or simply oil – had been a subject of interest financially and otherwise since the first commercial well was drilled in Pennsylvania in 1859. Oil had been known in America through seepages since prehistoric times. Indians in California used crude oil and asphalt to waterproof baskets and to caulk boats. Among Eastern Indians, particularly the Senecas, oil was esteemed as a medicine; and this admiration was shared by some white men – medicine show operators and other dealers in nostrums – who gathered it from the surface of springs from which it seeped, and sold it in bottles gorgeously labelled 'Seneca Oil', advertising it as a cure for almost any malady known to man.

But the industrial Revolution was in full swing. Whale

oil was insufficient to grease the wheels of manufacture, and various vegetable oils, such as that from the castor bean, proved equally inadequate to meet the growing demand. If some plentiful and cheap lubricant were not discovered, machinery could never run in the mighty harmony of industry that was bulding up.

The invention of the kerosene lamp, and the discovery that petroleum could be broken into numerous by-products of commercial value, at once gave a vast impetus to the oil industry and provided a solution, at least potentially, for industry. Lubrication could be brought from the bowels of the earth. If only enough of it could be discovered, it was the answer. Over the country spread the search for oil.

Petroleum had been known in small quantities in the vicinity of Nacogdoches, Texas, since 1887. In Corsicana, the city fathers in 1894 decided to drill an artesian well for a municipal water supply. At 2,480 feet the well suddenly filled with oil. Citizens of Corsicana were quite bitter about the 'failure' of the well and the 'waste' of money on it, and the city fathers who failed to get the water had a rocky political road to ride. But a few men saw value in the greasy substance, organized a company, and drilled another well, finding oil again. At first there was little market for it, but presently Eastern capital became interested, a small refinery was built, and Corsicana became the first Texas commercial oil field.

So far the oil industry was puny. But Texas has a way of doing things in a fabulous manner. A retired Austrian naval officer, Captain Anthony F. Lucas (an Americanization of his original family name of Luchich) had ideas about finding oil arrived at through his experiences in drilling for salt. He believed that under the earth there were salt plugs about which petroleum might gather.

South of Beaumont, near the marshes of Galveston Bay, stood a low hill called Spindletop. Lucas obtained a lease and began to drill the hill, late in 1899. He found a little oil but ran into trouble and lost his hole, being forced to give up drilling in March, 1900.

Already he had put all his own money into the venture, and he and his wife, who was a member of an aristocratic Georgia family, lived in a shack, the furniture of which consisted of cracker boxes for chairs and a plain carpentered table of yellow lumberyard pine. Nevertheless, Lucas would not give up. Somehow he managed to get more financial backing and tried again, this time with the newly devised rotary drilling method.

What followed is history – perhaps the most important event not only in Texas oil but anywhere in the nation's petroleum industry. On the morning of January 10, 1901, the men working in the derrick on Spindletop saw mud coming up from the well. They fell back. Suddenly, with a roar like an express train, a column of liquid driven by terrific pressure shot four tons of pipe out of the hole and clear up through the crown block of the derrick, spraying the ground about for scores of yards. It was oil, heavy and green, a stream six inches thick, spurting more than a hundred feet over the top of the derrick, and spouting an estimated 75,000 to 100,000 barrels a day.

The famous Spindletop strike, the first immense oil gusher in America, was the genesis of many things. It solved the lubrication problem for industry. More importantly, the theory and methods it proved assured a veritable ocean of petroleum, which meant the beginning of the liquid fuel age and therefore the introduction of the era of the automobile and airplane (there were 5,000 motorcars in America in 1901, where there are 50,000,000 or more today). It revolutionized warfare on land, on the sea and in the air, and made it infinitely more terrible and devastating to civilian populations as well as combat forces. It ushered in a new era for the oil industry itself, and created overnight fortunes the like of which the world had hardly ever witnessed before. It changed the whole way of life of America and much of the rest of the world.

From the day the Lucas well blew in on Spindletop, oil became the biggest thing in Texas. Other great fields quickly were discovered – Sour Lake and Saratoga in 1902, Batson in 1903, Humble in 1904, and so on – each boosting the state's production of oil until in 1905 it produced 28,136,000 barrels.

And still Texas found more oil. Across the vast state geologists, lease hounds and wildcatters went. The oil fields straddled the state. Out in the Panhandle – where Coronado once rode drearily in the belief there was no treasure to be found there – great oil and gas fields were discovered. Westward, almost all the way to El Paso, another vast producing area was developed. As if all this were not enough, the East Texas field was found near the Louisiana border – the biggest yet. In less than nine years that single field produced 1,281,226,000 barrels – more than the whole of Europe (excluding Russia), together with Africa, Japan and assorted other countries, had produced in all of history. And back and forth between these outposts, hundreds of separate fields spread out – an incredible outpouring of wealth and useful resources.

Scrofulous little shack towns sprang up in the new fields, and crime and vice flourished as always in such communities, whether in cow towns, mining camps or oil dumps. And wars were fought for titanic stakes – for oil leases and drilling rights, for distribution areas, for refinery sites, and for competitive markets – interests that ran into the billions of dollars and dwarfed any other quick wealth in the world's history. Yet physical violence played no part in these property wars. A new kind of fighting had come in. There was skulduggery of countless varieties : cheating by slick lease men to get control of fields; money barons selling each other out to ruin; cut throat price wars on the high national marketing levels; a whole new and complicated network of legal tactics, precedents and statutes, the astute oil lawyer slashing his opponent with suit and counter-suit as remorselessly as ever a Spaniard slashed an Indian with his sword for gold, real or imaginary. It is said – and probably quite accurately – that far more men have been ruined in oil than have profited from it. But the public has gained unquestioned mighty benefits.

The oil craze lapped over into New Mexico. In 1922 the Hogback field was found in the northwestern corner of the state, and on the Navajo reservation west of the famous natural landmark, Shiprock. But the real play developed in the southeast corner – the old stamping grounds of Billy the Kid. First the Artesia field came in near the Pecos River, on what was once part of the old Chisum cattle barony. Then, almost on the Texas border, the Eunice, Jal and Hobbs fields were discovered. New Mexico became a major oil state, producing more oil than her parent, Old Mexico, and ranking sixth in the nation in spite of self-limiting her production.

But Texas was, and is, first. She produces nearly a quarter of all the oil in the world, over twice as much as all Russia produces, and about a third of the nation's entire production – something around half a billion barrels a year. Today oil derricks sprout like strange forests all the way from Texarkana almost to El Paso and from Dalhart to the gulf coast. The Texas oil millionaire has become a recognized form of fauna as typical of the state as the Texas cowboy. Nor is the Texas oil epic nearing an end. It may be only beginning. Each year new fields are discovered, new reserves mapped out. And the celebrated tendency of the sons of the Lone Star to speak with some exaggeration of their native state and all it does hardly can keep pace with the reality of this modern miracle.

Out of what the oil wells represent came a factor which did more than all the six-shooters and sheriffs' badges to tame the Southwest – the motorcar and the paved highways which lace across the open spaces, bringing every ranch and hamlet to comparatively near companionship with the rest of the nation. The breezy son of the Southwest considers a man who lives a hundred miles away a near neighbour and thinks no more of clambering into his car and scooting fifty miles over smooth concrete or blacktop to eat breakfast with a friend than if that friend's house was next door. Airplanes skim the skies, and radio and television echo the banalities of crooners and soap operas in shanties and oil kings' palaces alike, bringing their contribution to the homogeneity which makes forever impossible the return to the old, wild days.

No longer is it a test of courage and physical ability to venture out into the country of mesas and deserts, Indians and cattle, vivid colourings and strong sun. The Southwest has become one of the nations favourite playgrounds. Instead of lifting scalps, Indians – particularly Navajos and Pueblos – are prime tourist attractions in the great railroad stations and the observation cars. At countless places in Texas, New Mexico and Arizona, luxurious hotels and dude ranches do a thriving business in tourist trade, besides providing, on occasion, gaming devices for the quick abstraction of money from their guests.

All this is recent, and it is part of another kind of history than this. But there is a final chapter that belongs here.

On the night of July 15, 1945, thunder and lightning rumbled and flashed, and rain fell in the dark hours, as if all nature were ominously concerned over what was taking place. The United States was at war. Germany had yielded, but Japan still fought on in the Pacific. In an old ranch house at the Alamogordo proving grounds in southern New Mexico, a tense group of men, dressed in dungarees or jeans, watched the cool, methodical work of one of their number, bending over an odd contraption.

In spite of their rough garb, these were scientists – American, British, Canadian, and refugees from warring European nations – the most brilliant experts in chemistry, physics, explosives and weapons who could be mustered. With them were important military officers, as gravely concentrated as any of them, perhaps more so.

Not one of those men was sure what was in store for him in the next couple of hours. But every one of them was certain that what was about to occur might be of near cataclysmic import. They were watching the final assembly of the first atom bomb in history by Dr. Robert Bacher, of Cornell University, after the parts had been devised and manufactured under the direction of Dr. Robert Oppenheimer, nuclear expert of the University of California. It was to witness the explosion of that engine of dreadful portent that they were gathered.

Once something jammed – a vital part of the mechanism. There was a catch of breath by the watchers. Unruffled, Dr. Bacher reassured his colleagues and went on with his work. Presently he freed the mechanism and there was a long sigh as he stepped back and announced that the preliminary assembly was done. The bomb, whose potentialities no man could surely foretell, was ready for its detonation.

Like a smoothly oiled machine, the team of top experts now took over their predetermined roles. One oversaw the setting of the timing mechanisms. Another gave his attention to the delicate task of mounting the bomb on a steel tower which had been erected for it. Others checked instruments, already in place, to record the effects of the explosion.

Zero hour was near. Scientists and military personnel went to their assigned observation posts, which were placed at distances ranging from five to ten miles from the tower. Following carefully rehearsed instructions, they donned dark glasses and lay flat on the wet ground with their feet toward the tower, to protect themselves from the blinding flash and other manifestations expected from the bomb.

Rain beat down on their faces and thunder echoed over the desert, with lightning now and then luridly lighting the mountains and momentarily revealing nearer countenances, queerly drawn and intent as the final instant approached. What would happen? Would the result of this experiment with cosmic forces by puny man be outside of and beyond all calculation?

There was a line of speculation to the effect that the discharge of the atom bomb might set off a chain reaction of inconceivably wide-spread and disastrous effects. The scientists here present discounted that, but it represented one extreme of thinking. At the other extreme lay the possibility that, after all, the bomb might perhaps not work – and all the great effort and treasure poured into it would be wasted. Somewhere between these poles of thought was the very real sense of personal danger experienced by each man. Nobody knew the extent of the coming explosion or how it would behave. They could only wait and see.

With hearts perhaps beating a little faster than usual, they listened as the voice of Dr. Samuel K. Allison, of the University of Chicago, heard over radio speakers placed near every observation post, counted off the time lapse.

'Minus fifteen minutes . . . minus fourteen minutes . . . minus thirteen minutes . . .'

At minus forty-five seconds a robot mechanism took over.

Minus thirty seconds . . . minus ten seconds . . . minus three seconds . . . minus two seconds . . . minus one second –

Every watcher held his breath.

Suddenly there was a brilliant flash of an intensity beyond any description. At Albuquerque, more than a hundred miles away, one account said 'the night sky blazed noon-day bright'.

The flash was instantaneously followed by the bursting out of a luminous, expanding sphere, several hundred feet in radius from its centre – the fire ball.

Then came chaos – a numbing, mighty detonation – a sustained roar of sound, shaking the earth, the greatest voice ever loosed on this sphere, up to that moment.

And with that the blast wave, levelling everything in its immediate periphery – followed by a tornadic wind, greater than the fiercest hurricane, screaming out in every direction.

Gasping, awed, almost stunned by what they themselves had set into action, the observers gazed up and saw – *the cloud*.

Gigantic. Incredibly malignant and towering. Coloured with the brilliant polychromatic hues of every form of heat – whitehot fury, dull red, oranges, yellows, ultraviolets – swirling with awesome turbulence and charged with radio-active death in amounts beyond comprehension, it tore its way up, through the overcast, into the stratosphere where the now familiar mushroom top spread itself forty thousand feet above the surface of the ground.

Where the steel tower had stood was a prodigious crater and the tower itself was utterly vaporized by the heat of the explosion, fierce as at the centre of the sun.

Slowly the scientists crawled to their feet and stared at the dreadful pillar, held motionless for the moment by awed fascination as they tried to measure in their minds this titan of catastrophe. Perhaps after that came the feeling of triumph – followed almost instantly by speculation, even fear, of the future.

The first atom bomb had been successfully exploded. The war with Japan already was as good as ended, for two of these bombs, dropped on the cities of Hiroshima and Nagasaki, would swiftly bring that empire to its knees. And the most important problem facing the human race was posed – how to control this new giant of atomic energy, both as a destructive and as a constructive force.

It was thus that the Southwest, which had witnessed so much of violence and change in its four hundred years of strife, became once again a frontier of vast consequence : the theatre for the launching of what has been called 'the second epoch in history'.

Today many things are changed in the Southwest, but even with the coming of the atomic age many things also remain individually and harmoniously unchanged, and in this is a feeling of comfort to the human heart. In the deserts and canyons the Navajo still watches his herds of sheep and his wife croons as she weaves the brilliant and beautiful rugs for which their people are celebrated. Pueblo farmers labour in their irrigated fields or make pottery and silver jewellery of rare charm and elegance. *Vaqueros* still ride the range and the voice of the coyote is heard at moonrise of nights. Guitars and soft singing voices sound from little adobe *cases* in Mexican villages in the darkness, and when the dawn comes the mountains and deserts are illumined by a wonder of sunrise such as is seen almost nowhere else on this globe.

You will be greeted, often as not, with a flashing smile and a Spanish *'Buenos días,'* when you meet one of the people of the Southwest upon the road.

And when you part, you will hear the old beautiful Spanish farewell : *'Vaya con Dios* – Go with God.'

Some Books to Read

THE list of sources used in preparing this volume is long, and he who wishes to embark upon the Spanish and French archives, to say nothing of those written in English, could well devote many years to them. For him who has less time, but wishes to read further, I suggest here a lesser list of books which I can endorse both for interest and for a general background of information.

The starting place for one who wishes to steep himself in the history of the Southwest is Coronado, and of the books on Coronado's grand exploration the best for general purposes is *Coronado on the Turquoise Trail*, by Herbert E. Bolton, a great scholar on the early phases of the Southwest's exploration. Similarly, Bolton's translation and editing of *Kino's Historical Memoir of Pimería Alta* is the best available English version of that remarkable missionary's adventures.

For the period of early Spanish colonization I commend *After Coronado*, by Alfred Barnaby Thomas, a translation and excellent editorial summary of important material from the archives of Spain, Mexico and New Mexico. A handy volume covering the suppression of the Pueblo Revolt is *Diego de Vargas and the Reconquest of New Mexico*, by Jessie Bromilow Bailey.

Concerning La Salle's tragic effort on the Texas coast, nothing better has been written than *La Salle and the Discovery of the Great West*, the classic account by Francis Parkman. On the whole French episode – and the Spanish also – the monumental works of Hubert Howe Bancroft are almost fundamental, particularly his *New Mexico and*

Arizona, and the two-volume *North Mexican States and Texas.*

The rise of Texas and its struggle for independence are well told in a number of historical works. Among these, Henderson Yoakum's *History of Texas* and William Kennedy's *Texas,* although differing from each other in some particulars, are close to the times. Francis White Johnson's *Texas and Texans* is interesting also, as containing much of the early Texas correspondence and papers. In this connection I strongly recommend the reading of *The Raven,* Marquis James's magnificent biography of Sam Houston.

The period of the Mexican War has been thoroughly covered in many histories of the nation, but Bernard De Voto's discerning dissection of the period, *The Year of Decision,* is fascinating reading. An earlier and highly interesting account of American operations is *Doniphan's Expedition,* by William Elsey Connelley.

The War of the Rebellion, an Official Compilation of the Records of the Union and Confederate Armies, available in most important libraries, is diffuse and hard going, but gives the gist of the operations in New Mexico and Texas during the Civil War. As for the long Indian difficulties, the reader cannot go wrong on *Massacres of the Mountains,* by J. P. Dunn, *Carbine and Lance,* by Captain W. S. Nye, which deals with the Comanche-Kiowa-Cheyenne wars, *The Apache Indians,* by Frank Lockwood, and my own *Death in the Desert,* republished recently with a companion volume, *Death on the Prairie,* under the new title, *The Indian Wars of the West.*

For general reading concerning the Southwest, J. Frank Dobie's writings are a mine of entrancing information. *Coronado's Children,* telling of the lost gold and silver mines, *The Longhorns,* and *The Mustangs,* all by Dobie, will introduce the reader to this peculiar kingdom of fact and folklore.

The chronological story of the cattle industry is told in my own book, *The Trampling Herd,* and there is an infinitude of works dealing with separate facets of that fascinating phase of history, including *Historic Sketches of the Cattle*

Trade, by Joseph G. McCoy, and *Cattle,* by William Mac-Leod Raine and Will C. Barnes.

As to the period of the range wars, there are innumerable books, but to name only a few of the best, I suggest: for the Lincoln County War, *The Saga of Billy the Kid,* by Walter Burns; for the struggle to bring law to Cochise County, *Wyatt Earp, Frontier Marshal,* by Stuart Lake; and for the Pleasant Valley War, *Arizona's Dark and Bloody Ground,* by Earle R. Forrest.

This is only to touch the surface of the literature available. It is my hope that it will stimulate the reader to delve more deeply into the fascinating story of the Southwest.